D1590355

The Better Brother

TOM & GEORGE CUSTER AND THE BATTLE FOR THE AMERICAN WEST

The Better Brother

TOM & GEORGE CUSTER AND THE BATTLE FOR THE AMERICAN WEST

Roy Bird

TURNER

Turner Publishing Company

445 Park Avenue, 9th Floor
New York, NY 10022

200 4th Avenue North, Suite 950
Nashville, TN 37219

www.turnerpublishing.com

The Better Brother: Tom & George Custer and the Battle for the American West

An earlier edition of this book was published in 2002 under the title
In His Brother's Shadow: The Life of Thomas Ward Custer

Library of Congress Cataloging-in-Publication Data

Bird, Roy, 1952-
  The better brother : Tom & George Custer and the battle for the American West / Roy Bird.
     p. cm.
  Includes bibliographical references and index.
  ISBN 978-1-59652-770-6
  1. Custer, Thomas Ward, 1845-1876. 2. Custer, George A. (George Armstrong),
1839-1876--Family. 3. Soldiers--United States--Biography. 4. Brothers--United States--
Biography. 5. Indians of North America--Wars--1866-1895. 6. Indians of North America--
Wars--West (U.S.) 7. United States. Army. Cavalry Regiment, 7th. 8. Little Bighorn, Battle
of the, Mont., 1876. 9. West (U.S.)--History, Military--19th century. I. Title.
  E83.866.C968B57 2011
  973.8--dc22
  [B]
                                    2010051911

Printed in the United States of America

11 12 13 14 15 16 17 18 — 0 9 8 7 6 5 4 3 2 1

For Laura, Cody, and Paul,
and for my forbearing wife,
Luann

Then hurrah for our brave commanders,
Who lead us into fight.
We'll do or die in our country's cause
And battle for the right. . . .

—Garry Owen

CONTENTS

INTRODUCTION

Arguably, more books have been written about the Custer family and the exploits of its members than about any other topic in the history of the American West. The bibliography of books, pamphlets, articles, theses, and dissertations devoted to George Armstrong Custer is seemingly endless. By judicious and partisan selection from this wealth of material, one could "prove" nearly any theory about Custer and his family that one might care to propose. The most a single historian can hope to do is to reach individual, informed conclusions about the Custers, and this has been my goal here.

Many readers may ask, Why another Custer book? And, especially, why a biography of the famous George Armstrong Custer's younger brother, Tom? I hope this work will offer some speculation about the younger brother that may make some difference in the current regard in which George—a man who has lately come in for more than his fair share of criticism—is now held. I believe these opinions can be supported by reasonable deductions from some facts about Tom's character and his conduct. A close scrutiny and study of Thomas Ward Custer may clear up some misconceptions about George. For instance, George allegedly fathered a half-breed Cheyenne boy called Yellow Bird or Yellow Swallow, in reference to the light hair inherited from his father. Yet Tom had as much access to Yellow Swallow's mother, a girl named Monasetah, and he had light hair, so he could just as easily have been the young boy's father. If, indeed, either Custer sired the child.[1]

The Seventh Regiment, U.S. Cavalry has been more lionized and has had more mud slung at it than any other unit of the American Army during the period of the Indian Wars. To a large extent, the weight of this reputation has fallen on George's shoulders, but it would not be remiss to shift some of the responsibility for the Seventh's rowdiness, particularly in the officer cadre, to the shoulders of the wild and reckless Tom. The famous arrest of Rain-in-the-Face, ordered by George, has been made notorious because of the threat that the Sioux warrior would cut out the heart of the Seventh's commander. Documentation indicates that the threat was actually made against Tom Custer, because it was he who locked the chieftain in the calaboose.[2] Some historians ridicule this idea, relegating the story to short footnotes in otherwise sound histories, as though it could be dismissed as untrue. They base their beliefs that the tale is a myth chiefly on a letter denying the veracity of the story written by a lieutenant of the Seventh Cavalry shortly after the battle on the Little Bighorn. A substantial amount of evidence, however, is persuasive that the story is not merely a fabrication. It should be remembered that, although his heart was not removed, a severe sort of revenge *was* taken by the Indians on Tom's remains.

Had Tom Custer not been overshadowed by his more famous

brother, he might well have become one of the more notorious rascals and military officers in the American West. On the other hand, had it not been for brother George, whom the family and intimate friends affectionately called "Autie," it is also possible that Tom would never have risen as high in the military ranks nor the corps of the well known as he did. Despite the legendary feud between Tom Custer and Rain-in-the-Face, along with the ever-popular story about Tom's shooting scrape with James Butler "Wild Bill" Hickok in Hays City and many other tantalizing incidents, Tom has taken a backseat to Autie in the minds of readers and has held but marginal interest for historians.[3]

To complicate matters, there was a good deal of competition between Autie and Tom, perhaps indicative of sibling rivalry. The traditional belief that there necessarily exists a spirit of rivalry, jealousy, and hostility among siblings dates from the biblical story of Cain and Abel. Alfred Adler turned this belief into a formal psychological concept. A young sibling—in this case, Tom—may feel envious and resentful of an older sibling's size and strength during childhood. Adler theorized that such an attitude, carried over into adulthood, produces a similar rivalry between the brothers as men. But jealous as siblings are, they normally care for one another as well. The love-hate relationship is a key to comprehending many incidents in the behavior of siblings toward one another.[4] In hunting, in military skills, in relations with the fair sex, Autie and Tom definitely competed; at the same time, the elder Custer went out of his way to bring Tom under his benevolent, protective wing throughout both men's military careers and continually wrote his wife that he worried and watched over "Brother Tom." For his part, Tom idolized George. At their end on a Montana battlefield, Tom abandoned his troop of the Seventh Cavalry to die beside his brother.

In the years since the demise of Autie, Tom, and the Seventh Cavalry at the Little Bighorn, the image of George Armstrong Custer has swerved wildly from that of hero to that of villain, and the appearance of Tom Custer has fluctuated in a similarly obtuse manner, when he appears in literature at all. What follows is not a chronicle of a nineteenth-century scandal but rather a serious attempt to understand one member of a multifaceted family that made a huge impact on the history of the American West. The intent here is first to tell the interesting story of an overlooked character in history; second, to turn some new sod in the fertile field of Western history; and, finally, to examine the famous by shedding some light on one of the not-so-famous persons behind him.

When research on this project was first taking shape more than twenty-five years ago, Dr. Lawrence Frost, a noted authority on the Custer family, pronounced Tom to be a "rough one to research" and wrote that "there is very little about Tom available."[5] Frost was quite correct on both counts. It may seem that my selections from the extensive literature of this period of history are unduly partisan and designed to expose the unpleasant or scandalous side of Tom's nature, but glimpses of his better profile are also provided. Whatever the case, few will deny that in order to uncover the true character of the subject of any biography, the seamier side must be revealed. Otherwise, the results of the effort are of negligible utility. To research Tom Custer, a variety of resources have been tapped, although very little of this material discusses Tom in detail. This study relies on an outgrowth of legend, a compilation of some of the available information, and a careful selection of data to form the foundation of most of the conclusions I have reached.

This work also follows the example of previous writers in the field of Western history too numerous to mention. What isn't the overt expression of a historian's subjective opinion—which in the final analysis is the essence of all history—or for which no reference is provided within the text or by footnote, can be found by consulting the resources listed in the bibliography.

1
THE FORMATIVE YEARS

The year 1845 was not of special note, historically speaking, to Ohio. The National Road, which crossed Ohio, had been completed five years earlier. The smoke raised by the "Toledo War"—brought on a decade earlier when Michigan, applying for statehood, claimed as its southern boundary a line roughly south of Toledo, which provoked the militias of both Ohio and Michigan to mobilize—had cleared. Two canals that connected Lake Erie and the Ohio River had been started in 1825; the Ohio and Erie Canal from Cleveland to Portsmouth was completed within six years, but the Miami and Erie Canal, stretching from Cincinnati to Toledo, was not finished until 1843. The first steam railroad was introduced to the state in 1837, and by 1845 there were lines in use or nearly ready for use from Cincinnati to Cleveland and from Cleveland to Pittsburgh, Pennsylvania. Early industries of the era in the state were the manufacture of glass, pottery, and paper, and meatpacking, but the majority of the population of Ohio was actively engaged in agriculture or agriculturally related pursuits such as milling, harness-making, or blacksmithing.[1]

One member of the latter profession, a blacksmith named Emmanuel Henry Custer, was about to become a father for the sixth time around the middle of March, 1845. The birth of another child into an already large family did not seem extraordinary to Emmanuel. Indeed, bearers of the family name of Custer were widely distributed throughout the United States, even though Emmanuel could not be certain that all of them were descendants of a single common ancestor. The earliest antecedent of Emmanuel was Paul Custer, who migrated from the Rhineland in Germany in 1684 as a member of an intrepid band of Mennonites that constituted the second company of immigrants to settle in William Penn's new American colony. The family grew and expanded westward, scattering from a central nucleus in Pennsylvania westward and somewhat southward to western Maryland, where Emmanuel's grandfather and namesake settled. Despite a frequently repeated claim that the elder Emmanuel was a Hessian officer in "Gentleman Johnny" Burgoyne's invading British army during the American Revolution, the old man was actually peaceable, more inclined to farm than to fight, to work than to make war. Old Emmanuel married Mary Fadley in 1778 and a few years later made Cresaptown, Maryland, his home. He still lived there in 1845, and he anxiously awaited word of his sixth great-grandchild from Emmanuel.[2]

The revered old grandfather possessed amazing physical vigor. With it and the typical German virtues of practicality and fastidiousness, he carved a tidy, prosperous farm from the Appalachian wilderness. His second son and Emmanuel's father, Jacob Custer, was born at Cresaptown on February 26, 1782. Shunning the plow,

Jacob instead turned to making plowshares as a blacksmith. He was tremendously successful at smithing. In fact, in an era when a prospective bridegroom required a large dowry before securing a wife—often not marrying until nearly middle-age—Jacob wedded Catherine Vallentine in May, 1802. In sturdy Pennsylvania Dutch fashion, he bedded Catherine, fathering another large family, numbering eight children all together, at Cresaptown.[3]

Of those eight children, Emmanuel was the third eldest. He was born on December 10, 1806. He spent eighteen years learning his father's trade, but rather than working in his father's business in Cresaptown he forsook Maryland and moved to New Rumley, a small hamlet in Harrison County, in east central Ohio. The migration was not a major one, less than a hundred miles. A good-sized group of Pennsylvania Dutch resided in the area already, and older members of the Custer clan preceded him there. An uncle, also named Jacob Custer, had laid out New Rumley about 1812. Steubenville lay almost straight east of the village, and there were so many Germans in that region that there was even a neighboring town called Germano in Harrison County.[4]

Establishing a home on the Ohio frontier required little in the way of accoutrements. The farmers around New Rumley owned one or two oxen or horses for tilling and transportation, a few useful household articles, a wagon and a plow, and a handful of agricultural implements. These few basic necessities were all that were needed to set up housekeeping on the frontier. New Rumley never developed beyond the hamlet state (the town gets no more than scant notice on road maps or atlases today), but Emmanuel had a flourishing trade with the Harrison County agriculturists. He was the only smith for many miles around.[5]

Young Emmanuel prospered so quickly and so well that, like

his father before him, he was able to marry at an early age. Only four years after setting himself up in business, he tied the knot at the age of twenty-two. He married Matilda Viers on August 7, 1828. Little is known of Emmanuel's first marriage other than that during the six years it lasted three children were produced and that Mrs. Custer died an untimely death sometime in July of either 1834 or 1835. Only one of those three children, Brice W. Custer, outlived his father.[6]

The lot of an unmarried parent on the frontier was difficult, with that of a widow even more so than that of a widower. Thus it was that Emmanuel married Maria Kirkpatrick in 1836 or 1837. She was a recent widow and mother of two children, and she also lived in New Rumley. Her maiden name was Maria Ward. Born in Burgettstown, Pennsylvania, on May 31, 1807, and of Irish heritage, she first married at the age of sixteen to Israel R. Kirkpatrick. She wed Emmanuel Custer when he was thirty or thirty-one and she was twenty-nine or thirty years old.[7]

The newlyweds began a new family a couple of years after their wedding. Although they had several children already under their roof, they were to parent five more. In practical effect, George Armstrong Custer was the oldest of the progeny of Emmanuel and Maria's marriage, because the first two died in infancy. George was born on December 5, 1839. Nevin J. Custer, a quiet, reserved little boy, was born on July 29, 1843. Apparently, the pair of recent additions had little effect on either of the parents' first broods— Brice Custer and David and Lydia Kirkpatrick, brought together under unique circumstances, took no exception to their younger half-brothers. So harmonious were domestic affairs in the Custer household that in later years it was only through serious conscious effort that the children could separate the identities of the three groups.[8]

Then, in June 1844, Maria conceived again. It was warm during the first few months of her pregnancy, but by mid-September the weather was cooling rapidly so that when winter arrived in full force Maria shivered for both herself and the child within her. Temperatures dipped below the freezing point nearly every day in January and February. While no pregnancy during the nineteenth century was easy, the conditions of this one must have been very hard for the second Mrs. Custer to bear. As March rolled around and Maria's baby commenced to kick inside her swollen body, temperatures warmed and the first of the spring rains that would bring about twenty inches of moisture to the state before the end of summer were falling. The snow of the previous winter had not been heavy, however, so the occasional disastrous floods that often worried settlers on the Appalachian plateau were not expected.

George was five years old and Nevin a mere twenty-one months when the third son of Emmanuel and Maria's marriage was born, on March 15, 1845. The infant was small, possessed deep-blue, capricious eyes and a ready smile, and a few sprigs of sandy hair sprouted from his bald baby pate. His small size failed to prevent his release of energy, for he exhibited constant activity and enormous physical strength in his powerful little fingers. Emmanuel allowed his wife to name the latest addition to their ever-growing family, and she bestowed the classic Irish "Thomas" as a Christian name for the baby with her own maiden name as his middle one— Thomas Ward Custer.[9]

Tom was a precocious baby, much as his older brother George had been. And George showed an unusual degree of interest in his new brother. As Tom grew, George kept a watchful eye on him. It gradually became apparent that the materialistic and relativistic standards of Emmanuel and Maria, which were typical of American society of the time, had some bearing on the form of a mild jealousy that George developed toward the baby.[10] Neither parent viewed this as exceptional, though, because having reared many children, they recognized the symptom as common among their children, just as it was common among the offspring of their friends and neighbors. The approval and resulting rewards from the Custers often depended upon how the child compared with the others, as well as how the children compared with him.[11]

In order to look good to his parents, and thereby be approved and loved in his own eyes, George had to see himself as better than someone else, so—with few other children in tiny New Rumley with whom to compete and with his half-brothers and half-sister as much as a decade older than himself—George saw Tom as his rival. Nevin had always suffered from poor health, lacked physical vigor, and was unwilling to join in George's rough-and-tumble play; besides, George was only two years older, so he was too close in age to Nevin to feel much rivalry.[12] But not so with baby Tom—it was not long before the infant competed with his older brother in multiple ways.

The newcomer received much of the attention that up until his arrival George had received. Their mother now split her time between the infant and Nevin. George accepted the large amount of care dedicated to Nevin because he had become used to having Maria cater to the needs of his sickly sibling, but he probably failed to comprehend why Tom, who seemed perfectly healthy, received so much of their mother's attention. George felt urged to compete with the baby for Maria's affections. If he were loved for himself and if his achievements were measured against some absolute standards, he would have had less reason to be jealous of his infant brother. As it turned out, however, George had to settle for half as much care as that to which he was accustomed.

All the young Custers grew up at New Rumley. Harrison County's population consisted of two widely divergent groups of people—the Pennsylvania Dutch and the Virginians, of Scotch-Irish and Cavalier English stock. Tom Custer's early life and ancestral background were both completely rural, but because his father was Pennsylvania Dutch while his mother was Scotch-Irish it may be surmised that he was exposed to a certain amount of cosmopolitanism in his native county. It is safe to guess that his family had less than an appreciable amount of association with the Virginians. Historian Milo Milton Quaife pointed out that "as for Yankees, they were so rare in the county as to be an unknown species."[13]

Even the Pennsylvania Dutch and the Virginians were few and far between. Little Tom had few playmates outside his brothers and sisters. He remained the baby of the family until he reached three years of age, at which time Boston Custer was born on Halloween, 1848. Even then, Tom was always smaller than George. Nevin seldom joined in their games, leaving George and Tom to entertain themselves together. In the late 1840s, their games were often inspired by the recently concluded war with Mexico, the two brothers being as infatuated with the glory and excitement of war as most lads are.[14]

Both George and Tom were endowed with great physical energy and an overflowing love of life. As Tom grew he demonstrated something of the Irish in his gaiety, much of the German in a certain tenacity of purpose. In an all-boy pair of siblings such as George and Tom, the older of the two tends to choose games in which achievement is through skill, the younger selecting those in which achievement is by power.[15] George was older, stronger, and developmentally more coordinated than Tom, so the latter had to play catch-up, at which Tom probably became quite tired.

Still, research studying two-child relationships has found that the younger sibling is generally happier and more generous than the older one and that on average the older child remains more jealous and selfish no matter what type of training he receives, even if he is treated more indulgently than his younger brother or sister.[16] It therefore becomes possible that George continued to be jealous of Tom in spite of any type of training whatever, whether severe, moderate, or indulgent. Such treatment was unlikely to eliminate George's sense of having been replaced by Tom and having lost some of his parents' love.

On the other hand, the traditional belief and formal psychological concept expressed by Alfred Adler, the Viennese sociologist, that there exists an innate spirit of competition, undoubtedly influenced young Tom. He could not help feeling resentfully envious of George's size, strength, and experience, any more than any other so-called little brother can. The children were close in age and their contacts at home were most likely marked by bickering and bantering during their play. They also did the chores required of farm boys on the Ohio frontier. As the older of the two, George often assumed the role of mentor to Tom. Sometimes this was welcomed, sometimes not. The baiting and battling of family life was not absent from the Custer household.[17]

The emphasis of the common concept of sibling rivalry has been on the dethronement of the eldest—George, in the younger group of Custer kids—from his place of unique eminence by the arrival of younger offspring. Tom was assisted in this dethronement when another brother, Boston, came along on October 31,

1848, and when a sister, Margaret Emma, appeared on the scene on January 5, 1852. The result could well have been a mutual, if mild, animosity between George on one side of the coin, who was jealous of the three replacements in his group, and Tom, Boston, and Margaret on the other, who were all trying to displace George in their parents' affections.[18]

Jealous as siblings are, however, they generally love one another as well. This was particularly true of the Custers. They often felt ambivalent, tugged in two directions. Among George's more admirable characteristics, both in youth and in his adult life, was his devotion to his family, which during his life continued evident and conspicuous. Tom became his brother's favorite. Throughout their lives the two brothers were exceedingly close.[19]

Emmanuel and Maria, aware of the turbulent aspects of their children's relations at home, were often thoroughly startled and pleasantly surprised to note how their youngsters banded together when one of them was threatened or abused. In reference to Tom, George may have used the term "kid brother" disparagingly, but it carried a considerable amount of affection, too, perhaps more so than with Boston and Margaret, and he was certainly closer to Tom than to his older half-brothers and half-sister. The affection was casually masked from the other children. It should also be noted that the responsibility that George felt toward Tom was usually coupled with a real authority over him. It is possible that the wielding of such authority was intrinsically satisfying in its own right. It fit well with George's drive for independence and enhanced his identification with his parents and their segment of nineteenth-century society.[20]

What all the explorations into the psyches of George and Tom boil down to is a simple interdependence. George relied on Tom to be the recipient of his frustrations brought on by anxieties, to share his escapades, to be a student and companion, and to accept his authority. Tom needed his older brother for guidance, to take the blame for his own actions, to get him out of scrapes as all big brothers are expected to do, and as support in most of his efforts, not to mention for companionship and to have someone to emulate. Gauged against typical brother-to-brother relationships, the one between Tom and George was outstanding.

By the early 1850s, Emmanuel Custer had approached the half-century mark in age. In the mid-1800s, this was on the downhill side of a man's life (even though Emmanuel's grandfather lived to the ripe old age of "about 100 years"). He wanted to enjoy his last years and saw the marriage of his step-daughter, Lydia Ann Kirkpatrick, to David Reed of Monroe, Michigan, as a God-sent opportunity to relieve himself and his wife, Maria, of the burden of raising the younger children of the family. Thus, Lydia's relationship with her siblings became more that of a second mother to George, Nevin, Tom, Boston, and Margaret. Tom finished his growing years in Michigan and throughout his adult life considered Monroe his hometown.[21]

Although it was Michigan's second-oldest settlement, Monroe never grew very much. By 1860, its population numbered less than four thousand, and though it became the seat of Monroe County, it remained a rural community.

Save for his experiences in Monroe, Tom's background was that of any other farm boy, but if the five-year-old expected to be allowed to roam the countryside around the small town footloose and fancy-free, he was disappointed. Lydia Reed was a strict task-mistress—probably even more so than his real parents. Chores were distributed evenly among the newly arrived children and school was mandatory.

Tom never liked school much. He started in Monroe shortly after his arrival at the Reed's home. He was usually barely promoted because his marks were average or below. He was often switched with the schoolmaster's rod. Lydia planned to send all five of her wards clear through the eight grades, which would provide them with a solid background in reading, writing, arithmetic, history, and geography. Education at that time seldom extended much beyond that point for the offspring of a blacksmith, but George talked about teaching or perhaps attending the military academy at West Point, New York, even at that early date.

Nevin held no greater aspiration than that of becoming a farmer. As for Tom, he sincerely hoped that he would not have to go to school other than the eight grades Lydia required of him.[22]

And as for Boston and Margaret—well, they were too young to worry about such matters. Actually, Tom seldom saw the pair when they did not have ample amounts of Lydia's homemade jam disguising the features of their faces.[23]

Before Tom reached the age of twelve, he really had no idea what he intended to do with his life. George wanted to be a soldier, Nevin a farmer, Tom undecided. Since George was his primary playmate, Tom gravitated toward the same hopes as the Custer boy who was "a born soldier" and who could spout and carry out the militia's manual of arms like clockwork.[24]

Unfortunately, Tom followed in the wake of his much-admired brother. While George was quick to learn but lacked scholarly patience, Tom faltered in school and was forced to work desperately to keep up with his classmates. Tom continually found himself compared with George, who was the strongest wrestler, the best rider, and the fastest runner. To put up with the criticism and teasing, Tom became a roughneck and a practical joker.[25]

He all too often found himself in deep trouble on account of his unsettled, restless nature. In school, in the community, even at home, his efforts to match the achievements of his brother brought him much grief. But through it all Tom learned to fight and he learned to be brave. Whereas Autie could be smug and aloof in his self-assurance and quiet about his accomplishments, Tom pressed himself to equal the amount of attention Autie received.

As Tom engaged in high-spirited practical jokes and antics, he sprouted from a stocky, blond little boy in short pantaloons into a lanky, wiry farm boy. Adolescence left him even more unsettled. Nevin swung readily into the life of a farmer. Autie worked diligently toward finishing school, then teaching awhile, ever talking vaguely about becoming a soldier. But Tom still wondered a great deal about what he wanted to do with his life. To compound matters, Autie beguiled the girls around Monroe, something else that Tom—just developing an interest in the opposite sex himself— envied.[26]

Tom tried and tried to bridge what he perceived as a gap between himself and Autie. George was inclined to lay in bed longer than was expected of a youth on a Michigan farm, pampering himself because he and everyone else knew that he could get his chores finished long before he left for school.

Not so with Tom. He would often wake at dawn. He dressed swiftly and crept downstairs, hoping not to rouse anyone else in the large household. When Lydia invariably said, "Good morning, Tom," he would start. There was his older half-sister in the tidy kitchen, putting a pan of bread into the oven or stirring up breakfast or doing one of the many other things that were the lot of women of the 1800s. How puzzling, Tom thought, that no matter how early he got up, Lydia was always up earlier. Sometimes he figured she never slept at all.

Lydia was darker-haired and of darker complexion than any of the younger group of Custer children, smiling and cheerful. Tom thought she looked just right in her starched apron and clean dress. She was not one who patted or fussed over her children or younger brothers or sisters—but they all knew that she loved each and every one of them just the same. Tom loved her greatly in return. He believed that if he ever married it would be to a woman much like Lydia. It would be quite natural to establish a home and family like that of the Reeds in Monroe. He loved Lydia as if she were his real mother and often imagined a wife like her. Her example would prove to be one that no other woman in Tom's life would ever match.

Monroe's first citizen was Judge Daniel Stanton Bacon. Tom soon heard about Autie's first encounter with pert, dark-eyed Elizabeth Bacon, the only surviving child out of three born to the awe-inspiring judge. Swinging on the front gate of her father's yard as Autie strolled down Monroe Street, she had smiled impishly before calling out, "Hi, you Custer boy!" and dashing into the safety of the house.[27] Autie swore Tom to secrecy but reticence failed to prevent a private covetessness on Tom's part. Neither boy realized then how intertwined their lives would become with that of Libbie Bacon. The desire for a relationship similar to that between Autie and Libbie would prove to be another factor in Tom's bachelor life.

Throughout his early teenage years, Tom wrestled with those two problems—what to do with his future and what to do about girls. Old Emmanuel believed he held the solution to his growing son's first question. Tom was old enough by then to visit New Rumley each year with Autie and Nevin. Harvest time found the brothers back at their parents' home, usually delivering a month's wages, about twenty-five dollars, to their folks for safekeeping. Emmanuel and Maria occasionally visited Monroe, too. Emmanuel became the topic of gossip whenever he appeared in the town, simply because there was never such a talker in town—he would spout Democratic politics to anyone who would listen. He even kept up a standing argument with one conductor—an ardent Whig—on the through train as it passed Monroe. They shouted at each other every time it went by.[28] He created quite a stir in a town that was predominantly Whig or held membership in the new Republican Party espoused by that upstart from Illinois, Abraham Lincoln.

Emmanuel advised Tom to take up the family blacksmithing business. It was an honest, profitable way to make a living, Emmanuel often told him. Settlers swarmed west like a plague of grasshoppers. They poured over the roads from New England and the Tidewater into the new states and western territories. And they all needed blacksmiths—for horseshoes, for nails, for iron mongering for dozens of different purposes. When Emmanuel retired, the smithing business could be Tom's. Neither Autie nor Nevin expressed any interest in pursuing the family business. Tom always listened in silence. He would not hurt his father's feelings for any reason. But he would never enter such a mundane profession as smithing.

The problem of girls seemingly had no solution. Tom was still in school when Autie finished and started teaching. Shortly after he took a part-time teaching position and began studying literature at McNeely Normal School in Hopedale, Michigan, Autie told Tom about his first affair d'amour. Mary ("Mollie") Holland, the daughter of an affluent farmer, caught Autie's fancy; he soon shared a trundle bed with Mollie on the Holland farmstead.[29]

Tom probably turned green with envy upon finding out about

the liaison. He typified the aspiring romantic. He used every trick he observed Autie use to attract the young ladies. He cultivated a youthful Casanova image, and his wit and striking good looks served him well. None of his experiences, however, came near to this one of Autie's. Even when Mollie and Autie were caught red-handed, as it were, in the trundle bed by Farmer Holland—and the romance cut short—Tom felt somewhat left out.

Autie's affair with Mollie Holland indirectly produced a favorable effect on Tom's love life and, just as indirectly, on his lifetime career as well. For it brought on Autie's final decision to attend West Point. The military institute appeared to be a stepping stone to the glamor, the excitement, the greatness of a life in the army. Not only that, cadets at West Point could not marry—and Autie had had his fill of women, for the time being.[30]

West Point was supposed to be able to make gentlemen out of boys from any station of life. It exerted some influence on Autie while he attended the academy, even though his effervescent nature overcame his common sense on many occasions. According to the records covering Custer's stay at the Point, which devote six closely written double pages of foolscap to his misdeeds and cover a wide variety of military inadequacies, he smoked while on duty, drank too frequently, and in one instance while he served as officer of the guard, rather than halt a scuffle between a couple of plebes, he cleared the area so that they could fight out their disagreement. He collected so many demerits and studied so infrequently that, in 1860, he barely graduated thirty-fourth in a class of thirty-four.[31]

Meanwhile, back in Monroe, Tom filled Autie's shoes, at least for a time. He became the local Romeo. Having completed school, as much of it as he was to complete, he worked on the Reed farm and at his parents' home in New Rumley occasionally, but he sneaked off from the fields repeatedly to visit girls or smoke, drink, gamble, and carouse with his fellows. He associated with numerous of the more unsavory characters around Monroe. In short, he was considered the black sheep of the Custer family for the four years—from 1856 to 1860—that Autie was away at West Point.[32]

Tom remained frustrated, however. Old Emmanuel gave Autie his blessings for the latter's endeavors at the academy, although Maria harbored misgivings about such a bold decision. But Emmanuel still urged Tom to take up smithing. Whenever he visited New Rumley with Nevin, Tom went into the blacksmith shop where his father told him how happy he was or extolled the financial benefits of hammering horseshoes. Tom thought of Autie, who the family had believed destined to be a scholar and who was now to be a soldier, and assumed that again his brother had one-upped him. While the rest of the Custer household showed nothing but enthusiasm for Autie's success, Tom felt once more in the wings.

Even the low standing of Autie in his class of cadets failed to dampen the family's admiration for the prospective officer. This, along with the desire to be close to his brother, probably decided Tom's mind regarding his own career. He saw how the Custers thrilled over their soldier son, so he determined to serve in the military, too. Of course, his chance would not come until the Civil War broke out.

Of all the mysteries in Tom Custer's life story, his childhood is the most difficult to fathom, for little is documented about his early years. Born a few years after Autie, and with little competition from Nevin, Tom developed a mutual dependence with George. The latter was mildly jealous of Tom on account of attention their parents lavished on the younger boy as a baby, and he considered Tom his rival because he had to feel better than someone to feel approved by the older Custers. On the other hand, Tom was jealous of Autie for the latter was stronger and developmentally more mature than he was. Autie also served as Tom's teacher in the ways of life, a standard to live up to, and guardian on the occasions when his help was required. At that same time, the two boys cared deeply for each other. The result was a mixture of rivalry and closeness that would last to the ends of their lives.

2
MILITARY LIFE

Homer's *Iliad* immortalized the tale of Greek hero Achilles' choice between a long life of commonplace obscurity and a few brief moments of glory as a warrior and a guarantee of infinite renown. George Armstrong Custer drank danger like fine old wine, finding a peculiar, barbaric comfort in mortal combat that overcame all his fears. When his younger brother Tom gained a chance to enter the American Civil War, a single individual in a whole generation of young men who, through no fault of its own was destined to fight in the dreadful war, Tom hastened into the ranks to become a soldier like Autie. His unflagging courage and great physical stamina served him well. Like a few who were not given Achilles' choice between glory and oblivion but rather followed a special star, Tom found a strange beauty and a certain sort of stable happiness in war and in the army.[1]

Tom was only sixteen years old when the war erupted in 1861. President Lincoln's first call for 75,000 volunteers to fill the ranks of a small regular army included some boys his age, but like many other Americans, Tom's father believed the fighting would be of short duration, so Tom was kept at home in Monroe.

That did not prevent him from hearing glowing details of the army from Autie. Although he graduated last in his class at West Point with so many demerits that if the war had not broken out when it did he might never have received a commission at all, Tom's brother became a second lieutenant in the Second United States Cavalry regiment.[2] On a visit to Monroe in 1861, while he was on leave before joining his regiment, Autie really cut a dash in his cavalry uniform. He made a big impression on petite little Elizabeth Bacon. He also stirred up a hornet's nest when he commenced courting her, for shortly after he began in earnest, he was seen tramping down Monroe Street, boisterously intoxicated—a matter which drew the attention of both Libbie's father and his own older sister, Lydia Reed.[3]

Tom sniggered behind his brother's back after he heard what Lydia did when it happened. Being a strict matriarchal figure, not to mention being firmly opposed to the use of alcohol, she was so disconcerted about the incident that there and then she extracted a promise from George, on his word of honor as an officer and a gentleman, that he would never drink another drop of intoxicating liquor. Oddly enough, he never did after that day. That submission not only soothed Lydia but also helped to clear the way with the honorable Judge Bacon for George to court Libbie seriously.[4]

But not for long. Tom and Libbie were each sorry to see George step onto the train that would carry him out of Monroe and their lives and into the first major battle of the war at Bull Run. Autie left his loved ones already a hero in their eyes. Tom was probably the only one watching him leave who understood that Autie noted the characteristics that people expected of a hero and cultivated that image. George possessed all the qualities of greatness admired by nineteenth-century Americans, and during the next few years he would use them to best advantage. He was faced with social and economic barriers to success, but in classic Horatio Alger style he overcame these walls, believing that individualism was the most important part of his own abilities. He mastered his environment and other men through his domineering will. No one, not even Tom, stood impervious to his authority.[5]

When Autie entered the Second Cavalry he was a broad-shouldered six-footer with a slim waist and muscular legs, known as one of the best riders in the Union army. In little time, he became known as "Cinnamon" because of the cinnamon-scented oil with which he liberally anointed his curly yellow hair; he let it grow longer so the locks glistened, and he donned a show-off, foppish combination of uniforms that included a tight hussar jacket and golden lace trim on black trousers. A staff officer in the Second Cavalry once caustically commented that he looked "like a circus rider gone mad."[6]

His outlandish appearance did not hinder a phenomenal rise in the ranks. He served gallantly at the First Battle of Bull Run in July 1861, where he gained the attention of old cavalry campaigner Phil Kearny.[7] Kearny placed the swaggering second lieutenant on his staff, a move that lifted Custer above the regular officers to set him on the road to the stars of generalship.

The next leg on that path was the impression he made on the new commander of the Union forces around Washington, D.C., George B. McClellan. Custer caught McClellan's eye when the general, accompanied by his staff, rode up to the bank of the Chickahominy River of Virginia during the Peninsula campaign of 1862. McClellan remarked, "I wish I knew how deep it is." His staff sat their horses, shrugged their shoulders, and thoughtfully began to make estimates about the depth of the dark water. The brash Custer, however, muttered "I'll damn soon show him" to a man mounted beside him, then spurred to the bank and rode his floundering steed into the swirl till he reached the middle of the river. He then swiveled in his saddle and called out, "That is how deep it is, General." McClellan, awed by the junior officer's audacity, soon added Custer to his staff, although he remained a second lieutenant.[8]

Autie's innate courage urged him to make himself an example to the troopers he commanded. During a minor cavalry engagement, in which a higher ranking officer was killed, Custer, by then a captain, took over command and led a full-blown, saber-swinging charge that not only carried the day but also won him a brevet brigadier generalship. He received a command with a brigade consisting largely of Michigan regiments, so he quickly dubbed his riders "Wolverines." The Michigan brigade marched and fought with the Army of the Potomac throughout its campaigns against Robert E. Lee in Virginia, including the battles at Fredericksburg, Chancellorsville, and with distinction during the Gettysburg campaign.[9]

Back in Monroe, Tom followed his brother's early exploits proudly and avidly. He dearly longed to join "big bub Aut" in the Northern cavalry, but Emmanuel and Lydia kept him firmly tied to their farms during the first year of the war. All belief that the war would be short-lived had long since dissipated, but Emmanuel remained adamant about Tom joining the army—he wanted only one soldier son.

Tom, however, was not to be denied. Most of the other boys, childhood playmates of the Custers, had enlisted in volunteer regiments. Tom gave no thought to the military regimen, with strict regulations, tootling bugles and banging drums from dawn to dusk, long marches and short rations, harsh officers, even the possibility of horrible wounds or death. The war to which he looked forward was the same one that big brother Autie, the swashbuckling cavalry officer, fought. He ignored any opportunity of attending West Point when his father Emmanuel brought up the subject. Tom was sure that his father would soon forget about the military academy because he was so reluctant to have more sons than George in the military. Tom was also sure Emmanuel would become reconciled to his enlistment as a private soldier when he was still only sixteen years old.

Tom tried to enlist at that young age, but he was sent back home. Finally, with Emmanuel's grudging permission, he tried again at seventeen, and on September 2, 1861, he was sworn in as a private in the Twenty-first Ohio Volunteer Infantry regiment. Although this regiment participated in the Chickamauga, Chattanooga, and Atlanta campaigns, historian Charles M. Robinson III says Tom's only battle with the Twenty-first Ohio was at Stones River, Tennessee, in December 1862.[10]

Tom did not want to displease his father, but he did not plan to miss out on the chance to grab some glory. He wanted a uniform with brass buttons and to fight rebels on battlefields with fluttering banners, flashing sabers, and raucous noises. The ensuing months saw him learning the manual of arms, his place in the army, and how to march.

One night in 1864, Tom sat inside a large twelve-person army field tent, writing a letter to George. He had removed his snappy forage cap and the short blue jacket called the blouse of his uniform. With a lantern set on the writing table, through the open flap of the tent he could see the flicker of candles and lanterns in hundreds of similar tents. He could see the flames of many campfires and hear the sounds of army night life as it rustled quietly around him. Two letters written by one of his mess mates of Company H, Liberty P. Warner, who shared the tent with Tom in late 1861 and early 1862, describes their life during that period. One of these letters even provided an accompanying plan of their tent accommodations with a key to where each soldier slept.[11]

At that time armies of the Union and of the Confederacy were fighting in the narrow Shenandoah Valley of Virginia. Although this strip of the Southern state was nominally controlled by the federals under General Phil Sheridan, Rebel general Jubal Early, a hard-hitter with a smaller force of veteran Southerners, challenged the Yankees. Tom's brother, George, was now a major general of volunteers with command of the Third Cavalry Division. He was Sheridan's favorite cavalry officer.

At first it seemed that Early, who had already been beaten twice, was whipped. But on the morning of October 19, 1864, just as Sheridan prepared to return to camp, Early launched a sudden attack that took the Union troops completely by surprise. Sheridan barely staved off utter rout by personally turning retreating federals around and leading them back into the fray.

Tom's pen scratched rapidly. He was missing out on all the fighting, and with it his chance at glory. He hoped Autie could do something about the matter.

General Custer's devotion to his family, which would reach full fruition a dozen years later, showed itself when he learned that Tom wanted to join him. Tom, who entered the Union army as a private soldier, attained a commission through his brother's influence. He fostered a flamboyant, hell-for-leather horseman image, that of a man who, like his famous brother, possessed the great basic virtue of liking to fight.[12] Thus, when the Army of the Shenandoah under Sheridan, including George Armstrong Custer's Third Division, wintered at Winchester, Virginia, Custer sent for his new wife, Libbie Bacon Custer, on October 28, 1864. The first of the next month also saw the arrival of Tom.

Tom joined Autie on a trip back to Monroe. It had been several years since the brothers had seen each other. Autie had been home on his leave from West Point during the summer of 1859 and again in 1861 before joining the Army of the Potomac before the first battle at Manassas Junction. Tom had been no more than a mere stripling those times.

When Armstrong picked Tom up on the way back home, the sleeves of Tom's uniform boasted the chevrons of a corporal, and the forage cap setting jauntily on his blond head displayed the emblem of the Twenty-first Ohio. Like George, he demonstrated restlessness and energy. In the years since the older Custer had left for the military academy, Tom had grown older and changed so much that Autie barely recognized him. And when Autie found that Tom had not been home since he enlisted, mischief formulated in the minds of the brothers.

Mother Custer was informed of the planned prank upon the boys' arrival. To everyone else, family members included, Tom was passed off as "Major Drew." Even his own father failed to recognize him as his son Tom, and Mrs. Custer especially enjoyed the confusion of poor, mystified Nevin.[13]

On their return to the military life, Tom joined General Custer's volunteer cavalry division as a new lieutenant. He had not been there a full week before, on November 8, 1864, Autie appointed Tom his new adjutant general on the staff to replace an old friend of his, Jake Greene, who was held prisoner by the Confederates. George followed a precedent with his appointment of Tom to his staff. Seeing that no less than General Phil Sheridan himself had similarly assigned his own younger brother, Mike, to his staff, no one could gainsay Custer the privilege of following the nepotic example. The day Tom joined the staff was a rainy, dismal one, and that same day, Abraham Lincoln was re-elected president of the United States, indicating that the North did not want to change horses midstream. Tom cast his vote in camp but failed to remark about the election. He seemed too awed by his new assignment, about which he later wrote, "And if anyone thinks it's a soft thing to be a commanding officer's brother, he misses his guess."[14]

Tom was mustered out of the Twenty-first Ohio on October 10, 1864. He accepted the commission of second lieutenant of the Sixth Michigan Volunteer Cavalry soon after. Once Tom was in the cavalry corps it was a simple matter for his brother, the general, to request permission to add Tom as an aide. Custer's friend and colonel of the Sixth Michigan, James H. Kidd, made room for Tom so that a commission was available. It was then that Secretary of War Edwin M. Stanton ordered the discharge of Tom from the Twenty-first Ohio with the clear understanding that he must accept the commission or remain a noncom in the infantry, short of which he would be considered a deserter.[15]

His was a hard place to be for sure. Tom was the new swain and practical joker in the division's winter quarters. He was now a blue-eyed, flaxon-haired, bean-pole-tall, nineteen-year-old second lieutenant, second youngest of the general's three kid brothers. As such, he envied and emulated "big bub Aut" with ambitious devotion. And his new sister-in-law Libbie wrote to her parents that "Aut's brother Tom has received a commission in a Michigan Regt.

and is with us. Such an open-hearted boy, he adds much to our family circle—for such I consider the Staff. In fact, dear Father and Mother, no happier woman lives than your devoted daughter."[16]

Indeed, Tom fit in well with the "family circle." With his fellow staff members he strummed away on an old jew's harp, sneaked pipes of tobacco, swilled liquor behind his tetotaling brother's back, gambled heavily—occasionally using money he did not really have—and generally got on famously with the other staff officers.[17]

In public, Tom and Autie maintained a strictly formal relationship, but in their own quarters—especially during the winter of 1864 when there was little else to do to entertain themselves—they helled about in horseplay, rollicking boys again, noisily trying to outdo each other with pace-setting pranks and hilarious jokes. Libbie tried to appear indulgent toward the childish actions, but the very first night that the two brothers were with her in camp they set the example that would become familiar.

Libbie looked on horrified when her husband, the general, and the lieutenant began to wrestle. Soon they were tumbling on the floor, rolling over and about, while Libbie, virtually helpless with a serious case of the giggles, tried to keep her distance from wildly swinging arms and flailing legs. Autie abruptly stopped the game saying, "Wait—let me put Libbie in a safe place." Tom and he separated briefly while the general caught her up and hefted her to the summit of a contraband chest of drawers in Autie's tent. He left her there while they resumed the fracas. They separated once in a while to call to her before rejoining the contest. The top of the highboy thereafter became a barless jail for Libbie whenever the brothers wanted to tease her. Because she was small and delicate there was no way she could scramble down. Also, she had no reason to want to. So she would wait there until either George or Tom was willing to lift her down.[18]

Libbie and Armstrong were deeply and irrevocably in love. Between them there was no room for anyone else—with the exception, of course, of Tom. But as one biographer of Libbie Custer has implied, Tom had his army life and Autie had Libbie. He wrote, "There was rarely a day that Tom, Autie and Libbie did not have their romps. This display of boyishness had been evident after each engagement during the Civil War and Autie had married. The exhibition was quickly transformed into a scene of official or domestic tranquillity when a caller was announced."[19]

According to D. A. Kinsley, a biographer of George, "When off duty, General and Lieutenant were frolicking brothers. At all other times, the contrast was startling. No familiarity, no favoritism. Tom knew his place and kept it—or suffered severely for breach of discipline."[20]

Still, for both his brother and sister-in-law, Tom's presence in the division was a pleasant diversion from regular army routine. Libbie wrote:

We could not help spoiling him owing to his charm and our deep affection. When Tom came in to report he was the most formal of them all standing at attention anodizing a tone of voice that betrayed no signs of anything but the strictly disciplined soldier. The two called each other "Sir" and until I had become accustomed to this I used to think that Tom had surely been offended by some distinction and I prepared to take his side and plead his case whatever might be the right or wrong of the case. As soon as the report was made and the commander had said, "I have no more orders, sir, for the present," Tom flung his cap off, unbuckled his saber and the two were calling each other by their first names and with some teasing words in the midst of a scuffle as vigorous and rollicking as when they were boys on the Ohio farm of their childhood.[21]

The familial fraternization between Tom on the one hand and George and Libbie on the other lasted through part of the winter at Winchester right up until the womenfolk with the Army of the Shenandoah were sent away in preparation for the campaigns of 1865. Libbie was supposed to go with other army wives to Washington, D.C. "Lonesome and anxious," she remembered how she had excitedly written to Judge Bacon and her mother in Monroe on December 4, 1864, that "I am the only lady in the Army. The wives of officers have been ordered out. Gen'l Sheridan thought women interfered with soldiers' duties." However, Autie had somehow arranged things with Sheridan so that his "dark-haired loveliness" could linger until serious fighting began again. Libbie added in her letter that "Tom is a fine boy. He has improved so much." She had taken Tom into her heart and mothered him just as Lydia had when he lived with her in Monroe.[22]

Many of his revelries while at Winchester took place behind Autie's back, and almost all of them without Libbie's knowledge, partly out of Tom's respect for her as a mother figure. As with Lydia in Monroe, Tom began to see Libbie as the kind of woman with whom he could settle down. He determined that since he could not have his sister-in-law and surrogate as a wife, he would look for one almost exactly like her. Her gentle attempts to reform him completely became something of an inside joke with the impish junior officer and his older brother. In one instance, Autie allegedly asked, "Has the old lady taught you to say your prayers yet, angelface?"[23]

His adaptation to military life finally seemed to suit Custer's parents, too. They evidently felt more secure in the knowledge that at least Tom would have the premier member of the family to look after him. They always understood when Tom spoke about his service with the army because it made them feel proud of him. Years before, they would have been so ashamed, so worried about what would happen to him in the future. Now they knew. By turning into a hard-working, successful soldier he had exonerated himself in their opinions. He had desperately wanted to redeem himself; he felt guilty about not becoming a blacksmith. Was that why he never wrote to them about the seamier side of soldiering—about women, liquor, and gambling among the officers and men? He felt now as though he was some kind of soldiering machine with no soft spots, no desire or need for love, possessed by only the hard drive of ambition. Surely there was more for him than that, and yet that was what he had let himself appear to be in his parents' eyes in order to justify his existence and atone for youthful mistakes.

Then, in the early spring of 1865, when the campaigning resumed amid frequent showers, roads that were no more than quagmires of sticky mud, and hailstorms of minie balls from "Marse Robert's" Army of Northern Virginia, Tom met the opportunity to make himself as important in the eyes of the family and friends as the adored and envied Autie. That spring at long last brought on the collapse of Lee's army and its escape from the extended trench warfare around Petersburg. General Ulysses S. Grant, the highest-ranking officer of the Union army, and General George Gordon Meade, hero of Gettysburg and commander of the Army of the Potomac, had caused their troops to fight in the trenches throughout the fall and winter of 1864 trying to weasel Lee out of Petersburg to capture Richmond. When Lee finally abandoned the Confederate capital and headed west, Sheridan's Army of the Shenandoah received the assignment to stop him. Sheridan sent Custer's cavalry division to obliterate the last desperate Confederate gamble.[24]

The two forces clashed on March 2, 1865. Custer dismounted most of his division and attacked the enemy's flanks with carbines sputtering. Then he took the Eighth New York and the First Connecticut Volunteer Cavalry regiments and drove them straight down the Confederates' throats—charging in a galloping column of fours, bugles blaring in the blustery March air, straight into the middle of the line commanded by his old nemesis, Jubal Early. Right over the hastily thrown up barricades went the mounted troopers, flankers broke in the ends of Early's line, and all resistance ceased.[25] Custer had impetuously attacked Early in the shadow of the Blue Ridge Mountains with a mere fifteen hundred troopers of his mud-delayed division. Tom gallantly led the final charge himself, chasing Early into the hills of Virginia. "Old Jube" was last seen by the Custers and their boys swimming the South River to obscure safety—accompanied by the cheerful din of hoots and jeers by the victors. Tom was awarded a citation for bravery and a brevet promotion from first lieutenant to captain for brave and meritorious service by his enthusiastic brother.[26]

After this battle George and Tom returned to their headquarters to celebrate with the rest of the staff. Later, Tom learned that some squadrons of the division rode roughshod through the streets of a nearby town called Waynesboro, sabering rebel fugitives as they tried to escape.[27]

While those stories disgusted and sickened him, Tom discovered a certain exquisite joy in the thrill of fighting. He felt born to soldiering. And his greatest martial experience of the Civil War was yet to come.

On April 3, 1865, during a brisk, violent cavalry skirmish with some of Lee's outriders at a place called Namozine Church, Tom singlehandedly emulated the exploits of "big bub Aut" who was by then glamorized all over the North for personally leading glittering saber charges. The fray was vicious, as had been the fighting on the two preceding days. One horse had already been shot out from under him.[28]

On this day, Tom rushed to the attack, outriding his fellow cavalrymen and leaving them far behind. As he approached a small Confederate force, the new horse that he had acquired only the day before was also shot from under him. But the stubborn new lieutenant persisted. He captured the enemy colors, three officers, and eleven enlisted men alone![29]

For this act of heroism, Tom was awarded the Congressional Medal of Honor. This decoration had been authorized in 1862. On February 17 of that year, Senator Henry Wilson of Massachusetts rose on the floor of the United States Senate to introduce a resolution creating an Army Medal of Honor for presentation to private soldiers of the Union armies who distinguished themselves in combat. The resolution went through an amendment procedure before receiving the signature of President Lincoln on July 12, 1862. It was not until the following year that Congress saw fit to pass another law providing that commissioned officers as well as noncoms and privates could be recipients of Medals of Honor. Like brevet commissions, which were awarded primarily "for gallant conduct or meritorious service," the chief requirement to win the award—at that time the only medal conferred by the United States government—was "gallantry in action."[30]

For many years the Medal of Honor was the only military decoration authorized for any service of the armed forces of the

United States, so Tom thought it curious that no one had ever considered bestowing a dozen or so Congressional Medals on his idol, Autie, for his sundry and diverse accomplishments. The pretty little things had been distributed like gimcracks ever since their authorization in 1862. When questioned about his not having the decoration, George answered flippantly, "I never asked for it, so nobody ever gave it to me." He then typically added, "To prove to you how much I value and admire my brother as a soldier, I think that he should be the general and I the captain."[31]

Before the first week of April had passed, Tom, flamboyant and overconfident because of his first award, led another charge. He galloped ahead of the other cavalrymen, distinguished now by his immaculate service uniform kept uncommonly clean, his tousled head of sandy hair and beardless cheeks, and his hard, expressionless eyes. For his action that day he would win a second Medal of Honor and another brevet promotion.

George Armstrong Custer, with his own gaudy uniform, his cinnamon-anointed curls, and equally sharp eyes, had received a report of a Rebel wagon train winding through the mountainous terrain, the white canvas covers visible occasionally through the raw, bleak forests glistening from spring showers. He called his squadrons to the attack at a dead run with sabers swinging. Some of the Confederate infantrymen protecting the train routinely fell into line along a stream called Sayler's Creek to repel the attack. However, a large gap in the moving train opened up ahead because the Rebels at the head of the column did not realize that their fellows had halted. Armstrong's cavalrymen went pouring through the hole, effectively stopping half the wagon train, cutting the traces to the wagons, chasing away the teams, carving up drivers with their flashing swords, chopping up wheel spokes with axes, setting fire to what was left, and creating general havoc in any other way they could think of.[32]

The supply train was that of Confederate General Richard Ewell's corps. And Ewell was a fighter. So while some of Armstrong's division committed mayhem with the wagons, much of it found itself engaged with Southern infantrymen. Tom Custer led a mounted assault on another part of the train along with his older brother. Tom was the first man to jump his horse over barricades of crates and boxes and into the midst of the enemy, which poured a continuous and deadly fire of lead into the attackers. Tom seized the regimental colors of the Second Virginia Reserve Battalion, at the same time crying out for their surrender. At that precise instant, the Confederate color-bearer heaved up a huge Le Mat revolver and shot Tom point-blank in the face.

The pistol ball ripped through Tom's left cheek and tore its way out through the back of his neck. Burnt powder speckled his face like a handful of black pepper. The resolute young Custer grasped the standard in his left hand, dropped his saber, drew his own Colt Army revolver with his right, and shot the color sergeant, mortally wounding him.

General Armstrong cleared the barricade shortly thereafter. Instantly, his steed was shot out from under him by a rapidly retreating rebel. Scrambling to his feet shakily, Autie was confronted by the grisly specter of his younger brother, blood coursing down his powder-burned countenance in thin, red rivulets. Tom gasped, "Aut! The damn Rebels shot me, but I got their flag!"[33]

Tom then hauled on the reins of his charger to hurry on, but Armstrong clutched the horse's headstall, calling out in return, "Where do you think you are going?"

"After Ewell!" came the quick reply.

"You damn fool," said Autie, "can't you see you're bleeding like a stuck pig? Get to the rear and find a surgeon before you drop dead!"

"Is that an order?"

"That's an order."

The general then turned to his orderly-lieutenant, a Lieutenant James Christiancy. "Jim," he said, "conduct Captain Custer in arrest to the nearest ambulance. If he tries to get away, shoot him!"[34]

Chastised, Tom sullenly obeyed and probably by going to the rear to be patched up he avoided bleeding to death. Tom was, however, amply rewarded for both his conspicuous bravery and his compliance with the general's order. Winning his second Congressional Medal of Honor, he was breveted to a major in the cavalry division. Thus Tom was awarded two Medals of Honor, single-handedly seized two Confederate battle flags, and had two horses killed beneath him within one week's time—a Civil War precedent. He remains one of only nineteen American soldiers ever to win two Medals of Honor.[35] One researcher has compared Tom to other, better-known American war heroes: "As the only man to receive the Medal of Honor twice for separate actions, he was therefore the highest-decorated soldier of the Civil War and was to the Civil War what Alvin C. York was to World War I and Audie L. Murphy was to World War II."[36] He was also breveted again before the war ended to the rank of lieutenant colonel—almost as spectacular an ascendancy as that of his brother, relatively speaking.

After his brother's amazing feats, Armstrong wrote to Libbie in Washington: "When Tom first joined me, I was anxious concerning his conduct. But now I am as proud of him as can be, as soldier and brother. He has quit the use of tobacco, is moderate in drink, is respected and admired by officers and all who come in contact with him."[37] He was right on the last count, about the respect and admiration given to Tom, but wrong about the smoking and drinking—and it should be noted that he completely ignored little brother's gambling and interest in the numerous female camp followers.

Just as relations between Autie and Tom were more than cordial, relations with other officers and enlisted men were fairly good as well. The men were deferent toward the general's younger brother for his accomplishments and honors. Much to his liking, he received due respect from all in his own right—and not because he was the general's brother.

The young soldier bravely managed to get into the fight. Sayler's Creek was the last real battle of the war in Virginia. Witnessing the rout from high ground in the rear, Lee remarked grimly to an officer, "General, that half of our army is destroyed."[38]

The end came on April 9, 1865, at a little crossroads community named Appomattox Court House. Union troops had positioned themselves in front of Lee's line of march with other overwhelming forces on his flank and a large body of infantry pressing his rear. Marse Robert had fewer than 30,000 men with him by then, not half of whom were armed or in suitable military formations. The remainder were worn-out soldiers pathetically doing their best to keep up with the army but who could hardly be counted on in a battle.

Just as "Old Curly," as Autie was known by his men even though he was only twenty-five years of age, prepared to make a final, crushing blow on the sadly thin lines in Lee's front, out came a Confederate horseman, a white flag fluttering at the end of his staff, and an unexpected quiet settled on the field.

Armstrong, with the recuperating Tom mounted at his side, accepted the white flag of surrender from the Army of Northern Virginia.[39] While soldiers in both armies stared blankly at each other, unable to conceive of the fact that the fighting was actually over at last, Generals Grant and Lee made their individual ways into the little town to settle things for good.

For Thomas Ward Custer, the end of the War Between the States was anticlimactic. He had trained for over a year in preparation for distinguishing himself on the battlefield. Suddenly, just when he actually began striking some blows at the enemy, the fighting abruptly ceased.

At any rate, he seemed to take the shock to his system quite well. Like everyone else in the country, he felt relief that the horrible war that had split the nation had finally reached a satisfactory conclusion. He had a brevet lieutenant colonel's commission in his possession—a rank that seemed impossible when he enlisted as a private soldier a few years before—and a pair of medals jingling on his dress uniform. And he was a member of his famous brother's staff.

As such, his first assignment was to accompany Autie to Richmond where the division was stationed as soon as the Confederacy's surrender became final. At Armstrong's headquarters outside Richmond, Elizabeth returned to her husband. She was enthusiastically welcomed once again by Tom, the other staff officers, and hordes of grinning, jubilant troopers.[40] A rousing, joyous round of celebrations broke out to commemorate both the end of the war and the reunion of the intimate Custer family group. Old Curly, Libbie, and Tom were toasted and touted by adoring soldiers.

President Lincoln's assassination dampened but did not deny the American public their victory celebration. At the Grand Review in Washington, Autie rode at the head of his division. His mount, a recently acquired, high-strung thoroughbred named Don Juan, suddenly carried the gangling yet garish young major general, replete with his gaudy uniform, his anointed curls, and his deep-set blue eyes, into a headlong, unscheduled run. Some accused Custer of purposely riding at breakneck speed along the route of the Review, but it was entirely accidental. Armstrong at last calmly regained control of the animal and returned to the head of his division with subtle elan to quietly complete the march through the nation's capital city. Tom grinned unabashedly at Autie when the latter returned to the head of the division.[41]

After the Review, Libbie, the general, and his staff returned to their camp for a farewell review of the Third Cavalry Division. The cavalrymen cheered the boy general for a long time, until tears ran unashamed down his cheeks. Then they gave their other Custer hero a round of cheers. Finally came a resounding cheer for "Mrs. Custer!" Tom broke ranks to join his sister-in-law. "Ride forward, Libbie, and acknowledge it," he urged her good-naturedly. She lifted her horse's reins and the horse started up, but she suddenly checked her mount. "Oh, Tom, no! I can't bear it!" she whispered to him, her voice breaking imperceptibly. "It's sweet of them, but they mustn't see me crying so foolishly. It's all for Autie, anyway."[42]

The last was a proud but bitter pill for Tom to swallow. Although he was a hero as much as Autie, the division's cheers were primarily for his brother. The last review of the Third Cavalry Division became the close of the Civil War chapter of Tom's life. He had waited almost three years to join the glory-hunters while Autie grabbed a good share of the glory. When he finally joined his brother's command, Tom had only the final week of the war to gain renown of his own, but he took pride in his rapid accumulation of luster and public praise. He spent a year discovering that he truly enjoyed the life of an army officer, especially basking in the limelight cast by his general brother. For a time he would be satisfied with his portion of adulation.

3
INTERMISSION AND INTROSPECTION

Following the crisis and excitement of the Civil War, the late spring of 1865 served as a break in the life of Tom Custer. From wild charge to wild charge, the adventures of the Third Division headed by the boy general filled the Northern media. Powerful friends and favorable coverage in the press, however, were not the sole reasons for George Armstrong Custer's meteoric rise in rank. Tom's brother was a tenacious and fierce warrior. Because of his leadership, the division had captured 111 pieces of artillery, 65 battle flags, and almost 10,000 Confederate soldiers during the last six months of the war.

Tom was no less lost at the end of the fighting than his brother. He, too, was utterly fearless and desirous of more glorious conflicts. Directly after the end of the war, what remained of the Federal regular army was not demobilized. Instead, the upper echelon turned their attention south of the border to Mexico, where Benito Juarez and Porfirio Diaz determined to rid their homeland of Emperor Maximilian. More fighting was possible.

General Phil Sheridan had been appointed military governor of the Fifth Military District, the military division of the Southwest and Gulf encompassing Louisiana and Texas, with his headquarters at New Orleans. His orders were straightforward—protect this region where the rebellion was dying a slow death from the imperialistic ambitions of Louis Napoleon's puppet, Maximilian. In defiance of the Monroe Doctrine and taking advantage of America's all-but-suicidal altercation called the Civil War, the French had attempted to coerce Mexico into their empire. In addition, General Ulysses S. Grant, the highest-ranking American officer short of President Andrew Johnson, ordered his reliable old friend, Phil Sheridan, to "restore Texas and that part of Louisiana held by the enemy to the Union in the shortest practicable time, in a way more effectual for securing permanent peace."[1]

George Custer was the recipient of no end of offers because of his position as a war hero. A seat in Congress, the governorship of Michigan, all manner of places in private business, these were just a few of the honors offered by the grateful nation. Libbie was elated and Tom urged his brother to accept several of the "blushing honors" of public office.[2]

But Autie was less enthusiastic. A paladin, a chivalrous adventurer who missed the age of medieval knighthood, he respectfully declined to don any laurels other than those he won in battle to restore the Union. The red-tape honor of public office was simply not his cup of tea.

Nor was an army staff appointment in Washington. Even though offered by no less than General Grant himself, Autie had no desire or ambition to become a "featherbed soldier," any more than he had wanted to be an armchair officer during the war.[3]

Libbie was disappointed at first that her husband failed to accept one of the political appointments so lavishly laid out before him. Such jobs would have opened the way to endless rounds of parties, balls, and social life to which she had grown accustomed while she awaited Armstrong's call to her from Washington. She changed her tune, however, when her father, Judge Bacon, stepped in and admonished her after reading several of her complaining letters. "My Child," he wrote, "put no obstacles in the way to the fulfillment of his Destiny. He chose his profession; he is a born Soldier; there he must abide."[4]

Tom Custer was not so easily appeased as his sister-in-law. To him, Autie's acceptance of a political position or assignment to staff duty in Washington meant an answer to his own fervent, aspiring prayers. More than anything, he wanted to remain in the army. Like everyone else, he had obstacles to overcome. He assumed that he had to make his situation work for him as a whole person, not just in an isolated part of his life, like a career. But for everyone who told him that being the brother of a successful, famous person was not an obstacle, Tom wished they would try it for a while.

In the meantime, Tom had the opportunity to bask a little in his own fame. By the end of April 1865, he was home in Monroe on medical leave, where he was celebrated as "quite a hero in his own right." Libbie's father, Judge Bacon, took Tom under his wing. He wrote the general on April 13 that he took great pride in Tom's heroism and had gone to Mother Custer and Lydia Reed to dispel their fears about their boys in blue. A week later he wrote to Libbie:

"Tom, the young hero, has gone to the [Grand] Rapids to see Rebecca [Rebecca Richmond, a close girl friend of Libbie from Monroe]. I wanted him to go with me to Detroit on Monday but he declined. He is the lion of the day for one of his age and rank.

Many inquiries are made about him personally and by letter. He was made for the army and I hope he may be continued in service with a command and promotion."[5]

Rebecca Richmond and Libbie corresponded constantly. In a letter dated May 30, Rebecca described Tom's visit to Grand Rapids as well as her pleasure in meeting and getting to know him. "He is going to be much like Armstrong," she observed. "Under his air of abandon and carelessness he has great thoughtfulness and ambition. . . . He feels his lack of schooling and would make a devoted student could he once overcome the natural reluctance to entering school at his age."[6]

Tom wasn't the only attraction to awe the residents of Monroe. The day after Lee surrendered to Grant at Appomattox Court House, General Sheridan presented to Libbie the table on which the terms of surrender were written and signed. Judge Bacon also wrote, "The table is feasting on the eyes of many. Even the unlettered French look upon it in the light of an antiquarian." Apparently, Tom had carried the surrender table home with him from the war.[7]

He was not really driven to get ahead in the army. He wanted to be a great soldier, but he questioned his talent, even when Armstrong covered him with praise for his martial skills. He would have liked to be an important figure in the American military complex, but he did not have the ambition to make that happen. He preferred the comparatively soft, easy life of an army officer.

On May 14, 1865, the Judge wrote Libbie that Tom would leave Monroe early the next week. "Like all other soldiers he is restless and uneasy and wants to be with his command."[8]

Then, in the full-scale peace offensive about to be conducted by Phil Sheridan in Texas and Louisiana, General Custer was appointed chief of cavalry, Military District of Texas. Tom was pleased when he was picked to tag along as an aide-de-camp.

The Custer trio—George, Libbie, and Tom—followed "Little Phil" into the wild and woolly Southwest. George hastened to Texas to help Sheridan, "who desperately needed a man of mettle to help him clean out the hornet's nests of bounty jumpers, jayhawkers, moss troopers, brushwhackers, and scalawag carpetbaggers who were flagrantly riding roughshod over the lawless yucca country," as one historian wrote. Everyone in the upper ranks agreed that Custer was the man for the job. "I mean to endorse Gen'l Custer in a high degree," wrote General Grant to Secretary of War Edwin M. Stanton. Sheridan's sentiments were a matter of public record. "Custer, you're the only man that never failed me," he once said openly.[9]

Tom's devil-may-care attitude was often in evidence. On one occasion during the last week of June 1865, the steamboat chartered by the army to carry cavalry mounts, freight, and horse soldiers up the Red River into Texas was getting ready to depart its river quay. The skipper, a Captain Greathouse, put some officers and men on the cuff until they received the traveling expenses allotted them but not yet paid by the government.

"Tom, who had but 26 cents to his name, jingled it against a knife in his empty pocket and put on an air of affluence as the captain approached to offer his invitation. Before the offer could be made Tom majestically asked as to the cost of the trip because, he explained, it was his rule to pay in advance. This was too much for Autie. Hurriedly he left so that his laughter would not be viewed by the hospitable captain."[10]

The long journey from Monroe, Michigan, to Texas was a revitalizing vacation for Autie and Libbie. Tom looked upon it more as an extended, frolicsome adventure. They went by train from Monroe to Louisville, Kentucky, then by steamboat to New Orleans and Alexandria, Louisiana. While his brother and sister-in-law spent quiet, uneventful evenings together, Tom could be found down in the steamer's saloon, drinking and playing cards with the riverboat gamblers. He ran into one slick card sharp who used a highly polished, smooth-surfaced ring to observe what cards he dealt the pigeon of an army officer across the table from him. Tom learned a valuable lesson about poker that night.

While Autie and Libbie enjoyed their trip together, the general also made time for his little brother. Autie and Tom amused themselves by taking pot shots at the numerous alligators sunning themselves on the riverbanks. Every morning and each evening they would have a shooting match. Autie fired a new rifle purchased for him by a Washington, D.C., friend in honor of his wartime accomplishments. Libbie wrote to Rebecca Richmond that although she did not approve of their hunting, Autie was pleased with his new gun after he managed to put a ball right behind the eye of one of the gators.[11]

When the boat stopped and blacks formed long lines to carry ricks of already chopped wood on board to fuel the big boilers, Tom often took the opportunity to go ashore, especially when a town was nearby. Almost invariably there were young Southern belles from plantations in the vicinity and always local female entertainment in the riverfront villages, servicing the boatmen and itinerant travelers. The twenty-year-old had grown susceptible to the wiles of women when he observed the camp followers during the war, and there seemed no better way to humble the defeated Southerners than to level attention on their womenfolk who had been set up on pedestals during the antebellum years. Not a few of those called upon by Tom and the other Yankee officers had been plantation-bred ladies before the war.

Former Southern belles were not the only remnants of plantation life that the Custers witnessed in the deep South. In early July, 1865, Armstrong wrote to Judge Bacon from Alexandria at the conclusion of the steamboat trip:

When the wagons are loaded we will start for Texas. . . . This country is wholly unlike Virginia. It is more like notions formed from 'Uncle Tom's Cabin.' Slavery was not as mild as in States whose proximity to Free States made kindness desirable to prevent the enslaved from seeking freedom across the border. The knowledge that runaways would have to traverse hundreds of miles of slave or hostile country placed slaves at the mercy of their owners, in the Red River country, and every plantation had its Simon Legree and humble Uncle Tom. In the mansion where I now write is a young negro woman whose back bears the scars of 500 lashes given at one time, for going beyond the limits of her master's plantation. If the War has attained nothing else, it has placed America under a debt of gratitude for all time—for removal of this evil.[12]

Southern womanhood and the horrors of slavery presented two aspects of the remnants of the war that Autie and Tom confronted in Alexandria. A third soon raised its ugly head. While provisioning his new command, the Second Volunteer Cavalry Division, elements that swore he would never reach Texas alive challenged Custer and his staff. Alexandria seemed to Tom to be a vermin and varmint ridden pesthole. Some of the varmints turned out to be soldiers of the division. They were seasoned, veteran cavalrymen of the Union armies in the West and Trans-Mississippi West, accustomed to the loose discipline of the commanders of those forces. Just when most of the other soldiers of the North were going home, these men had been exiled instead to the dull routine of border patrol along the Rio Grande River, the Texas-Mexico boundary, or to restoring law and order to Texas after the collapse of the Confederate government. Smoldering ferment erupted in outbursts of insubordination—in one case, Tom just barely escaped a fistfight with an enlisted man—and desertion. A full-scale mutiny of Sheridan's cavalry forces seemed imminent until Custer put his small-booted foot down.

Part of one regiment, the Second Wisconsin Cavalry, became a mob bent on mayhem. A crowd of troopers aided by several officers assaulted the regimental commander, threatening him and demanding his resignation. Custer arrested sixteen officers and reduced seventy-six noncommissioned officers to the ranks.[13]

Another problem was with troops who took advantage of the civilian population. Texans feared their Yankee protectors more than those from whom they were being protected. Custer and his officers adopted severe measures to control this lawless element. One of his orders was an example of the heavy discipline: "Every enlisted man committing depredations on the persons or property of citizens will have his head shaved, and, in addition, will receive twenty-five lashes on his back, well laid on." Many in the North denounced him for "flogging men who had fought for their country, while favoring those who had turned traitor to it."[14]

Desertion was another problem. Fully supported by Tom, if not by other more lenient staff members, George arrested an insubordinate sergeant and a recaptured deserting private, both of the Third Michigan Cavalry regiment. The pair received summary courts-martial with sentences to be shot. The regiment threatened Custer with death if the sentences were carried out.

Tom encouraged the general not to be present on the day set

for the execution or, failing that, to at least carry a revolver for self-defense. Not only did George refuse both suggestions, he ordered Tom and the regimental staff to appear unarmed, too. Custer rode nonchalantly before the tense, glaring regiment assembled in the town square. The prisoners were prepared. Custer shouted: "If any man of you has a mind to take my life, let him do so now." Taken aback, the troopers made no response. "Very well, Major," he said, turning to the provost marshal, "carry out the execution." At the last possible moment, he personally jerked the sergeant out of the line of fire, letting the private fall into his grave.[15]

The grisly lesson made an impact on the impressionable minds of the soldiers. The Texas experience developed into nothing more than occupation duty, with occasional policing actions thrown in for good measure. The primary military excitement sprouted from lengthy route marches "through reeking pine barrens, over dust-gagging flats and hog-wallow prairie" by some of the sullen forty-five hundred men of the Second Cavalry Division.[16]

The ordinary Texas citizens reconciled themselves to the occupation forces so long as the Yankee troops protected them and their property from freebooters from both the North and the South. So Tom rode and learned from his brother to be merciless to his men and animals on campaign. He did not seem to notice that Armstrong pushed himself as hard as he did his troopers and horses. Instead, Tom reveled in his position of authority.

When he was in garrison, Tom had—as Libbie wrote about Autie—"fine opportunities every day for making a fortune in land, or cotton, or horses, or in buying Gov't claims," but the general advised Tom against investing while he remained in the service. With little outside his commitments as Armstrong's aide, he fell back on his old habits of gambling and escorting young women to entertain himself. Traits such as these did little to endear Tom to the common soldiers of the command.[17]

In these pursuits, Tom had plenty of company. Most of the Civil War staff accompanied them to Texas—George Yates, a friend from Monroe, was an officer along on this duty, as he would be to the end. Throughout their lives, the Custers liked to surround themselves with friends and relatives.

As the division trotted out of Louisiana and east Texas bayous and onto the flat, dry prairie, new entertainments replaced the younger Custer's vices. Rabbits increased in size and number, and hunting them with one or more of Autie's hounds was great sport.[18] "Horseback riding is one of our chief pleasures," George wrote, although it is hard to imagine taking pleasure in riding before or after a day's march across the hot, insect-ridden Texas plains. Tom and other staff officers rode with the general and his lady, which sometimes caused their embarrassment. About Libbie her husband wrote, "You should see her ride across the Texas prairies at such gait that even some of the staff officers are left behind."[19]

At Hempstead, Texas, the division established a semi-permanent camp. "Here Lieutenant Jacob Greene and his new bride, Nettie Humphrey, joined up," wrote historian Stephen E. Ambrose. "Nettie was Libbie's old friend from Monroe; Greene had served with Custer during the war and was glad to be back in the Army after failing in civilian life as an insurance salesman. Together with Tom, George Yates, and other Custer hangers-on, they went on late-afternoon hunting parties, held dances, played jokes on each other, and generally did their best to enjoy the situation."[20]

Because he liked surrounding himself with family, George summoned the boys' father from Michigan to the Lone Star State as forage master for the division of occupation. The old man apparently had never outgrown his pioneer spirit, so he quickly fit in with the group with "little to do and fine pay," which was a splendid reason for fulfilling his wanderlust.[21]

Forage master Emmanuel Custer, General George, and Aide Tom began on the prairie around Hempstead a custom that lasted throughout the brothers' careers on the American Great Plains. They rode to the hunt with those noisy packs of Autie's hounds. Beginning early in the morning, the family set out in search of game. For the space of perhaps half an hour after dawn, the world stood bathed in morning's freshness, in its coolness, in its bright cleansing light. For that half hour the Texas horizons were sharp lines in the distance. Then the coolness went away and a faint heat fog began to rise, the enveloping dust settled on the hunters, and the excitement of the hunt took control. Antelope, buffalo, deer— any sort of big game was fair game.

Once, overcome with the thrill of chasing his prey, Tom accidentally shot one of Autie's beloved dogs—and was never allowed to forget it. Said brother Autie, "Oh, Tom's a good shot, a sure aim. He's sure to hit something!" Contemporary newspaper reporters saw the humor in the situation. Clippings appeared on Tom's dresser, too, pertinent to the accident. For instance, "An editor went hunting the other day, for the first time in 22 years, and he was lucky enough to bring down an old farmer by a shot in the leg. The distance was 66 yards."[22]

Poor Libbie detested hunting. She managed to condone the bodies of dead animals only through sheer willpower. Yet she philosophically reconciled herself to Autie's hunting habits. She realized that dogs, horses—as well as the army—would always rival her for the general's attentions. Tom sympathized with her regarding the matter. He agreed with the black servant, Eliza, whom the Custers had picked up in Virginia and brought along with them to the Southwest, when she said, "You keer more for those pesky, sassy old hounds than you does for Miss Libbie. I'd be 'shamed if I was you. What would your Mother Custer think of you now?"[23]

Tom tried to shield Libbie from the results of the expeditions in Texas. He was not then so callous as to tease his adorable sister-in-law with dead game.

The fall of 1865 found the Second Cavalry Division moved to Austin. Hunting gave way to horse-racing. "Now, Father, don't wrinkle up your brows when I tell you that we race horses," wrote Elizabeth. "Autie is considered the best judge of a horse here. . . . We now have 3 running horses and a fast pony, none of which has been beaten."[24] With horse-racing, Tom found a new, enjoyable method of gambling away his lieutenant colonel's pay. Autie had the time of his life while at the same time meeting the challenge of taming Texas, pulling the "erring Sister" back into the fold. His conspicuous dress, his fearlessness, and his endurance made him a celebrity in both the Division and Texas. The provisional governor, Alexander J. Hamilton, recounted the general's "wise and efficient conduct of an affair as much administrative as military." His superior, Sheridan, recommended that he be made a full major general in the regular army.[25]

When George's enlistment ran out in January 1866, he returned to his regular rank of captain. With no one to support him in his army vocation, Tom was also to be mustered out. He and Emmanuel headed back to Monroe to contemplate their next moves.

Contemplation was something that Tom did a lot of while in Texas and afterward. The families of famous persons have a tougher life than meets the eye. To the inexperienced observer, Tom's existence seemed all glitter and ease, free from worries, but he knew the struggle and pain of understanding himself outside the strong identity of Autie, whose image was dignified by success, fame, and a special aura that virtually bordered on royalty. The fight to define himself outside Armstrong's sphere of influence left scars.

Choosing a career in a field other than the army might have helped the younger Custer separate himself from his famous brother. He could then have met the challenge with spirit and willfulness to discover who he was. Tom, however, still felt influenced by the sibling rivalry of childhood and still believed that he had a model of some sort in Autie that had to be followed or discarded— or some combination of the two. He should instead have searched for his own separate, unique identity. If he were ever to break out of Autie's sphere of influence and create a life of his own, the year immediately after the end of the war was the time.

Had young Tom Custer given up his connection to allow others to approve him, he might have followed his own path. After all, being a hometown hero and having another hometown hero as a brother was not something he had arranged, but he chose to stay close to his brother, now the leader of the family. He used Armstrong as a connection to get himself where he wanted to be. The connections got him there, but, as he learned when he was home on leave before boarding the steamer for Texas, they didn't keep him there. Instead of giving him an urgent confidence, realization of that fact left him at loose ends. He chose to remain in Autie's circle. Many soldiers still in the service and many veterans and their families resented his use of the general as an advantage. As a result, sometimes even his best efforts were berated.

Tom's self-esteem was further belittled by his recognition that being the second-to-youngest son of the Custer brood lowered his family's expectations of him. George's perfectionism dampened the ardor which Tom could have put to use bettering himself. Rather than letting his self-esteem be more important than his need for approval, he strove at times to outshine the general. He would never feel secure unless he was the best, to his disappointment, because outdoing the great boy general was a desperate goal throughout Tom's entire life.

Brooding about his problems only made them worse, of course. Since he indicated to his superior that he wished to remain in the army, Tom awaited further word about an appointment. By the middle of 1866, little more than a year after the end of the war, the military establishment had been all but dismantled. The authorized strength of the army was only 54,641 officers and men. The actual strength of the regular army was a mere 38,540.[26] Tom returned to small Monroe to lollygag around with his old cohorts while Autie was ordered to Washington to appear before the Joint Committee on Reconstruction. George gave testimony that Southerners in Texas and Louisiana were unrepentant and required military control to maintain order.[27] Unlike Tom, George then set off on a fortune-hunting trip to New York City, hoping to find something to help him spend his time profitably until he got a new assignment. He had a wife to support, after all, and Libbie had come to expect to be supported in high style. Armstrong could hardly afford to do so on the meager wages of a lowly captain.[28]

While in Washington, Autie asked for regular Army commissions for Tom, George Yates, and Jacob Greene. He was unable to secure a commission for Greene, who returned to the insurance business. "In the case of George W. Yates he was more successful," wrote Lawrence Frost, one of the most thorough Custer biographers. "Yates had been breveted a lieutenant colonel. On March 26, 1866, he was commissioned a second lieutenant in the 2nd U.S. Cavalry."[29]

Tom had been breveted lieutenant colonel during the war, too, and his commission actually was approved nearly a month before that of Yates. However, when his commission as second lieutenant came on February 23, 1866, it was a little disappointing. Secretary of War Edwin Stanton honored Autie's request but appointed Tom a second lieutenant in the First U.S. Infantry.[30]

Unfortunately, although his reputation stood unblemished, Autie's reputation in his old military academy class prevented him from claiming a higher rank than captain. This was the case, even though two of the three former Confederates to later hold the rank of general in the United States Army—Fitzhugh Lee and Joseph Wheeler—had also graduated at the bottom of their respective West Point classes. Additionally, many of the officers who had risen to the brevet rank of major general of volunteers—such as Benjamin Grierson and Andrew J. Smith—were given the ranks of full colonel and their own regiments to command. The nation had grown weary of the military during four long years of war—it was now more interested in cutting back the army, not worrying about reserving honorable places in it for their heroes. Tom was lucky indeed to have a commission at all.

Nevertheless, society and the business and political circles of the country began to revolve around George Armstrong Custer. He was a personality, a name everyone knew, and a crush of other celebrities flocked around to wine and dine him. All the while he longed to be in the saddle at the head of cavalry troopers again.

Near the middle of May, 1866, Tom enjoyed none of the attention Armstrong received. The better part of a year had passed and still no word came about his future with the infantry. His glowing tales of the bloody battles that earned him two Medals of Honor and a scar across his cheek, which he often tried to conceal by keeping a left profile to photographers, grew thin with their telling and retelling. He became too nervous with anxiety to enjoy himself with his typical pastimes. Then, on Friday, May 18, he was summoned urgently to the home of old Judge Bacon, where Libbie stayed while George gallivanted around in the East. The judge died suddenly of heart disease—Tom was all the Custer family Elizabeth could call upon immediately to ease her despair.

It took him next to no time to get to her side. After grieving for a while over Judge Bacon's remains, Tom and his sister-in-law stepped outside to get some fresh air. There for a moment both stood silent, thinking of three small graves and one larger one in the shaded cemetery not far away. The Bacons' two tiny daughters had died in infancy and later a fine, promising young little boy passed away, too. Libbie's mother had also passed away a few years before. Now with her father gone, she had only the Custers as family. She had been the Bacons' sole surviving child and as such all their devotion had been centered upon her. Tom gently put his arm around her to comfort her a moment more before hurrying to the telegraph office to wire Autie.[31]

Armstrong rushed to Monroe for the funeral. The whole town, it seemed, mourned with Elizabeth Bacon Custer the loss of her father and the town's most venerable citizen. The hero's homecoming after mustering out was darkened by the gloomy shadow that shrouded the town with the passing of the judge.

After her father was laid to rest, Libbie sat at a writing desk illuminated by a glass-globed oil lamp to write in her diary: "I would be far more miserable but for Armstrong's care. He keeps me out-of-doors as much as he can. I do not wear deep mourning. He is opposed to it. . . . Armstrong is thinking of going to Mexico. The Gov't there offered him handsome inducements. I am opposed to it. I do not want him ever to go into battle again. But if he goes, I shall go with him."[32]

So would Tom. The two tight-knit brothers talked with ever-increasing enthusiasm about heading south of the border to join the fighting with Mexican revolutionaries Benito Juarez and Porfirio Diaz, especially since it appeared that after six months there was slim chance of their seeing any action in the American army. The "handsome inducements" Libbie mentioned consisted of an offer of a commission to George as major general of caballeros, adjutant general of the revolutionary armies in Mexico, and an annual salary of $16,000 in gold—a princely sum to entice a self-appointed prince. This was guaranteed provided that Custer bring with him no fewer than a thousand mounted volunteers, the expense of which would fall upon the provisional government of Juarez.[33]

Tom eagerly told the general that they would have no trouble rounding up a thousand recruits—why, there must have been that many of the old Wolverine Brigade willing to join them in Michigan alone. They became even more enthusiastic when George received a wire from the boys' former commander, fire-eating Phil Sheridan. Ulysses S. Grant had sent a recommendation for Custer to Don Matias Romero, the Mexican ambassador in Washington.

Captain Custer applied for a twelve-month leave of absence for "special duty in Mexico as military attache . . . to the army of independence and deputy defender of the Monroe Doctrine."[34] Once more, political chicanery cooled Armstrong's heels. He was granted a leave of absence but was forbidden to leave the country.

Tom, who had planned to apply for a leave of his own as soon as Autie's arrived so that they could trek to Mexico together, was left high and dry. He still awaited orders. His spirits rose somewhat when George informed him that Secretary of War Stanton offered him the colonelcy of one of the ten new cavalry regiments of the increased regular army—the Ninth U.S. Cavalry, a regiment of African-American enlisted men—but Tom was nonplussed to discover that the ambitious Armstrong had bigger fish to fry. He applied for appointment to the post of Inspector General of the United States Cavalry.[35]

Well, after some consideration, Tom decided that that would be all right. After all, if he could use Autie in the capacity of colonel of an all-black regiment, how much more useful would he prove to be if he held such an influential political as well as military position?

The fortunes of life, however, frowned again. Political hacks in Washington concluded that Captain Custer would best be preserved in a subordinate (and hence politically safe) role. Tom's hopes were shot down again.

July came and was nearly over, and Tom was losing all confidence about his destiny with the army. He was nearly resigned to serving as a second lieutenant in the infantry. On July 28, thanks to the persuasive powers of General Grant, George accepted a commission as lieutenant colonel—Tom's brevet rank—of the recently raised Seventh U.S. Cavalry regiment. He got orders to report to Fort Riley, Kansas, where the outfit would organize in the fall.

When Tom heard this, without getting word of anything for himself, he reached the depths of despair. He became as depressed with his life as he ever would. The next few days were uncertain, anxious days of readjustment, drifting, groping, and grasping.

Without the blazing glory of war he was haunted by a hazy sort of grandeur left over from his achievements of over a year before. He felt as though he was fast becoming a has-been, an anachronistic although youthful soldier. He even considered resigning, as so many others already had.

At last, in August, a telegram arrived from Washington. Thomas Ward Custer had been transferred and was to join his brother in the Seventh United States Cavalry regiment.

The period from May 1865 to August 1866 was a time for reflection for Tom Custer. He examined in his own mind his tempestuous decline from war hero in his own right to shadowy introvert. From the hunting trips on the plains of Texas to a graveyard in Michigan, from a lieutenant colonel and aide to his brother the general to prospective Mexican filibuster, he reexamined his thought processes as well as his past and his future. It became for him one of the few interludes of his lifetime when, even while he was physically close to George, he had to fend for himself. It might have been the time for Tom to break away from Autie's influence and make his own way. Instead, it became clear to Tom just how loyal he was and how much he depended on his brother for security. He had not looked forward to being a junior officer in an infantry regiment, far removed from the aid and abetment of Armstrong. Now he could look forward to being a cavalry officer with his brother.

4

INTO KANSAS AND BACK
TO THE SERVICE

In the early autumn of 1866, Libbie Custer resided in a native limestone house on the Kansas prairie. She sat at one of the small writing tables on which General Robert E. Lee had signed the surrender at Appomattox in April 1865. The table was a gift to her from General Phil Sheridan. She wrote:

As I had heard more and more about Indians since reaching Kansas, a vision of the enclosure where we would eventually live was a great comfort to me. I could scarcely believe that the buildings, a story and a half high, were all there were at Fort Riley. No trees and hardly any vegetation except Buffalo grass that curled its sweet blades close to the ground as it protected the nourishment it held from the blazing sun. The plains as they waved away on all sides of us, like the surface of a vast ocean, had the charm of a great novelty and the absence of trees was at first forgotten in the fascination of seeing such an immense stretch of country, with soft undulations of green turf rolling on, seemingly to the setting sun.[1]

Mrs. General Custer penned this description of her first impression of Kansas after her arrival at Fort Riley on October 16, 1866. The Custers enjoyed the acclaim of the populace of Kansas, including the newspaper of the nearby town, the *Junction City Union.* Equally glowing descriptions undoubtedly reached Tom.[2]

Tom had re-entered the army on February 23, 1866, as soon as his original enlistment expired, and impatiently waited for orders. He was less than satisfied to find himself assigned as a second lieutenant of the First U.S. Infantry. After much complaining to his superiors and to Autie, matters changed rapidly in the early summer of 1866. George, second-in-command of the Seventh Cavalry, knew very well that an officer had ways of doing things, as Ralph Andrist has said, so that if black could not be made to appear white, it could at least be given a gray tinge. Thus Tom was allowed to resign from the First Infantry on July 27, 1866.[3] The next day Autie appointed him first lieutenant with the Seventh Cavalry.[4]

George had hoped to be posted at Fort Garland in the Rocky Mountains where the hunting was said to be excellent, but he went as ordered in late October to Fort Riley. He and Libbie arrived at the post on October 16 according to the *Junction City Union* of October 20, 1866. He reported for duty on November 1. He told Tom to be at the fort shortly thereafter.[5]

Tom took the train to Topeka, Kansas. The railroad had only just been completed the previous summer as far as Fort Riley, so connections were still unsure from the state capital of Kansas to the military post. A state coach carried him the remainder of the distance.

Occasionally the stage rolled and slid down the sides of ravines along the military road, struck rocky bottom with jarring impact and tilted forward, throwing Tom and his fellow passengers around in their seats. The military road stretched from Fort Leavenworth to Fort Riley and was one of the several similar byways that spread an army web over Kansas connecting the numerous military enclaves scattered throughout the state. Because of the quirks of the Kansas climate, although it was November a dull warmth clung on with the sinking sun, and the dust was a screen through which the passengers blearily viewed one another. The dust dampened normal breathing; it coated the faces of all, and presently those faces turned slick with sweat and a wetness that grew gray and streaked as it formed small rivulets. The smell of the coach became rank with the odors of bodies rendering out their moisture, and the confinement changed from mere discomfort to cramped pain.

The young lieutenant who finally stepped from the coach at the end of the ride was a man of light complexion who spoke with a gentle, seductive voice rather than that of an officer. He wore a blue shirt of the U.S. cavalry, and over his skinny shoulders stretched a pair of yellow braces (Yankees called them that—Southerners knew them as suspenders), which held his trousers high on his waist. On top of his wavy blond hair set a forage cap, tugged low on his forehead. A blue blouse, as the short jackets were called, kept him warm against the coolness of advancing evening.

When he stepped down, sharp-scented dust rose beneath his booted feet and the fragrance of the earth was strong—"the harsh and vigorous emanations of the earth itself." Tom, from a farm background, realized why settlers wanted to wrest the land from the nomadic Indians.[6]

He reported for duty with the Seventh Cavalry on November 12, 1866. From that point forward, his fate was cast as surely as if it were in bronze.

Before being reunited with Libbie and Armstrong, Tom found his bunk in the officers' quarters and got outfitted properly. At the commissary or the suttler's store he picked up all he would need as a cavalryman: underwear, socks, field boots and garrison shoes, two wool shirts, blue officers' blouse and blue pants with the yellow stripes of the cavalry down the outside seams of the legs, forage cap and campaign hat, his saber and its scabbard, carbine and sling, Army Colt revolver, ammunition, cartridge bandolier, canteen, mess kit, saddle bags, bridle, hobbles and picket pins and McClellan saddle, an overcoat, a rubber poncho with a hole in its center, wool gloves and a pair of collar ornaments with the cavalry's crossed sabers, the regimental number seven above and troop letter "A" below. His striker would later collect the incidental items such as entrenching tools, housewife kit, lariat, soap, comb, blankets, a straw tick mattress, a box of shoe polish and a dauber, curry comb, and brush for Tom's horse.[7]

As soon as was possible, the new lieutenant crossed the parade ground of Fort Riley to visit his brother and sister-in-law and become familiar with his surroundings. He found Autie and his wife firmly ensconced in their quarters. He also discovered an addition to the household—Libbie had persuaded one of her childhood chums and schoolmates from Michigan to make the trip to the plains with her. She was a gay, curly-haired blonde who preferred to be called by the fashionable name "Diana," although her real name was Anna Darrah. She had been the reigning queen of Monroe, so it was natural for Tom, the twenty-one-year-old bachelor, to strike up a friendship with her.[8]

When he entered the Custer residence at Fort Riley, Tom saw the interior as Libbie described it in a letter to her cousin, Rebecca

Richmond, in Grand Rapids:

Our houses are not built side by side, but they are double except the Commanders house next to ours. The halls of each house are at the end so we are separate from each other as need be. The houses all have wide verandas. Our house has a large parlor, my bedroom back of it and dressing room next to that at the end of the hall. We have a back entry and Eliza's [the African American servant from Virginia] room at the rear. Four chambers upstairs. Anna's the front room with a dressing room off from it.[9]

It did not take Autie's most powerful persuasive efforts to persuade Tom to abandon the officers' barracks in favor of the comforts of the Custer house. Tom moved into a room at the head of the stairs.[10] Directly below was a large kitchen and spacious dining room, both of which were the pride of Elizabeth's life at the post, because none of the other officers' wives had either in their quarters. The house was cheery and pleasant, and sunlight brightened the parlor all day long. As Libbie said, "As yet, we have not a house *crowded* with furniture, but enough to be comfortable."[11] When Tom moved in, the Custer household was complete once more.

William Tecumseh Sherman, famed for his march through Georgia and now commander of the Military Division of the Missouri, may have been one of the first to welcome Tom to his new home. Sherman had been present to greet George and his female entourage. He remarked upon meeting Libbie, "Child, you'll find the air of the Plains is like champagne."[12]

One man that Tom surely met his first day at Fort Riley was the colonel of the Seventh, Andrew J. Smith, who arrived the same day as Tom. Smith had graduated from West Point in 1838 and gained a good deal of experience in the West during his early service. He had been a close friend of Stephen Kearny, who had started Armstrong on his rise during the war and with whom Smith marched to California during the Mexican War. In the Civil War, Smith made a distinguished although not outstanding record. He commanded a corps and was one of Sherman's trusted officers. He served at Vicksburg and on Bank's Red River campaign. He had led both cavalry and infantry. Two things about Smith rankled with Autie: his brevet rank was major general, the same as that of Custer, yet he commanded the regiment and Custer was his subordinate. Second, Smith was one of the few men to defeat the great Confederate cavalry leader Nathan Bedford Forrest, a feat which he accomplished during the battle at Tupelo, Mississippi, on July 14, 1864, and for which he was as well known in the army as Armstrong was for all his accomplishments. Smith assumed command of Fort Riley as ranking officer, was designated commander of the District of the Upper Arkansas, and headed up the Seventh.[13]

Getting familiar with the new regiment, Tom and Armstrong soon found that the enlisted men at Fort Riley were a mixed lot. The soldiers they found on the post were regular army or volunteers whose enlistments were fast running out. They were not crack troops. They were men stationed too long in a backward, desolate world where discipline and training relaxed concurrently with morale. Of the recruits filling the ranks of the Seventh, a few veterans re-enlisted but many of the others were recently arrived immigrants, healthy and sturdy enough but able to speak very little English. Another large contingent was formed from a core of veteran Confederate soldiers who were sensitive, critical, and resentful of the Yankee hero's authority. Many of them joined up chiefly to secure free transportation across the country to the West seeking their fortunes; some of these men planned to desert at the first opportunity to hurry on to the Colorado gold mines around Denver, opened in the late 1850s and early 1860s. Few of the recruits had any cavalry experience, and the first mounts that arrived for their use proved to be largely wild and unbroken mustangs. The Custer boys set to work nonetheless with undaunted energy. George told Libbie, "I'm going to make this into the best regiment on the plains."[14]

Tom became familiar with the Seventh's officers as well. They arrived at the post one by one to take the places of those who departed after being transferred to other posts. One man that Tom was elated to find in the Seventh was George Yates, a friend and officer from Civil War days. Others among the new officers were Captain Louis Hamilton, a grandson of the famous American, Alexander Hamilton. Another was Captain Myles Keogh, a jovial Irish-born soldier of fortune who had once served at the Vatican, and there was also Lieutenant Nowlan, another Irishman. Canadian-born Lieutenant William Cooke was an expert shot, with the most luxuriant Dundreary sideburns in the command; Cooke would eventually become one of the central figures in "the Custer gang," the intimate circle of the Seventh's officer cadre that supported and depended upon Autie. Mike Sheridan, brother of General Phil Sheridan, was among the officers, too. Lieutenant Myles Moylan shared duties at Company A with Tom.[15]

Three bugbears that would haunt the future of the Custers also existed in the ranks of the Seventh's officers. Captain Frederick Benteen, who was a brevet brigadier general and cavalryman in the Trans-Mississippi West during the war, was white-haired and fresh-faced, but with a sharp and sardonic tongue. He was an efficient officer—he had audaciously arrested his own father, a Southern sympathizer, early in the war—and from the first he was critical of George Custer, six years his junior, partly because Autie outranked him but also because he believed Custer to be over-ambitious, under-cautious, and very unmilitary.[16] The senior major was Wyckliffe Cooper. He has been described as a "Kentuckian who had served with distinction in the Federal cavalry, had been a manic depressive, and had drunk himself into a fool's paradise."[17] Major Joel Elliott, who came to be a respected member of the Custer gang, would become the third of the Seventh's officers to stalk the lives of the Custers.[18]

The events involving these three men rested in the near future. For the first few weeks, Tom should have settled into the routine of regimental life. It would be spring before the Seventh demonstrated any unit solidarity, so the officers spent a good deal of their time whipping their companies into shape.

The worst error a new lieutenant could make in an outfit was to try to be popular with the troops. Also, the long-service noncommissioned officers—and even with the Seventh, most of them had plenty of service—expected respect, and they got it. Apparently, Tom knew a sergeant who scared hell out of new second lieutenants. He could reply "sir" to them in a way that made it a reprimand and left them squirming.[19]

Like most officers, Tom came to loggerheads with such noncoms and his troops as well. But generally, accustomed as he was to being separated from the enlisted men, he kept to his side of "the line." The line was the invisible but very real barrier that separated officers and enlisted men who were not sergeants. In garrison, sergeants had their own separate rooms in recognition of their status apart from the corporals and privates, who shared the company quarters.[20]

The privates' first loyalty was to their company, not to their officers. These soldiers of Tom's company were the men with whom he would sleep and eat, march and fight and if need be, die. They enlisted for five years, all of which time would normally be spent in the company to which they were originally assigned. Promotions were made by "the old man," or company commander, and hard-core soldiers occasionally re-enlisted to serve additional years in the same company. The company loyalty and rugged regimen of the time spent in garrison duty fostered a crude combination of individualism and group identity. Lieutenants Myles Moylan and Tom Custer confronted the uncowed troopers mornings and afternoons in drill and training.[21]

During the day, Tom was an officer in Company A, but during the evenings he became the gay, light-hearted younger brother of the Seventh's famous lieutenant colonel. Although the Custers by no means enjoyed overt luxury, they were financially better off than they had ever been before. Elizabeth elaborated in her letter to Cousin Rebecca:

I have bought Autie a lovely black cane seated and backed arm chair.... I have an oak and green carpet—a green and black tablecloth on a round table and albums, card basket, book rack, etc. on it; another round table we use for a writing table. Our chairs are quite comfortable and the wood fire in the place makes the room very cheerful. I have lace curtains like mother's and put up like hers. My easel stands by one of the windows and I am just finishing a picture for Autie when he returns, of a bulldog smoking a pipe.[22]

Into this cozy atmosphere, Cooke and Elliott and others of the

Custer enclave entered frequently for sociable evenings. Less often, all the regiment's officers were invited to the Custer home.

There was probably a positive correlation between money and authority on one side and achievement by both Custer boys on the other. Their assignment to Fort Riley put them back to work and back in their element. Armstrong had scratched his way to a command that would eventually see action; he contrived to bring brother Tom to Kansas, too. Each had money coming in and a relatively soft life. Modern research reveals that offspring of large middle-class families do as well, achievement-wise, as children of smaller middle-class families. No evidence supports the popular belief that large family size has a negative effect on the ability of the children to excel. George and Tom exemplified this fact. It was a simple case of the more they got, the more they wanted; therefore, the harder they tried to get it.

Paul I. Wellman, authority on the American West during the 1930s and 1940s, relates that "because the Cheyennes and Sioux went north to carry on their warfare, the summer of 1866 was comparatively quiet in Kansas."[23] The spring of 1867 brought the Indians back to the central plains. Early that year, General Winfield Scott Hancock, an older officer known to the Custers through his wartime service in the Army of the Potomac, prepared to show the red warriors that the "government is ready and able to punish them if they are hostile, although it may not . . . invite war."[24]

Unfortunately for Tom, he would not be going with Hancock and the Seventh. He began suffering from the severe pains of rheumatism. He had recently undergone the examination before the army examining board in Washington and had passed, but he had not been well for some time. While in Texas he contracted breakbone fever, an infectious, eruptive, tropical disease transmitted by mosquitoes that manifested its presence by a high fever, sore throat, and severe pains in all muscles and joints. Tom and Libbie both had attacks of the fever, the former suffering occasional inflammatory rheumatism for more than a year afterward. Now it flared up again.[25]

Rheumatism may also have run in the Custer family. Old Emmanuel sometimes suffered from its effects, but that was usually attributed to his age. More substantially, Nevin Custer, the only brother who did not join the army, was afflicted with chronic rheumatism. He had responded to the call for volunteers during the late war but to his relief had been rejected at the Cleveland recruiting office because of his affliction. Rheumatism may have saved his life, because he was the only male member of the family to survive into his twilight years.

Exhaustive research has failed to turn up much information about Tom's health with the exception of a casual remark by Libbie in a letter to Rebecca Richmond: "Tom is now quite sick, he is lame with rheumatism. But the Doctors think he will be around in a few days."[26]

In spite of Libbie's optimism, he evidently grew progressively but slowly worse. He remained on duty with Company A throughout the month of December 1866. The Fort Riley post returns of January, February, March, and April, 1867, list him on sick call but do not specify the nature of his illness.[27] However, he was not so seriously ill as to necessitate hospitalization; he was not admitted to the post hospital, nor does his name appear on the registers of sick and wounded for the Seventh Cavalry. Garry D. Ryan, Chief of the Navy and Old Army Branch, Military Archives Division, National Archives, has suggested that "perhaps he was treated privately in his quarters instead of at the Fort Riley hospital, this accounting for the lack of specific information."[28] Since rest and large doses of quinine were the treatment, and because there was an important connection between who one knew or to whom one was related and how many privileges one received, it can be assumed that Tom was indeed treated at the Custer residence.

At any rate, Tom was too incapacitated to leave with his company when the Seventh departed for its first campaign, commanded by General Hancock, in the spring of 1867. The column, eleven hundred strong with the Seventh and other outfits, left in April and marched and counter-marched, chasing elusive Cheyenne. George accompanied Hancock's expedition for part of the early spring against those Indians of the southern plains who were harassing the crews constructing the transcontinental railroad in Nebraska and the Kansas Pacific in Kansas, not to mention the narrow link of the Butterfield Overland Dispatch that connected Denver with the East along the Smoky Hill River trail.

During that time, Tom was laid up in the Custer house at Fort Riley. Libbie, Diana, and Eliza tended his needs and wants. Libbie was especially attentive when the inflammation and pain in his muscles and joints troubled him. Beside his bed she sometimes sat with her hands folded in her lap, pleasantly reposed. Tom appreciated her concern when she sat with her hair lying darkly back on top of her head, exposing dainty and delicate ears with small pendants, fretting about his health and keeping him company. Photographs of Elizabeth during this period show that she had a cool reserve in her eyes. The shadow of strength and intensity behind her smile greatly intrigued her visitors and was not overlooked by the young lieutenant.[29] Anna Darrah, on the other hand, was enjoying herself to the fullest, for there was no female competition at the fort. Almost all other women on the post were the wives of officers or of enlisted men. Both Anna and Tom lived with the Custers, Anna planning to spend the winter there. She had already made one conquest—Tom's friend and fellow officer of Company A, Myles Moylan, had succumbed to her charms.[30]

For his part, Tom tried to comfort Libbie while he rested in his room. Of course, she had been separated from Armstrong before, but as Lawrence Frost has pointed out in *General Custer's Libbie,* "In each instance, the time of separation and the capacity of the enemy was known."[31] With George now riding all over western Kansas, she grew despondent. She had obviously hoped that she had heard the last of war at Appomattox, but knowing better when Hancock's expedition marched onto the plains, she had only Tom with her at Fort Riley and Autie's letters to ease her mind. The correspondence between her and Autie was apparently endless.

The Seventh's light colonel somehow managed to get off almost one lengthy letter per day. Omitting military affairs as much as possible, Autie wrote his little wife about the game he hunted, camp life, and his plans for their reunion. Libbie did not write as frequently, but she sent an epistle out on every stagecoach. She was concerned because Hancock did not intend to allow wives of officers under his command to visit their husbands in the field that summer. For a while she limited herself to passing along the gossip at Fort Riley, but she commented in her 1895 book, *Tenting on the Plains,* that her attitude changed in late April. She was anxious, because distressing news about the Indian campaign and the stir created by a rare, mild earthquake that rocked central Kansas agitated her to the point of pleading with him to meet her.[32]

Tom did his best to relieve Libbie's anxieties. His illness kept him close to his room in the family residence, so he had plenty of time not only to encourage her but also to reflect on his situation. He longed to be mounted in the field with his regiment, but rheumatism kept him out of the saddle.

In those days, the higher commanders of the diminished regular army were generals and colonels like Autie who had traveled the road to the top by way of the hard school. Having learned how to efficiently kill their white brothers, North and South, they would now have little mercy on their red brethren. They had fought one war to mend the country and they were still committed to that line. On one main count, however, most of them fell short. They knew little or nothing about the Plains Indians or their methods of making war—the soldiers would make many mistakes and pay too high a price for lessons learned the hard way.[33]

While General Grant was still the number-one soldier in the nation, with the illustrious William Tecumseh Sherman as the second-highest-ranking officer, the army itself which they led to victory was gradually suffering a decline in public opinion polls. Sherman, and later Phil Sheridan, would follow as first officer of the regular army. But the common soldier who had lately saved the Union was no longer a popular celebrity. Truth be known, he very nearly was to become an object of scorn. A change in the natural mood of the nation took place not unlike that which occurred exactly one century later during the Vietnam War.[34]

The frontier army, a part of which served in Kansas, including the Seventh Cavalry, was a rowdy one, more so than any other military force the United States has produced. Military historian S. L. A. Marshall has stated that a large portion of the enlisted men were habitual drunkards and very few of their officers would refuse a nip from the bottle themselves. Payday invariably resulted in a mass spree, developing into a forty-eight-hour disruption of business for that particular unit. To make payroll matters even worse for the soldier on a Kansas post, much of the recruit's stipulated uniform issue was paid for from his own pockets, and he had to buy them on half-pay. He stayed in debt most of the time, either to the outfit's craftiest card player or to the "sergeant-banker," who lent money to soldiers at usury rates, usually about 20 percent per month till paid, and always stood by for collection when pay call rolled around at the first of each month. Most proper commissioned officers such as Tom purposely overlooked these operations. Army pay in the latter half of the nineteenth century was thirteen dollars a month for a private.[35]

This army went long-haired, moustached, and bearded to war, most of the men and many of the officers. Rather than being uniformed by a strict quartermaster, individuals generally wore what they pleased within the limits appropriate for each particular mission, the bounds for every outfit being set by its commander at the time.

If this was allowed with the purpose in mind of uplifting the morale of the average soldier, it certainly fell short of its object. That it was anything but a contented army is demonstrated by the number of desertions that started abnormally high and got worse. If an enlisted man saw a better chance of employment in cattle ranching, buffalo hunting, or freighting anywhere in Kansas during his travels, he just up and left. Unlike many cases during the Civil War, these men did not leave to return at some later date but often left not to return at all. During the war, soldiers went home to visit the family or harvest crops but would rejoin their outfits at a later date so were not counted as deserters. The soldiers of the frontier army most likely had no family ties; they simply deserted because of boredom, illness, or a disagreement with a higher rank.

Sometimes, however, they would leave an outfit to obtain a civilian position which looked better at the time, only to become disillusioned and re-up with another unit along the string of posts throughout western Kansas or elsewhere on the frontier.[36]

Marshall has written that in 1860 the regular army had numbered sixteen thousand. By the time the Civil War reached high tide there were ten thousand more on the muster rolls, for a total of twenty-six thousand. After 1866, its line strength or combat elements comprised 630 companies of infantry, cavalry, and artillery, the average unit mustering seventy men. Thus the total of the fighting force should have been about 43,100. He went on to point out that Congress had authorized a paper strength of 54,302 while increasing the cavalry by four regiments, changes that say clearly enough that the main military policy of the country was aimed at the threat of Indians on the Kansas and western frontiers.[37]

The regular army appeared sufficient on paper, but volunteering dragged and the total for all branches of the service was closer to thirty-eight thousand, far less than what was authorized and fewer than the total of tribesmen it would confront. Beginning in 1867 scores of skirmishes were fought between red men and white soldiers, with the army more often than not operating ineffectually yet rarely losing a bout—and those it did fail to win were typically more widely publicized than a victory. In many minor clashes across the young state where Tom now served, soldiers were surprised, mutilated, and killed and the survivors in turn fought back savagely, in a vicious cycle of small engagements.[38]

Most of the company commanders were from ten to fifteen years older than those in the regular army today. Like Tom, most had held higher brevet ranks in volunteer regiments during the Civil War. In the new frontier army, military promotion was slow, and despite the push to settle Kansas, good jobs in civilian life were few and far between. Strong lieutenants and captains have inevitably proved to be the spine of military organizations, and in this respect the frontier army in Kansas in 1867 was wealthy.[39]

The younger Custer's inordinate illness improved by April, even though he remained on sick leave. He began making plans to join Autie in the field anyway. Both he and his brother felt that it was important for him to be with his company during the regiment's first campaign. Libbie told Tom that while on a train to Fort Leavenworth (rail service had been opened to Fort Riley since the railhead had by then reached Abilene, farther west) she had met Hancock. The general informed her that Armstrong was off on a fifteen-day reconnaissance in force, but when he returned he could return to Fort Riley to take her with him to Fort Hays. Hancock presumably relented enough under the lady's charm to permit her to join her husband in spite of his previous ban of officers' wives on the march. He also praised the Seventh's leader as a husband and as a military man: "I do not know what we would do without Custer; he is our reliance."[40] Tom probably hoped to join his regiment when Autie came to Fort Riley to pick up Libbie.

The days of lying around Fort Riley, although it was the most comfortable army establishment in Kansas short of Fort Leavenworth, grew tiresome for the young lieutenant. He felt cut out for the hard-riding voyages on the plains of buffalo grass chasing the rampaging red warriors with Armstrong. Sitting on his duff in the staid, safe bounds of the Custer house with three women consequently seemed dull indeed. He had hoped all along to serve with big bub Aut in a cavalry outfit, but no sooner had he joined his brother in such a regiment than he was laid low with his rheumatism and forced to play the role of wallflower, sitting out the very first set of operations forming one distinct stage of the Indian Wars on the Great Plains. Not only that, George was assigned to command all of the troops and posts on the route of the Butterfield Overland Dispatch along the Smoky Hill River valley. He established his headquarters at Fort Hays and placed five infantrymen at each stagecoach station along the route to complement the five well-armed company employees already there. This was good hunting ground, and Tom envied his brother chasing buffalo across rolling hills and shallow valleys.

Time was growing short, for rumors of a major march for the Seventh were in the air, although as yet Custer had received no official orders. Tom knew that when they did arrive he would have little if any chance of catching up with the regiment. Lawrence Frost has stated that General Sherman concluded that the area between the Arkansas and the Platte rivers should become a no-man's land. If the region could be cleared of all Indians, any who entered it would be considered hostile and treated accordingly. As soon as the country between these rivers was freed of the Indian threat, the railroad construction crews, the stagecoaches, and homesteaders could travel westward in comparative safety.[41]

The anxiousness of Tom, George, and Libbie combined to finally rejoin the trio, and Anna Darrah and Eliza as well, near Fort Hays shortly before the expedition was to leave. Autie had the ladies' tents moved to the highest ground he could locate. Big Creek, along which Fort Hays had been established, was known to flood, and he wanted his wife and her company to remain high and dry. The Custers set up a canvas household where Libbie and Anna could put up while the boys were gone. Libbie described it in *Tenting on the Plains:* a hospital tent was used as a sitting room; connected to it was a wall tent that served as a bedroom; a pair of smaller canvas covers were placed nearby, one for the kitchen and another for the striker assigned to take care of the needs of the ladies.[42]

Thus Tom managed to join the regiment for its expedition to the Platte River. He was surely glad to be back in an active, fighting organization once more. After all, for a man of action as he considered himself to be, two long years of inactivity—first on the prairies of Texas, then waiting for instructions at home, and finally suffering the pain and indignation of an inflamed body at Fort Riley for four months—were all but intolerable. He looked forward to the coming summer with the relish typical of the Custer family.

5

BACK ON CAMPAIGN AGAIN

There were twelve companies of the Seventh Cavalry in the Division of the Missouri according to the report of the U.S. Secretary of War, 1866-1867. This military division included Arkansas, Missouri, Kansas, Nebraska, and the territories of Colorado, Dakota, and New Mexico. There were also 150 Osage Indian scouts, many of whom were used in the division by the Seventh Cavalry.[1] During its stay in Kansas, which ultimately lasted four and a half years, the regiment performed every sort of duty that could fall to the lot of cavalry troopers. Its expeditions, marches, and scouts eventually extended from the Missouri River in the east to the Rocky Mountains in the west and from the Platte River in the north to the Staked Plains of Texas in the south.[2]

The summer sun baked the column of cavalry troopers plodding across arid, dusty plains as it toiled north toward the Platte River in Nebraska Territory. Armstrong recorded the note that his command was to "thoroughly scout the country from Fort Hays near the Smoky Hill River, to Fort McPherson on the Platte, thence describe a semicircle to the southward, touching the headwaters of the Republican and again reach the Platte at or near Fort Sedgwick . . . then move directly south to Fort Wallace on the Smoky Hill, and from there march down the overland route to our starting point at Fort Hays."[3]

The battalion, only 350 men strong, moving in the habitual column of fours, left Fort Hays on June 1, 1867. Television and motion pictures have led the modern public to believe that cavalry in the West marched in couples, two troopers and mounts side by side, but the army found that this was too cumbersome. Most commanders preferred formations four abreast. The battalion left without Autie; he stayed behind to ensure the comfort of his wife and her friend. He rode hard from midnight until 4:00 A.M. to rejoin the column. When reveille sounded at 5:00 A.M., Tom and Lieutenant Cooke convinced the other officers that Autie had been lost since 2:00 P.M. the previous afternoon, and the colonel himself supported that fabrication. Later the officers, seeing through the thin story, concluded that he had caught up with them during the night.

The first day's march was only fifteen miles because Armstrong wanted to acclimate the men and horses for the long march ahead of them. After that day the troops moved across the prairie at an average speed of twenty-five miles per day. Although the battalion was relatively small, the column must have stretched some distance along the trail. There may have been sutlers' wagons following the troops at a short distance. Sutlers were merchants licensed to travel with specific regiments. The same year the Seventh made the scout under discussion, sutlers were replaced by franchised traders who set up permanent stores at army posts. There were also Delaware

Indian scouts along, whom Armstrong praised in his memoirs. Some white scouts were with the battalion, too. Autie dwelt mostly upon James B. Hickok, whose glamorous appearance captivated the colonel. Hickok, however, was only employed before the detachment left Fort Hays, when he was sent to Fort Harker with the request that more forage be sent at once to Fort Hays in preparation for the excursion to the Platte.[4]

"Wild Bill" Hickok began his frontiersman career at the tender age of twenty years as a law officer in Johnson County, Kansas, in 1858. He served in the Civil War and took part in several shootouts in the next decade, building a reputation of his own that would loom as large or larger than that of the Custers and the Seventh. He was a little over six feet tall, wore his hair long and swept back behind his ears, and was endowed with great strength and agility. And he was inclined to be sociable and did not swagger or brag, though he was fond of story-telling and made no effort to contradict any invented tales of his feats. He was a popular figure among the officers and the soldiers of the regiment. He had been engaged as a government scout on January 1, 1867, and during May and June of that year he was listed in the records of the quartermaster general as "scouting with 7th Cavly in the field."[5] The Custers would have more to do with Hickok in the future.

For now, Medicine Bill Comstock became the chief white scout with the battalion on its march to the Platte. Comstock had moved from Kalamazoo, Michigan, to the plains when he was fifteen years old. He was a small, quiet man, an excellent rider, and familiar with the plains and with Plains Indians. He had two great desires in life—to meet George Armstrong Custer and to see a railroad locomotive. When he signed on as an army scout he was assigned to Custer's Seventh, and Custer took him to the Platte River where he saw his first huffing, puffing steam engine on the tracks of the transcontinental railroad being built across Nebraska.

George surrounded himself with friends like Comstock and with his own family as much as possible. Naturally, Tom was near-by most of the time; William W. Cooke, Mike Sheridan, Myles Moylan, and Joel Elliott were among other approving officers. But Custer was estranged from most of his officers and men.[6]

The commander of the Seventh did not really require any close friends among his officers and never solicited any. Those he enjoyed were those Tom brought into the Custer fold. Armstrong was the commander of the regiment at all times; his would have been a lofty and lonely position had he not had Tom around with whom he could relax; he assumed that distance had to be established and discipline maintained, including Tom. Whereas George was reserved when it came to his relationship with the regiment, Tom was outgoing, and he drew his own friends to his older brother. Ranking officers like Benteen, Wyckliffe Cooper, Robert West, and Albert Barnitz resented the barrier thus built between the commander and his troops, even though apologists for George Custer claim that they actually resented Custer's personality and the fact that he was a younger man ranking them as their commander.

Still, Custer had confidence in the men of his regiment. Enough so, in fact, that he neglected to take two new Gatling guns that the Seventh was issued along on his march to the Platte. Those guns caused some consternation when they arrived at Fort Riley early in the year. Lieutenant E. S. Godfrey had to confront the problem of training crews to operate them. "I wanted to have target practice," recalled Godfrey, "but was told I would have to pay for the ammunition. The commanding officer refused to authorize target practice for fear he would have to pay for the ammunition." Needless to say, the crews detailed to man the guns never fired them, nor were they ever used by the Seventh.[7]

In the matter of weapons, the Indians often had the advantage over the army. During the closing years of the Civil War, Union cavalry were equipped with repeating carbines. Among numerous different models, the 1862 model sixteen-shot, .44-caliber Henry and the famous 1865 model seven-shot, .56-caliber Spencer were in use after the war; some regular infantry obtained rifles of the same make, the difference being longer barrels and cartridges with heavier powder loads. The Plains Indians traded for civilian models of repeating rifles, generally of better quality than those issued to the army.[8]

As for the cavalrymen's six-shooters, they were often weapons with ranges up to about three hundred yards, but they were not accurate beyond fifty yards of their fixed sights, and the red warriors demonstrated a powerful aversion to fighting at such close range.[9]

The summer of 1867 proved troublesome thanks to the depredations of the Indians. The regular army was therefore joined by a volunteer unit of Kansans. A battalion designated the Eighteenth Kansas Volunteer Cavalry was recruited in the towns east of Junction City and marched to Fort Harker, near Ellsworth. Illness decimated the four companies of this battalion, and they were all but useless to the regulars—the only fighting they saw was a firefight at Beaver Creek in northwestern Kansas. Furthermore, Autie did not want to be saddled with volunteers—he had run into enough problems without having to bother with amateurs.

The battalion set out on Saturday, June 1, 1867, and marched for a week and had come within thirty miles of the Platte River when Armstrong's anxieties began. Tom had been delighting in the long, hard rides and the feeling that he was finally back in the role of a campaigning soldier. At his brother's request he had refrained from imbibing for the most part—barring, of course, an occasional nip with the boys. But he knew that the battalion's second-in-command, Major Wyckliffe Cooper, was drinking heavily. So Tom was not surprised as Cooper's giddy world was crushed when the teetotaling Autie confiscated his entire whiskey supply. To add insult to injury, the colonel threatened to have Cooper court-martialed for dereliction of duty—a fate worse than death for Cooper, a career soldier—unless he repented and gave up his vice. In a terrible fit of depression, Cooper committed suicide.[10]

As luck would have it, Tom was officer of the day on that fateful occasion. He was shocked when upon stepping into Cooper's field tent he discovered the body. The shock was doubly so because he had to be the one to find the corpse, and he knew that Autie would be blamed for Cooper's death.

Cooper's suicide marked the beginning of a long, bad summer for the Custers. Whereas Autie had tried to create a barrier between himself and his officers, suddenly the rift became an open split. Some officers of the battalion never forgave him, and his words spoken over Cooper's corpse only made matters worse between himself and the hard-drinking officers: "Gentlemen, this is not the death of a soldier. It is unnecessary, standing as we do in the presence of such an example, that I should say more."[11]

The column reached Fort McPherson on the Platte the afternoon of June 10. Cooper was buried on June 11. Custer wrote in his field book: "Funeral as quiet as possible, suicide not being entitled to military honors."[12]

What is remarkable about Armstrong's reaction to Cooper's suicide is that he did not attempt to collect or destroy all the liquor in the command. Had he done so he might very well have faced open mutiny on the part of officers and enlisted men alike. Even Tom and the officers in his circle would almost certainly have rebelled at the idea; though it may have crossed Autie's mind, he never acted upon it. Doing so among the two-fisted drinkers under him would have caused him more grief than he already faced.

Besides, he had more pressing matters at hand. The same day Custer's column reached Fort McPherson, Sherman wired General Grant in Washington, "The only course is for us to destroy the Hostile, and to segregate the peaceful and maintain them." He also instructed Custer in a separate telegram to await marching orders before leaving Fort McPherson.[13]

Colonel Custer violated his instructions throughout the 1867 expedition. He apparently did not agree with Sherman's policy at this point in time. On his own initiative he called for a peace council with a large Sioux band under the leadership of Pawnee Killer.

General Sherman arrived at Fort McPherson on the Platte by train on June 11, 1867. He told Custer, among other things, "The redman must be taught a lasting lesson. All who refuse to obey the whiteman's law must be killed." His verbal orders to Armstrong left little to the latter's imagination: "I want you to clean out that Augean stable of hostiles along the Republican River. Capture or kill all you can. Written instructions will follow."[14]

Custer took the comments offered by his superior, Sherman, to heart, because he set out on the next leg of his circular journey back toward Fort Hays imparting to any Indians he found the word that they obey civilized laws or else. But he could not run Pawnee Killer to ground. Instead, the Sioux chieftain found him.

Tom was again the officer of the day on June 14 when the column, by then saddle-sore and thoroughly exhausted physically from more than three weeks of twenty-five-mile-a-day rides, bivouacked on the north fork of the Republican River. It was well after dark by the time the battalion got their horses picketed, their tents set up, and settled down for the night. Armstrong—who constitutionally required little sleep—sat in his tent sometime between then and the break of day, when he was lifted to his feet by the sudden sharp crack of a carbine. Shortly afterward, Tom poked his head through the entrance to his brother's tent and exclaimed "They're here!" Pawnee Killer had found Custer.[15]

Autie dashed out of his tent attired in his red flannel night shirt, barefoot and hatless, carrying his carbine in his right hand and appearing in less than delicate form before Tom and the excited troopers—few of whom were any more formally attired.

The whole battalion waited impatiently until the first flush of daylight revealed a body of several hundred mounted Sioux warriors intent upon stampeding the Seventh's horse herd at the rear of the camp. The Indians demonstrated more patience than the cavalrymen, waiting stoically for dawn before beginning the offensive. Alertness saved the cavalrymen from becoming foot soldiers, for Tom's warning brought every trooper out of his tent and armed to the teeth in short order. Tom, Autie, and a few other officers watched vigilantly for Pawnee Killer to make his first move, and when he did the colonel sent Tom into action in a hurry with instructions to force the Indians back with a carbine volley.

When the hostiles withdrew across the north fork of the river, Armstrong sent out one of his interpreters to arrange a powwow. "It was desirable," he wrote, "that we should learn, if possible, to what tribe our enemies belonged."[16] The redmen agreed to meet the yellow-haired chief and half a dozen of his officers on the bank of the watercourse. Tom wanted to be a member of the *ex officio* peace commission, but as Armstrong recorded, "To guard against

84

treachery, I placed most of my command under arms and arranged with Tom that a blast from the bugle should bring assistance to me if required." Custer, six officers, a bugler, and an interpreter dismounted on the short grass of the river bank, unholstered their revolvers, and tucked them into the waistbands of their trousers. The bugler was delegated to hold the horses and told to "watch every move they make. Upon the first appearance of violence or treachery, sound the *Advance*."[17]

It should be noted here that Custer relied heavily upon his brother to carry out his orders. Tom was often given responsibilities such as, in this case, preparing to come to Armstrong's rescue, usually superseding a higher-ranking officer than Tom, still a lowly lieutenant. It was common for Tom to be officer of the day whenever a tense situation was imminent or anticipated. Custer demonstrated a certain lack of trust for his subordinates by doing so, and that only added to the resentment that they had commenced to feel for him. Much of the resentment filtered down onto Tom and his close friends.

The conference with Pawnee Killer accomplished nothing except to confirm Autie's suspicion that this was indeed Pawnee Killer's Sioux band. The theater of the Seventh's operations was the scene of plenty of hard-fought and well-contested conflicts with its red foe, but this was not destined to be one of those occasions.[18] Custer's battalion began chasing Pawnee Killer's band all over southwestern Nebraska, always maintaining contact but never quite catching up for a conclusive encounter. The wily Sioux played cat-and-mouse until Custer grew frustrated.

Having had little luck, Autie took time out to telegraph General Sherman at Fort Sedgwick for orders while the battalion rested briefly at the headwaters of the Republican River. The column suffered terribly from the march after the swift Sioux. One day the outfit traveled a total of sixty-five miles—a truly incredible distance even for a cavalry unit and one for which George was summarily dubbed "Iron Ass" Custer by some of his less respectful enlisted men.[19] Throughout the journey the troopers ate inferior and insufficient rations and, because of a drought on the plains of western Nebraska, consumed little or no water. Dogs with the column died of thirst, and on several occasions there was no water for the men, horses, or draft animals.

Captain Albert Barnitz wrote to his wife, Jennie, about the general on this campaign, "You would be filled with utter amazement, if I were to give you a few instances of his cruelty to the men, and discourtesy to the officers." Barnitz then adopted a more military tone when he wrote Jennie—a close friend of Libbie Custer—"They do say that he just squandered that cavalry along the road!"[20]

When no orders were immediately forthcoming from Sherman, Tom helped Autie decide to again wire Fort Sedgwick. As it turned out, Custer's campaign against the Sioux was less than successful, for despite the pursuit of the hostiles with great energy a promising young officer was lost. Lieutenant Lyman S. Kidder had long since left Fort Sedgwick with orders and dispatches for Custer, Sherman telegraphed back, with ten troopers of Autie's old regiment, the Second Cavalry, and the Sioux Indian guide named Red Bead. But since Kidder had not yet found the Seventh, Sherman instructed Custer by telegraph to go from the Platte to the Smoky Hill at Fort Wallace. Custer set out for the post in northwestern Kansas the next morning.

The column remained short of rations and water, but its colonel pushed no less for mileage and time. To his earlier derogatory sobriquet the troopers added "Horse Killer," as dozens of animals collapsed under the strain of the hard pace. Jacob Homer, a corporal with the Seventh Cavalry, later had this to say about Custer:

"He was too hard on the men and horses. He changed his mind too often. He was always right. When he got a notion, we had to go."[21] Autie believed that because he needed little rest, the men under him needed just as little. The officers with whom he did confer—Tom, Cooke, Elliott, and others of the Custer gang—were as young as or younger and as energetic as he was, so he neglected to discuss the matter with old campaigners like Benteen, who could have predicted what was to happen next.

Mass desertions began before dawn on July 7, 1867. At the 5:00 A.M. reveille that day, thirteen troopers shouldered arms and took off for the hinterlands. Not far from the Platte River, thirty-five more deserted within twenty-four hours.

Autie became desperate, and realizing that most of his officers would side with the men, he depended on members of the Custer clan to save the situation:

Not knowing but that the remainder of the Command, might leave as well, I felt that severe and summary measures must be taken. I therefore directed Tom, Maj. Elliott, and Lts. Cooke and Jackson, with a few of the guard, to pursue the deserters and bring them back to camp—dead or alive. Seven of the deserters, being mounted on our best horses, made their escape. Six were brought back to camp. Three were shot down while resisting arrest; these only wounded. The remaining 3, by throwing themselves on the ground and feigning death, escaped being shot. Wounds were treated, but did not prove serious. Anticipate no further trouble.[22]

Although he expected no more trouble, he got plenty. In fact, things were boiling to a head. Poor Armstrong must have glossed over the facts of both Cooper's death and the deserters for his own benefit. But when he reached Fort Wallace he found that the situation had gone from bad to worse. To begin with, he finally found the dispatches Sherman sent out with Lieutenant Kidder—he also found the remains of Kidder with those of his ten men and Red Bead, the Sioux scout. Cheyenne massacred the Kidder party about July 1, so when the Custer column came across the site the bodies were badly decomposed.

Fort Wallace had 339 officers and men and 120 civilian employees in the quartermaster department that July. Additionally, Companies I and G of the Seventh were camped nearby. The relatively small garrison was almost doubled when Custer augmented it with his battalion—Companies A, D, E, H, K, and M—on July 13. They arrived at Fort Wallace after marching 181 miles in seven days, a phenomenal rate for the mounted troopers.[23]

They found the garrison and Captain Albert Barnitz, commander of the Seventh's contingent there, exhausted by disease, starvation-level rations, and attacks by the same Cheyenne that had wreaked havoc with Kidder's tiny force. Both the stagecoach and freight lines, the chief communications links between Fort Wallace and the outside world, had been severed by the determined Indians. The last word into the post before the information flow was broken had it that heavy rains upstream flooded Big Creek at Fort Hays, causing a mass departure in favor of dryer Fort Harker. Autie found no instructions from Sherman or Hancock awaiting him, nor was there any word from Libbie or Anna Darrah.

Utterly upset, he turned to his aide—Tom—and his adjutant, William Cooke, but instead of asking their advice he gave an excited command, "Order out a 75-man detail on the best mounts we've got. All our empty wagons as well. We're riding to Harker for rations and medicine!"[24]

Tom saw the obvious need for a command decision, but he also rightly suspected that the real reason his brother wanted to go to Fort Harker was to personally assure Libbie's safety. There is no solid evidence, but the pair may also have suspected the worst about the physical condition of the garrison at Fort Wallace. They had arrived at Fort Riley the fall before, only two months after a severe cholera epidemic swept through Kansas. Cases at Fort Riley had been reported on August 30, five days after 384 cavalry recruits for the Seventh arrived at the post. Although the dread sickness had been confined to those recruits, fifty-nine cases were listed and twenty-seven deaths reported at the fort.[25]

One study of the epidemic of 1867 indicates that the cholera wintered in the civilian population and was spread through Kansas by the great immigration of civilians and the transport of goods for the military by civilian employees. It is doubtful that Tom and Autie knew that the first case occurred on June 22, 1867, at Fort Riley. Companies D, F, and K of the Thirty-eighth Infantry passed through that post on their way to Fort Harker; all of these troops suffered from diarrhea and a few infantrymen remained behind at the Fort Riley hospital, though none were diagnosed as having cholera. Actually, all cases at Fort Riley were among civilian employees, and not one among any of the military personnel there in 1867, probably because of the careful hygienic methods of Post Surgeon B. J. D. Irwin.[26]

Having no word from his wife and suspecting that cholera was again extant in Kansas, Autie's mind became fraught with fear for Libbie. He appointed Captain Louis Hamilton second-in-command of the 75-man detail. Tom insisted on accompanying the detail. Together they force-marched over 150 miles through the barren terrain of the Smoky Hill River valley in fifty-five hours. The small detachment reached Fort Hays about 3:00 A.M. on July 18.[27]

The detail probably left Fort Wallace just in time. Cholera broke out among members of the Seventh Cavalry there on July 22. The first victim was a trooper of Company H. The disease peaked only three days later, but ten cases were reported and four died.[28]

When Autie, Tom, and the others got to Fort Hays, they found that the cholera had been there before them. In addition to the flood, the explosive outbreak of cholera had helped to persuade folks there to evacuate. In fact, the only people the boys discovered at Fort Hays were on sick call. Autie called Hamilton, Cooke, and Tom together for a council at 3:00 P.M. Since the cholera had reached Hays, it was surely at Fort Harker. That thought really worried the colonel; duty urged him onward as well. He knew he had to get supplies back to the beleaguered troops at Fort Wallace. So he again split his force. "Rest the men till daybreak," he told Hamilton, "then move out. I'm going ahead to Harker. Supplies will be ready to load when you arrive. If any of the men give you trouble, don't hesitate to shoot. Shoot to kill!"[29] The forced march to Fort Hays had been costly to the regiment—twenty of the escort, pushed to their limits, deserted on the way.[30]

With that, Armstrong, brother Tom, Lieutenant Cooke, and two troopers who volunteered sprang into their McClellan saddles and dashed off in the direction of Fort Harker, sixty miles away. They made the distance by 2:00 A.M. on July 19—in less than twelve hours.

Armstrong and Tom expected a jubilant reunion with Libbie and Diana. They found out that the girls were safe, but they had packed up and left Fort Harker for the safety of the Custer house at Fort Riley. But as biographer Kinsley has noted, nothing would satisfy George except to see his beloved wife alive and well. A quick check at the railroad depot proved that he missed the train from Fort Harker.[31]

Instructing Tom and Cooke to wait for Hamilton and the empty wagons to catch up, load them with the vitally needed rations and medical supplies, and head back to Fort Wallace with all possible dispatch, Autie snatched the headstall of a fresh relay horse from the startled hands of a courier and galloped out of Fort Harker. Tom saw nothing out of character in his brother's actions. He knew that Autie's one thought at the moment was of Libbie, although military instructions made no provision for him to leave his command. Still, as the spanking horseman dashed across seventy-five miles of prairie to Fort Riley, it appeared completely unlikely that anyone would condemn Armstrong's unscheduled, solitary ride to his wife.[32]

Hamilton made Fort Harker shortly thereafter. Tom and he supervised the loading of supplies onto army wagons and headed back for the flagging troops at Fort Wallace with all feasible haste. Since heavily laden wagons did not move as swiftly as empty ones, and since the party no longer had the inexhaustible colonel along to badger speed out of exhausted men and animals, the detail did not resemble the flying column that had reached Fort Harker within record time. Instead, the procession made sure, commendable progress at its most acceptable speed.

When the caravan of vehicles pulled into Fort Wallace, the younger Custer discovered the troops of the regiment in a rebellious mood. They had subsisted for months on food unfit for human consumption and faced the threat of scurvy prevailing among them, weakening many to such a degree that if they had not already been exposed to it, they risked the deadly cholera. Among the officers, Armstrong's treatment of the Cooper affair still rankled; among the enlisted men, the treatment of the deserters simmered in their minds; and much of the abuse that might otherwise have fallen on his brother was heaped onto Tom because of his participation in both incidents. It was a case of guilt by association. He had been present, if he did not actually take part in it, at the shooting of the three deserters—and it was he who found Cooper's body after the latter killed himself. The news that the colonel had abandoned the regiment to be with his wife surrounded by the comforts of Fort Riley while the men under his command faced disease, privation, and hostiles made the complaints more frequent and more poignant.

While this was going on, Autie received a wire from Colonel A. J. Smith, commandant of the Seventh Cavalry, at Fort Harker. Some historians claim that Custer obtained Smith's permission to leave Fort Harker to visit Libbie, but this point is debatable. Whatever the case, Smith now ordered Custer back to the command immediately. Custer delayed, using as his excuse the erratic timetable of the railroad. Upon arriving at Fort Harker, after the wagon train and brother Tom had gone, Smith arrested him. Hancock, who had not heard that Custer failed to receive any orders at Fort Wallace, insisted that George be arrested. Smith charged him with being absent without leave from his command at Fort Wallace and with using army mules and ambulances from forts Hays and Harker without permission.

Elsewhere in the field, the summer was fast drawing to a close and the army had thus far accomplished nothing. Autie returned to Fort Riley to await his court-martial with his sympathetic wife. Tom joined them, leaving the other members of the Custer gang to contend with the righteous wrath of the Seventh as best they could. In less than a year, the Custers had managed to alienate themselves from the regiment with which they would forever be connected. Tom could thank Autie for being in the mess.

Early in September they transferred to Fort Leavenworth, considered by the military to be the finest, most desirable post in the West. Autie and Libbie were ecstatic over the knowledge that General Phil Sheridan and his staff would shortly join them at Fort Leavenworth. Tom was pleased to be away from the criticism he suffered, not only because he was the light colonel's brother but also on account of his staunch defense of Autie and his role in the reprehensible affairs of the summer. Besides, since Fort Leavenworth was situated on the west bank of the Missouri River he was mighty close to the dens of iniquity—saloons, gambling halls, and such—normally associated with either a military establishment or a riverfront town.

The Custers anticipated no great problems at Autie's court-martial. The most they expected was an official reprimand. Hence all three were totally shocked when they entered the courtroom on September 15, 1867. One of the Seventh's company commanders and a friend of Wyckliffe Cooper, Captain Robert M. West, brought the complaints of the regiment before the nine-man jury in formal charges.[33] West had been one of those to run afoul of the abstaining Colonel Custer. A capable officer and Indian fighter, West drank a great deal. When the Custer battalion reached Fort Wallace after Cooper was laid to rest, Autie appointed him officer of the day. Before assuming this assignment, the tired captain tossed off a few drinks to wet his whistle after the hard march. Unfortunately for West, Custer caught a whiff of his breath while he was on duty; Custer arrested him and ordered his court martial for being drunk on duty while the post was besieged by Cheyenne.

The disgruntled officers of the regiment convinced Captain West to prefer charges against Custer. He became the prize witness for the prosecution and sacrificial lamb for the Seventh's officers.

Some of the latter assured West that they would also testify. Custer had so effectively established his dominance over the regiment, however, that many of his subordinates were afraid of him, West included. The day he was scheduled to testify West evidently drank himself into a stupor. He eventually testified that he heard Colonel Custer issue the following orders to Major Elliott on the day the three deserters were shot down: "Stop those men! Shoot them where you find them. Don't bring in any alive!"[34]

The most damning evidence came not from West but rather from Captain Frederick W. Benteen. He presented to the court's jury the comment he overheard his commanding officer shout to Tom and Cooke: "Bring back none of those men alive." Then Benteen expanded on the remark. "It was like a buffalo hunt," he said. "The dismounted deserters were shot down, while begging for their lives, by General Custer's executioners: Major Elliot, Lieutenant Tom Custer, and the executioner-in-chief, Lieutenant Cooke. . . . Three of the deserters were brought in badly wounded, and screaming in extreme agony. General Custer rode up to them, pistol in hand, and told them if they didn't stop making so much fuss he would shoot them to death."

That is the only reference available regarding Custer's threat to personally kill the wounded deserters. Obviously, Benteen exaggerated the circumstances by referring to Elliot, Cooke, and Tom as "executioners"—knowing that the enlisted men of the regiment were a wild bunch, and that they put up a fight rather than allowing themselves to be captured—but it was a well-known fact that Cooke was a deadly pistoleer.

The references to his role probably had Tom squirming in his seat. What he had expected to be a routine trial—in an army of about 38,000 men, no fewer than 13,500 men were court martialed during the Indian Wars—had become a serious situation for Autie with possible repercussions for Tom.[36] There were technical problems with the trial from the outset, and a huge amount of testimony was presented (Lawrence Frost's *Court-Martial of Custer* provides the verbatim account of the trial lasting 150 pages). Twenty-five days after the court convened at Fort Leavenworth the meetings concluded. It is a matter of record that Autie was found guilty of being absent without leave from his command. It was his good fortune to have plenty of friends in high places—through a fair amount of manipulation he escaped being convicted of the charges leveled by West, Benteen, and others. Nevertheless, Custer was sentenced to be "suspended from rank and command for one (1) year, and forfeit his pay proper for the same time."[37]

This failed to satisfy the anti-Custer officers of the Seventh—they wanted him demoted to civilian status. They cast about for something more to hang on Custer. That thing showed up shortly. The specter of Wyckliffe Cooper, who died because Autie relieved him of his booze. Smarting under the failure to bust Custer to an inglorious civilian, Captain West and his fellows—"a crew of drunken pick-pockets," as Custer called them—received the unanimous and outspoken support of the dead major's friends and family who blamed Custer for his disgraceful death. Custer officially listed that death as "from excessive drinking." The Coopers besieged the U.S. Department of War for satisfaction. When that failed, they went so far as to suggest that the "yellow peacock" had paid Tom, who first found the body, to shoot the major.[38]

West, Benteen, and the anti-Custer officers knew that this was no more than an attack on the characters of Tom and Armstrong and dissociated themselves from it. But the hint fooled some influential folks back east, and it started a slow but ever-growing anti-Custer movement that would later cause a backlash against Armstrong.

It had turned out to be a grueling summer, in more ways than one, when Tom finally got back in the saddle as a campaigner. In one way, it passed quickly, as time usually does when one is busy—and the long, fast-paced, wearying marches guaranteed that Tom was busy. In another way, it had been an eventful season. Cooper's suicide, the chase after Pawnee Killer, the conference with the Sioux chief, the chase after the deserters, the discovery of the Kidder party, the rush for supplies for Fort Wallace—all made an otherwise useless campaign interesting.

Finally, it was morally crushing. The court martial at Fort Leavenworth during which all the Custers' dirty military laundry was aired proved that even a national hero, whose star was becoming faintly tarnished, was not above rules. That was a lesson that would be hard for Armstrong and brother Tom to learn. As 1867 drew to a close, they did not look back to profit from their mistakes but looked forward to a future that would throw them back into the national limelight.

6
THE WINTER CAMPAIGN

The most picturesque figure in American military history and his wife spent the winter of 1867–1868 between Fort Leavenworth and Monroe enhancing his image. He had seen hard service on the plains, and he emerged as one of the cavalry's most capable campaigners. He told anyone who asked that his temperament was well suited to the merciless methods employed in subduing Indians and that he was champing at the bit to get back into action. In the meantime, the Seventh was busy fighting Indians. No one then knew that the upcoming battle would be counted among the most controversial in the history of the Indian Wars of the United States.

Always conscious of his impression in the public mind, Custer seized the enforced vacation of his suspension as the time to enhance his image. Forsaking the regal costume of his Civil War days, he adopted the buckskin coat of the frontiersman, an excessively wide hat in order to stand out in a crowd, and other individualized costume features which have remained a part of the Custer tradition. He wanted to be identified with the West, yet keep his striking figure on the pages of the contemporary media. Custer had a craving for theatrical display.

The army had been ineffectual against the Sioux and Cheyenne in the expeditions of 1867. But that summer was mild compared with the following summer of 1868. In two months that year, 117 settlers were killed and 7 women were carried off into captivity. There were at least 25 raids recorded during that time. As Paul Wellman has explained vividly, "The Cheyennes made a desert out of western Kansas."[1] Elements of the Fifth Cavalry, the Tenth Cavalry (an all-black regiment), several regiments of infantry, and of course the Seventh Cavalry operated on the plains—mostly in company groups—all through the spring and summer. Like the summer before, however, nothing was accomplished.

With his brother and sister-in-law absent, Tom participated in the beginning of a compelling human interest story involving the Seventh Cavalry. The uproar that rocked the regiment in 1867 had settled down, and Tom now got along fairly well with his companions. The Seventh, then stationed in central Kansas, had lost some horses in skirmishes with Indians that spring of 1868. To replenish the remount depot of the outfit, Tom went to Fort Leavenworth to obtain replacements. There he received forty-one horses, including the one that was later known as Comanche.[2]

The lean, fair-haired, twenty-three-year-old spent a brief time visiting friends in Leavenworth before looking after the business of picking up the wiry mustangs. The horses, captured on the plains, had been shipped to the big remount depot at St. Louis, then loaded aboard railroad cars and shipped west to Fort Leavenworth. At some point, either in St. Louis or at Fort Leavenworth, the horses were branded with a "U S" high on their left shoulders.[3]

On May 14, 1868, Tom left Leavenworth by rail for the Seventh's encampment just east of Hays, at Ellis Station. The Seventh needed the mustangs for the start of another campaign against the red warriors of the plains. Kansans hoped the cavalry would conquer the redoubtable tribesmen this time. The young daredevil who had won a pair of Congressional Medals of Honor during the war created a minor sensation among the gamblers and prostitutes who plied their trades in Leavenworth, and he managed to visit briefly with Armstrong and Libbie before he left for the Seventh's camp near Ellis Station. He always got along better with common folks than he did with high society. He supervised the loading of the buckskin Comanche with the other picked cavalry mounts onto stock cars. As the train pulled out toward the setting sun on the 14th of May, he grinned and waved his campaign hat at the Leavenworth station master standing on the station's platform.[4]

Those forty-one horses were the only remounts received by the Seventh Cavalry in 1868. The rest were needed by other units serving on the plains, as afire as the region was with strife between red men and white. Because of frequent delays, the journey from Leavenworth to Ellis Station took two nights and two days. It was important for the train to stop at regular intervals to feed, water, and care for the horses. It was also necessary for the steam engines and cars destined for the high plains to be switched onto sidings to wait for maintenance crews to finish what they were doing and clear the tracks or for other trains to pass by on their way east.

When the delay promised to be lengthy and the train had not stopped in the vicinity of a frontier settlement, young Lieutenant Custer ordered the mustangs driven down the wooden ramps out of the cars to give them time to stretch their taut, quivering muscles, to roll, and to graze on the lush, short buffalo grass, green yet in the late spring, that flourished along the railroad's right-of-way. A few of the horses had fretted themselves into a distemper and stood with drooping heads. Others wandered around aimlessly, uneasy and restless. The buckskin, though, appeared to accept the uncomfortable travel with good humor. Margaret Leighton wrote that he trotted briskly down the ramp on each occasion, snatching his muzzle full of grass and rolling on his back in the dust with as much energy as his admiring onlooker enjoyed.[5]

Tom may have commented favorably on Comanche, but to him buckskins looked far too much like the ponies of the Indians he had come west to whip. He preferred sorrels as better-looking animals, with light brown or red coloring, white blazes and forelegs, and longed to own one himself. Officers commonly purchased mounts from the army so that they could personally look after the animal or be certain that the creatures received preferential treatment. Tom was disappointed when Autie later mounted each company of the Seventh on matching horses because Company C got the call to ride sorrels, while he remained with Company A. The horses Tom took back to the regiment with him that spring, however, were sturdy little mustangs bred on the prairies—they came tough and they outlasted a good many better-looking critters on a march over rough territory. At least the regiment would be as well-mounted as the nomadic braves it was supposed to chastise when it resumed campaigning.[6]

Tom and his equine charges got a rousing welcome upon getting back to the outfit's camp. The men rested and relaxed among canvas barracks, mess halls, and storage tents in the shade of cottonwood trees before being ordered back into the field. They were eager for word from the East and, among those who had lost horses, to select new chargers. Captain Myles Keogh, the good-natured Irish commander of Company I, chose Comanche, and their names would be linked forever afterward. Keogh was a good horseman, better than any in the regiment except Armstrong.

Members of the Custer clan asked Tom anxiously what he had heard from the colonel and Elizabeth.[7] Tom concealed the emotions he felt behind a hard, darkened countenance. His friends noticed that he had remained close-mouthed about his brother ever since the court-martial nine months before. The suspension, still in effect, did not set well with Tom. He never admitted the justice of the charges. "Nothing but army politics and jealousy," he stormed, according to Leighton. The very thought of the trial still angered him, perhaps even more after dwelling on it for three-quarters of a year. "They're spending the summer in Monroe, Michigan," he answered the questioners stiffly, from behind his emotionless mask. "They seem to be having a gay time among their family and old friends."[8]

Indeed they were. As has already been pointed out, they treated the suspension from duty and pay more like a vacation. Armstrong also fell back on his ancient penchant for academic matters. Remembering his early teaching experience, he spent his spare time producing articles for various contemporary magazines in which he glamorized his achievements and incidentally popularized himself. In doing so, Armstrong exhibited a talent for writing.

Meanwhile, Phil Sheridan had assumed command of the military division of the Missouri. Viewing the failure of two summer campaigns, he decided that the best chance for ultimate success was to attack the Indians in their winter camps. His reasons for the decision were as follows:

Not less than eight hundred persons had been murdered, the Indi-
ans escaping from the troops by traveling at night when their trail

could not be followed, thus gaining enough time and distance to ren-
der pursuit, in cases, fruitless. This wholesale marauding would be
maintained during the seasons when the Indian ponies could subsist
upon the grass, and then in the winter, the savages would hide away,
with their villages, in remote and isolated places, to live upon their
plunder, glory in the scalps taken, and in the horrible debasement of
unfortunate women whom they held as prisoners. The experience of
many years of this character of depredations, with perfect immunity
to themselves and their families, had made the Indians very bold. To
disabuse their minds of the idea that they were secure from punish-
ment, and to strike them at a period when they were helpless to move
their stock and villages, a winter campaign was projected against the
large bands hiding away in the Indian Territory.[9]

Sheridan had tried several other experiments to combat the
"wholesale marauding" of the bold braves. Things grew so critical
that he took to the field in person. He quickly realized the futility
of attempting to follow the Indians, who knew the country like the
backs of their hands and could live off the land, with soldiers who
had to carry their own supplies, trust all too often to inefficient
scouts, or were otherwise handicapped.

The most unusual experiment Sheridan tried was a unit made
up entirely of frontier scouts, frontiersmen in every sense of the
word, from the western part of Kansas. Fifty-two of them were recruited under Colonel George A. Forsyth. They were assailed on
Beecher's Island on the Arikaree River, just across the border in
Colorado Territory, on September 17-25, 1868. In that celebrated battle many of the scouts were killed or seriously wounded in
standing off several hundred Cheyenne warriors. The plainsmen
proved their mettle in addition to killing a terror of the Kansas

prairie, the Cheyenne chieftain Roman Nose. But the little band of scouts failed to calm the flaming plains.[10]

Sheridan recruited more than the white scouts. Indian "friendlies" were often employed as guides. The Osage most frequently served on the Kansas expeditions. George Custer wrote in *My Life on the Plains* that the Osage were his preferred friendly scouts; indeed, he had had a great deal of contact with them at Council Grove, Kansas, where he owned several town lots and where the Osage had an agency, and in most of his plains campaigning.[11] George would be using Osage scouts again before he expected to. He was recalled by Sheridan for the winter campaign the general proposed.

Custer's reunion with his regiment was both a joyous and a disappointing one. There were a number of officers who maintained a loyalty to Custer and did many little things to demonstrate it. They were members of the Custer gang—the phrase often used in a derogatory sense spiced with envy.

One man who had been numbered among the friends of the Custers was Captain Louis McLane Hamilton, as noted before, the grandson of the famous American, Alexander Hamilton. Following the court martial, Hamilton apparently rethought his position within the ranks of the regiment, for he became a loner, associating with neither the Custer faction nor the anti-Custerites. Having seen the arrow-riddled remains of the Kidder party, Hamilton was also deathly afraid of capture by the foe. "When my time comes," he once said, "I hope I'll be shot through the heart in battle." His wish would almost be fulfilled.[12]

Another disciple of the Custers developed into an enthusiastic supporter and devoted friend. Canadian-born William W. Cooke was a well-built man, erect of carriage, standing about six feet tall.

His handsome features gave the young Canadian an aristocratic appearance, with brown eyes, brunette hair, and fuzzy side whiskers. He and Joel Elliott were Tom's closest friends, not to mention Autie's staunchest cohorts. In fact, it may have been their friendship with Tom Custer that ensured their loyalty to his brother. In this light, Major Elliott's eventual fate becomes most curious.

With the regiment once more, George was again in his element. He prepared for an energetic chase after the raiding Cheyenne. When one recruit reported to Company M of the Seventh in 1868, a friendly veteran informed him that it was a good idea to "feed up to the limit when you get a chance, for you will need a hump like a camel, to draw on, when you get in the field."[13]

The regiment's light colonel also began recruiting reliable scouts. He later wrote that the only criteria by which he judged his guides were, "Do you know the country thoroughly, and can you speak any of the Indian languages?" He took on a number of friendly Osage and made "California Joe" Milner his chief of scouts. This bearded, dirty, gabby fellow became the life of the campaign. His rough, plainsman-style humor kept the expedition in stitches but did not deter from his vast knowledge of the foe and the southern plains that the column would traverse. Custer told the white scouts that each would be paid $75 a month—a princely sum, considering the pay of regular army soldiers at the time—and a bonus of $100 would fall to the lot of the scout who located an Indian band.[14]

Custer was given the job of confronting the Indians on the warpath, but he had plenty of help. The Tenth Cavalry, the African-American regiment with Brevet Major General Benjamin H. Grierson, the highly regarded Union cavalry raider, as colonel, came to Kansas that summer. The unit immediately commenced subjugating hostiles and protecting settlers. Companies of the regiment stationed at Fort Wallace had rescued the besieged scouts at Beecher's Island. The officers of the Tenth were anxious to prove their African-American soldiers as good as any in the army, so they were "faithful, brave, and zealous." The regiment had already seen hard service in the summer campaign.[15]

Two other columns, General Eugene Carr with seven troops of the Fifth Cavalry and Colonel Evans with six troops of cavalry, two companies of infantry, and four small, mountain howitzers, operated on either side of the Seventh as beaters.

Custer was also to wait for another regiment, a Kansas volunteer outfit, to join him. Phil Sheridan approved the organization of this unit, the Nineteenth Kansas Volunteer Cavalry, upon the request of Kansas Governor Samuel J. Crawford. The governor had served as an officer in a Kansas volunteer regiment during the Civil War and promptly resigned his elected officer to fill the colonel's position in the Nineteenth. The regiment joined Custer and the Seventh in Indian Territory but missed all the action. Custer demonstrated a typical characteristic when he moved off against the Indians without waiting for the Kansas unit—he wanted all the glory of a victory to fall to the Seventh. The volunteers marched back to Kansas and were mustered out in April 1869. Both the Eighteenth Kansas in 1867, mentioned earlier, and the Nineteenth Kansas in 1868, were called into service primarily to relieve regular units from garrison duty to do more fighting. Naturally, since they were state units they also served in the federal service but at little cost to the federal government.[16]

George, Tom, and the Seventh moved out from Fort Hays early in November. The weather was fairly good for that late in the season and the march was relatively easy. Autie took time to write

Libbie about a humorous incident that took place in camp after a long day on the trail.

Cooke says Tom expects that I will bring some good clothes out he can borrow. He evidently needs them this time as his dog Brandy *caught a polecat and Tom, in rushing in to pull him off, got enough perfume to last him several months. This is not exactly the country to allow a man parting with his clothes as he can't very well go back several hundred miles to replace them. Tom partially turned the joke so hard on him on some of the other officers in the camp. As the mishap occurred to him about dusk, he with Capt. Hamilton concluded that they would call on the other officers in camp while Tom was so highly if not fashionably perfumed. So they started on their visiting expedition. They would enter a tent where probably half a dozen other officers were already crowded. Room would be made for them when a universal remark arose, "Some dog has been killing a skunk. I wonder where the damn brute is?" A third would reply, "It's evidently close about here you can bet!" So the conversation would run until Tom and Hamilton, nearly busting with laughter, would betray the secret. Then they would leave and enter another officer's tent where the same scene would be enacted.*[17]

In the middle of November, the leisurely moving cavalcade reached the point where Wolf and Beaver creeks join to form the Canadian River in Indian Territory. A small post called Camp Supply came into existence as a supply center and base of operations in 1868 for Sheridan's winter campaign. It was from here that the Seventh left to punish the Cheyenne.

On November 22, in the midst of a bitter cold snap, with a foot of snow on the ground, the regiment departed Camp Supply for the Washita River country.[18] Sheridan expected Custer and the Seventh to do the majority of the fighting, but Armstrong still had time to write a note of complaint to Libbie.

He said he wished that Eliza, the African-American cook and maid, was along with him to bake some real rolls instead of the "solid shot" his cook provided him. And Tom was pestering him for one of his beloved stag hounds because Libbie had told Tom he could have one of them. "I tell him they are my dogs not yours," Autie wrote irritably, "and that if you bring any out, you are at liberty to dispose of them as you see fit; yet I might as well talk to a mule. You have had some experience in determining how persistent a Custer is when seeking anything he really desires."[19]

Marching southward, scouts reported to Tom on November 26 that they had discovered the hot trail of a party of Indian warriors returning apparently from a raid on the Santa Fe Trail. Mail carriers between forts Dodge and Lamed using that thoroughfare, an old buffalo hunter near Dodge, and a pair of General Sheridan's personal dispatch riders, had been killed by a war party in the area, and the scouts believed that they had struck that band's trail. After hearing the news, the regiment did not stop. The troops streamed along the hoof prints of Indian ponies in the snow. Their equipment clanked coldly against their frigid leather saddles, metal buttons of greatcoats and weapons glinting in the bright winter sun rising overhead.[20]

Custer followed the track as rapidly as possible all day long. After a brief rest stop, Autie decided to continue the march through the night. Tom swung wearily into his McClellan, joined his troop near the head of the retinue, and listened attentively as scouts reported more and more Indian signs. He rode up beside his brother when the Osage scouts came upon the dying embers of a fire kindled by Cheyenne herd boys earlier in the day. Little Beaver, one of the best Osage scouts, sniffed at the coals. He told the officers that the camp was nearby. Tom stood by as Armstrong and Little Beaver ascended a ridge. On the far side lay a dark smudge in the snow, lit as it was by the bright moon—an immense pony herd.

In a brief conference Autie revealed that he had heard dogs barking in the distance, the sound of a bell from the pony herd, and the shrill cry of a baby on the far side of the hill. The Seventh had come upon a large camp—they knew they were very close to the main village of the Southern Cheyenne. As dawn approached, the colonel whispered commands to Tom and the other company commanders, then sent them scurrying through the crusted snow to their posts in the dark.

The village on the Washita was that of Cheyenne chieftain Black Kettle. But it was not the only village in the Washita valley. Kiowa, Arapaho, Apache, Comanche, and other Cheyenne sprawled their encampments the length of the river—there were at least two thousand warriors in the valley, although only a few hundred were with Black Kettle.

Those few hundred still smarted from an attack by whites four years earlier. Black Kettle had kept them out of trouble as much as the tribe of proud warriors would be. But some braves committed a few depredations. In retaliation, a posse of 90-day volunteers under ex-preacher John Chivington attacked Black Kettle's village in November 1864. Despite the fact that Black Kettle flew a white flag and an American flag above his tepee, men, women, and children were killed indiscriminately. The noncombatants were slaughtered without pity and their bodies left to rot.

Now, Armstrong divided his force into four detachments. He learned the lessons taught to Federals during the Civil War by

Thomas "Stonewall" Jackson and Robert E. Lee. Several times, the two Confederates had surprised and defeated the Yankees by dividing their smaller forces and striking their enemy in pronged attacks. Custer saw the strengths of unexpectedly splitting an array into separate lines of battle. So he gave Joel Elliott three troops, Captain Thompson and Captain Myers two companies each, and he retained four companies. The distinct units quietly surrounded the village. As the first glints of the sun rising above the horizon gleamed on the morning of November 27, cinches were tightened and freezing cold weapons were examined.

In the lead of Custer's detachment—which included Tom's A Company—fluttered two pennants—the guidon of the Seventh Cavalry and the stars and stripes of the American flag. A bugle sounded in the crisp dawn. A small regimental band, too, struck up as the array rode out. The tune was a lively Irish gig, the "Garryowen," which had become the regimental air of the Seventh. The regiment rode down on Black Kettle's doomed village from every side.[20]

There is small doubt that Colonel Custer was rash in attacking so large an encampment of Kiowa, Comanche, Arapaho, Apache, and Cheyenne without first carefully scouting. His judgment was sound, however; the division of his command seemed as much a surprise to the village as the attack in the winter; it was his good fortune that Black Kettle's band camped somewhat apart from the rest of the encampment. Considering the fact that no one counted on the Indians to be numerous or armed with good, repeating rifles, and since the army did not then believe that undisciplined Indians might be expected to stand and fight a modern cavalry unit in regimental strength, Custer's attack was not without justification.

One by one the companies came into battle columns, each company's guidon waving gallantly from the staff fixed in the socket of

the guidon corporal's stirrup. For a moment only the Seventh remained still, each trooper sitting uneasily in his saddle, heels well
down and back arched, carbine unholstered from the belt swivel
on his right, campaign hat pulled low to the level of his eyes to
protect him from glaring sun and biting cold air.[21]

One shot signaled the charge. The cavalrymen pounded down
on the unsuspecting occupants of the lodges. The brass band played
"Garryowen" until saliva froze in the valves of the instruments.

The charging troopers fired one volley from their carbines, then
they were among the tepees. Black Kettle and his squaw were killed
before their own lodge. Braves, naked save for their breech clouts,
leaped from their buffalo hide dwellings, sounding their war cries:
"Hey, hey, hey! Take courage! The earth is all that lasts!" Women
warbled the tremolo, cheering the warriors on. Their keening and
the screams of dying people and horses rent the morning. Many
men and women died in the village. Many others ran into the icy
Washita where they fought or tried to get away.

Nude men sprawled along the river bank, firing at the mounted soldiers while naked women tugged blankets or buffalo robes
around children to protect them from the razor-sharp edges of
the broken ice, although the river already ran red with blood. The
Cheyenne men at the river bank fought to the last man, all sacri-
fices so their families might escape.[23]

Armstrong and Tom rode into the village side by side, each
protecting the other. They picked off Indians with their revolvers
as their horses weaved in and out of the trees and lodges, spatter-
ing snow and slush and mud from their hoofs. The cavalrymen
around them yelled like buffalo hunters riding down on big game,
which just added to the confusion.[24] The brothers saw one Cheyenne woman run out of her lodge, dragging a white boy along by

his arm. She had adopted the child as her own, but rather than see him captured by the white men, she stabbed him with a knife. Before she could kill herself, she was shot dead.

Tom rode through the village oblivious to the arrows and bullets whizzing about him like angry bees. His courage, like that of his brother, was a triumph of his mind over physical fear. He knew fear, unlike Autie, who toward the end of the Civil War had become certain that he would not be killed. Autie was fully aware that he had the ability to rise within his chosen profession, and he determined to do so at all costs. He chose the position of danger invariably at the head of the charge because he knew it was the place to seize success; he knew that riding at the head of the column, he inspired his men with the confidence he himself felt, and thereby "made of each a hero," as Frederick Whittaker expressed it. Whittaker continues, "All this was the result of a deliberate plan. He had counted the cost of success and was fully prepared to pay it. He wanted honor and distinction among his fellow men, or death in the field."[25] Tom rode beside his brother at the post of danger because he overcame his fear and because he felt it his responsibility to be close to Armstrong at all times.

The battle at the Washita appeared to be at an end by 10:00 A.M. Although the village was destroyed, however, the Custers were surprised to find hundreds of additional warriors riding up the valley. It was only then that a captured Cheyenne woman informed Tom, Autie, and the staff that there were Indian villages extending almost ten miles farther down the river. Men hurried from these camps to assist the village of Black Kettle.

Seeing a small group of fugitive Cheyenne a short distance down the valley, Tom's friend, Captain Louis Hamilton, and fourteen troopers set off to round them up. The Seventh reformed and, menacing the Indians in the distance, prudently retreated. Events became confused at this point. Some say that despite the obvious danger, Custer ordered Hamilton, who had lately alienated himself from the Custer fold, to capture the fugitives. Custer himself was contrite. He wrote Libbie on December 6, 1868: "The sad side of the story is the killed and wounded. . . . Hamilton killed by a rifle bullet through the heart."[26]

Colonel Custer led his men a safe distance from the scene of the fight and set up camp. Tom immediately reported to the field hospital, where Dr. Morris J. Asch and his assistant surgeon were treating about a dozen wounded troopers. During the mad charge through the village, an Indian rifle ball had winged his hand.[27] It was his third wound after the two battle scars he had sustained in the last days of the Civil War almost four years earlier.

Incidentally, the Indian was generally a poor shot at long ranges. He lacked the self-control and patience to learn the correct use of firearms and he had no teacher. All that most braves learned was to save empty shell cases for reloading with powder and lead obtained from traders. But what he lacked in skill in the use of the white man's weapons he more than compensated for in his ferocity in combat when he chose to fight.[28]

At the hastily thrown up hospital, Tom heard the rumor that his old friend, Captain Hamilton, was dead, shot in the back. Rumor also had it that Cooke had shot him, but no one could at that time be sure. Cooke may have had motive to shoot the captain, if he believed that Hamilton was a traitor to the Custer cause, but he certainly never said that he killed the grandson of Alexander Hamilton, and Tom was loath to accuse one of his comrades of murdering another. At least Hamilton had not been captured by the Cheyenne, and had died shot in battle.[29]

Tom also heard in the hospital the story of a teenage bugler boy who sat on a stack of captured buffalo robes near where Dr. Asch was bandaging the young lieutenant's hand. The young bugler's face glistened with bright crimson blood, which trickled down his cheek from a wound in his face. A fleeing Cheyenne had shot the lad in the head with a steel-pointed arrow. The quarrel entered under his eye, glanced off the boy's cheekbone, and emerged near his ear. It looked like the arrow had gone clear through the teenager's head. The steel point, Tom learned, was barbed so it could not be pulled out. Dr. Asch cut the arrowhead off, then withdrew the shaft. He let the wound bleed while the skin stretched back into place before he dressed it. When asked if the bugler had seen the Cheyenne who shot him, he flourished a bloody fresh scalp of a Cheyenne. "If anybody thinks I didn't see him, sir, I want 'em to take a look at that!" he boasted.[30]

Autie later wrote about the regiment's losses in addition to Hamilton's death: "Major Elliott with but six men charged away from the command in pursuit of two Indians . . . not one escaped . . . Col. Barnitz was wounded by a rifle bullet through the bowels . . . Tom receiving a flesh wound in his hand from a bullet."[31]

The fact was, Hamilton and five men were dead, and Tom, Barnitz, a third officer, and eleven men were wounded. Elliott and his men were missing. Of the enemy, Black Kettle and more than one hundred Cheyenne including many women and children had been killed. Fifty-three women and children were captured. The Seventh destroyed a thousand buffalo hides, five hundred pounds of lead, the same amount of powder, four thousand arrows, all the tepees in the village, and seven hundred ponies.

The dismal effects of summer forays against the Indians had prompted Sheridan to recall Custer for the winter campaign.

The victory of the Seventh, although characterized as a massacre, proved a success and firmly established the reputation of the Custers and their regiment as great Indian fighters in the public mind.[32] And they were not yet finished with the winter campaign.

7

THE END OF THE WINTER CAMPAIGN AND KINDRED MATTERS

It was a cold afternoon in December 1868. Tom Custer sat astride his horse beside Myles Moylan at the head of Company A. Over his uniform he wore an army issue greatcoat and over his hands, Berlin mittens. In front of him the Osage and white scouts already moved out southward from Camp Supply. A tall, long-haired man atop a thoroughbred horse skittered about before the first company in the procession—George Armstrong Custer, the great Indian fighter.

Although his friend Elliott and the detachment of cavalrymen had not rejoined the regiment, Tom had concurred with the colonel's decision to fall back to Camp Supply. The huge number of Indians in the Washita Valley made it seem a wise decision. Within a few days the Seventh again marched south, on an errand of mercy this time. When the Nineteenth Kansas Volunteer Cavalry entered the temporary military installation, Colonel Crawford reported that two white girls, a Miss White and a Mrs. Morgan—the latter a bride of one month—had been captured by Cheyenne in raids along the Solomon and Republican River valleys in Kansas. Their capture aroused great indignation in the state. So the Seventh together with the Nineteenth Kansas set out to liberate the women.

The long caravan was led by the scouts, followed by Autie's headquarters squad. Tom gazed at the pennant with the two stars of a major general stitched into its blue field. This was what the elder Custer had been in the Civil War, but no longer was, although army protocol prescribed that he be politely referred to as "General." Custer also used the highest brevet rank of officers in both personal and military correspondence, so whenever Tom was mentioned in an official capacity it often was as Colonel Custer. In some officers' minds, the use by George of the general's pennant was mere showmanship. Benteen, for instance, whose mind always had an acid realism, stared at the flag with an unfavorable thought. In the captain's critical opinion the commander had no right to the use of the two stars. It was a display of vanity that he held against Custer, adding it to his sizable list of Custer's many other obvious faults. After all, Benteen had also been a general during the war, but he did not take advantage of the fact and was not called "general" by anyone.[1]

The Seventh boasted a lot of their experiences to the newcoming Kansans. The regular army troopers felt that each and every one of them was a hero, deserving of a Medal of Honor like Tom's two.

During the Indian Wars, however—a period which extended from 1861 to 1898—the United States army awarded only 416 Medals of Honor to its members. The method of delivering the award was generally informal. A commanding officer at a post, noticing a soldier in his command perform a particularly gallant or heroic act under fire, wrote a missal to the Secretary of War, upon which a Medal of Honor was occasionally issued. Typically, presentations, too, were informal. A dispatch rider would deliver a small, registered package to the winner. If the soldier happened to be gone on a patrol or other mission, the first sergeant would sign for the parcel and casually toss it onto the trooper's bunk. Only rarely was the presentation made at regimental formation. And until after the Battle of the Little Bighorn, in 1876, Tom remained the only soldier in the Seventh Cavalry to have won the only medal the country had to offer in the nineteenth century.[2]

The second march of the regiment during the winter campaign was bitterly cold. On December 7, 1868, despite the inclement weather, Custer took the same trail as he had earlier toward the Washita, with the volunteer Kansans and his own men. Upon their arrival at the now deserted location of Black Kettle's village, which they had destroyed, they learned the fate of Major Elliott and his men.

Those ill-fated soldiers had followed fleeing Indian women and children down the river. Three men were among the fugitives, one of whom was Little Rock, a Cheyenne chief. The three warriors stopped to fight to allow the women and children to escape. Little Rock was killed, but the other two escaped with their fleeing families.

Little Rock's brief, sacrificial diversion saved his people and was fatal to Elliott. Having failed to seize the refugees, Elliott turned to ride back to the regiment. He ran smack into a large band of the braves coming up the valley from the villages below. Elliott's detachment was cut off, surrounded, and massacred in the short fight that followed.

Custer was dejected at the loss when he came across the site.

Gory visitations of the Kidder party seemed to have reappeared. No sane leader could condemn a subordinate to do what Elliott had done. A journey so far from the main body of troops against such terrible odds should have been overruled even if the men were volunteers.

As it was, George and Tom found all but one of Elliott's force in a tight circle where they had fought back to back. The sole exception was a sergeant-major named Kennedy. The Indians later revealed that Kennedy was the last survivor and an attempt was made to seize him alive. Realizing that torture was in store for him—he, too, had seen the Kidder party—Kennedy went along with the red men, pretending that he was willing to surrender. Leaving the circle of dead comrades, he approached one of the suddenly quiet warriors with his hand outstretched in a token of friendship. But when the unsuspecting brave advanced, Kennedy swiftly gutted him with a saber, thus sealing his fate. The other Indians shot him full of holes. They also stripped, mutilated, and pincushioned all the fallen bodies with arrows—the usual method of dishonoring an enemy.[4]

Tom stood by with his hat in his hands and his head hung low in sorrow while Elliott's men were buried. Then he set out again for the chase after the renegade perpetrators of what he saw as a crime. He had a good stomach for a fight.

But the fighting was over for 1868. Farther south, Satanta and Lone Wolf, chiefs of the Kiowa contingent of the huge Washita village, had been met, arrested by another army unit, and used as hostages to force the Kiowa back onto a reservation. The Comanche disgustedly went south of the border into Mexico, the Apache disappeared into the New Mexico mountains, and the Arapaho settled down, which left the Cheyenne the only hostiles still in the field. Finally, the Seventh and the Kansans went into winter quarters at Fort Cobb, Indian Territory.

Not everyone was satisfied with the Custers' performance in the campaign, especially a few of the Kansans. In the first place, the two white girls were still captives, and their rescue was the reason many of the Jayhawkers signed up. Another factor appears to have been the harsh realities of Indian warfare and unnecessary deprivations at the hands of Custer men. Their opinions were best expressed by a youngster from Manhattan, Kansas, who reported regularly to the Manhattan *Standard* throughout his tour of duty with the Nineteenth Kansas. Alfred Lee Runyan, the future father of writer Damon Runyon, enlisted in Company M of the volunteer regiment in October 1868, resigning a position with the *Standard* to do so.[5]

Although Runyan saw no action during the winter, serving primarily as a mounted escort for supply trains from Fort Dodge to Camp Supply, he came to hold George A. Custer in contempt, and he wrote candid stories for his newspaper, one of which mistakenly claimed that more cavalrymen than Indians were killed in the fight on the Washita because of Custer's poor judgment. After his first few letters, Runyan purposely began spelling Custer's name incorrectly. His descriptions of the notorious Washita battlefield written in January 1869, are poignantly revealing:

On the 8th of December we reached our destination and camped about five miles from the battle field of Gen. Custer. The Nineteenth had not yet arrived, so we camped and prepared to make ourselves as comfortable as possible. The next day a party struck out to visit the battle field. Almost everything was burned. From appearances it looked as if there had been between forty and fifty lodges. Later accounts of the battle from eye witnesses, say that the 7th were very glad to get out of there, and that there were more of the cavalry than Indians killed. All the advantage they gained was in the first charge on the north side of the creek, where a few lodges were located. The cavalry had much difficulty in crossing a creek between them and the main part of the lodges, so that the warriors got a good position in the woods from which it was impossible to drive them. This was the "Glorious" victory of the 7th.[6]

Many of Runyan's remaining letters describe the boredom of riding in army supply wagons from Kansas forts to Camp Supply—most of the volunteers' horses had to be requisitioned by the Seventh—and young Runyan obviously chafed under the yoke of military protocol. Rather than the dashing cavalry charges against savages he had envisioned, he and his regiment were relegated to the mundane tasks of a campaign while the Seventh Cavalry and the Custer clan grabbed all the glory. But Runyan also pointed out to his readers back in Manhattan the traits of Custer as a military leader: he was among the first vitriolic critics of Custer's Indian-fighting career; he demonstrated the fact that Custer sought personal fame at the expense of his enlisted men; he proclaimed that Custer was a rabid believer in nepotism, filling the ranks of the Seventh with family and friends; and he implied that any accomplishments Custer showed as an army officer were due more to the highly touted "Custer luck" than to any real skill as a tactician, although the latter criticism was unfair.

Early in 1869, they again launched an array against the captors of the white women. Tom rode beside Autie as the colonel's aide, followed by the Seventh and the Nineteenth Kansas. Both outfits had become hard to handle, Tom and his friends especially causing

Autie some grief. Before leaving Fort Cobb, Custer wrote Libbie on February 9: "I have been very strict with the officers. Have no favorites where duty is concerned! I had had Tom arrested . . . also Yates, for drunkenness and disorderly conduct. George is 'huffy,' but I hope will soon get over it. Tom is cuter than ever, but he is becoming a little wild. A few more nights in the guard-house should tame him down. Nevertheless, his conduct grieves me."[7]

The knowledge that they moved to rescue the white captives calmed the Kansas volunteers, and the return to the field with prospects of action settled Tom and his friends down. The column, guided by a captive Cheyenne girl named Monasetah, located an Arapaho village in February. Autie chose William W. Cooke's sharpshooters to escort him. He selected Captain Sam Robbins, a Dr. Renick, and, naturally, brother Tom, as members of the council. Neva, a friendly and trustworthy Blackfoot who had scouted for John C. Fremont and married Kit Carson's daughter, went along to interpret. "I need not say that in the opinion of many of our comrades our mission was regarded as closely bordering on the imprudent, to qualify it by no stronger term," Autie remembered. Little Raven, the Arapaho chieftain, received the group without incident and agreed to return his people to their reservation. Cheyenne were nowhere to be found.[8]

After hunting high and low, Monasetah at last located a Cheyenne village. It would have been easy enough for the regiment to ride roughshod over the Indians as it had earlier in the winter. Instead, in order to keep the prisoners which the colonel supposed were there from being slain, as they had seen the white boy killed in the village on the Washita, Autie and Tom resolved to use diplomacy in place of force. They sent the girl guide to the encampment to make "good promises of peace." Medicine Arrow, a Cheyenne leader in his middle years, cautiously talked with the Custers' emissary before calling a council with "the Long Hair" and "Buffalo Calf"—Armstrong and Tom, respectively.

Armstrong, Tom, and their compatriots met representatives of the Cheyenne in a sacred lodge. There, Custer swore his peaceful intentions while Medicine Arrow smoked a pipe under the Sacred Medicine Arrows of the Cheyenne and emptied the ashes on the colonel's boots to bring death to whoever breached the promise of peace, in accordance with the Indians' ceremony of truthtelling. Thereafter, Tom listened, bored and impatient at once, for days. His brother flattered, cajoled, pleaded, threatened, and promised tediously, never believing the Cheyenne when they told him they had no white captives. At last, he exacted a promise from Medicine Arrow to follow him to the agency.[9]

Armstrong then took a bold step. After the Cheyenne started to the agency behind the two cavalry regiments, the colonel called a hasty council. The meeting was actually a trap. Troopers of the Seventh attempted to seize the Cheyenne leaders. Medicine Arrow escaped, but three Indians were taken, to be hanged unless the band surrendered the white prisoners immediately. These prisoners were with another band, but Medicine Arrow convinced his fellow Cheyenne to relinquish the white captives.

The colonel broke his word in the eyes of the Indians, once by capturing the warriors after promising peace in the sacred lodge. He did so again, not only in the eyes of the Indians but also in those of many of the anti-Custer officers, when, after the two girls were sent to him mounted on a single pony, he kept his own three prisoners. The captive warriors were taken back to Kansas where two were killed and the third wounded. Another strike was scored against Custer.[10]

The return of the white prisoners effectively concluded the winter campaign. With all the Indians on the southern plains presumably under control, General Sheridan went back East, and Armstrong and Tom journeyed to Fort Leavenworth with good news for Libbie. The Seventh Cavalry was to be camped near Fort Hays during the upcoming summer. She and Anna Darrah could join the regiment.[11]

Tom looked forward to getting back to the civilization of Hays City, crude as it was. The bewitching beguilements of brothels, saloons, and gambling salons enticed him, although Tom, like his brother, was basically quite religious. Old Emmanuel Custer believed his sons, as he himself did, should have deep religious convictions. He also assumed that they should hold deep political convictions—provided they were of a Democratic bent. If either Tom or Autie had any such political convictions, they were only temporary. The boys supported a political personage or principle rather than a political party.[12]

Tom carried a small four-by-six-inch volume, *The Words of Jesus,* with him throughout the recent campaign. Inside the front cover of the volume was the following inscription: "For Col. T. W. Custer, 7th Cavalry, U.S.A." On the flyleaf, in the same lovely, flowing penmanship: "Lulie G. Burgess, 405 Grove St., Jersey City, June 20/68." Miss Burgess was Tom's Eastern sweetheart. Some historians have evidence that Lulie Burgess eventually became Tom's fiancée, but little is known about her. Tom made a few references to her in letters written to others, but no letters between the couple have yet come to light. However, Tom made use of her gift. Many passages were underlined and numerous were the notations in Tom's own handwriting placed in the margins of the dogeared pages. Lawrence Frost, owner of the book, recorded "Prophetically he had written in it: 'For strangers into life we come, and dying is but home. Going home. Home, Lord, tarry not, but come.'"[13]

However, Tom Custer's lifestyle belied the words in his religious book. He was sometimes a hellion both during official military expeditions and in camp. He had good reason, too. For the common soldier and officer alike, life in the Kansas military installations usually consisted of sheer boredom. The red warriors seldom struck near more than one fort at a time, and the men at the other stations were seldom called upon for assistance. So they stayed at home. Drill on the parade grounds, stable duty for the cavalry, occasional target practice, fatigue duty, and manual upkeep of the forts consumed most of the soldiers' time. Troopers looked forward to patrols and campaigns as relief from the doldrums of post life, while buffalo hunts entertained officers. Leaves to the nearest town came about once a month, around payday. Soldiers in Kansas were a bored lot.

The Seventh would not have things quite so bad during their summer stay at Fort Hays. To begin with, the men were near enough to the town of Hays City to visit frequently when they were off duty.

Second, Custer and the Seventh were acknowledged to be the premier Indian fighters on the plains by Generals Sherman and Sheridan and the American public. Late in the summer of 1869 the new colonel of the regiment, Brevet Major General Samuel D. Sturgis, wrote in an official communication to his headquarters: "There is, perhaps, no other officer of equal rank on this line, who has worked more faithfully against the Indians, or who has acquired the same degree of knowledge of the country and of the Indian character."[14]

The Custer family returned to Hays where the regiment's former scout, Wild Bill Hickok, reigned as marshal. Hickok got along famously with George and Elizabeth. He and Tom had swapped tales of derring-do in narrow, sawdust-floored bars. A new personality had been initiated into the Custer gang, too, one whom Tom found interesting. The veterinary position in the regiment had been left vacant since the outfit was activated in 1866. It was not until May 1869, that Dr. John Honsinger, a German national but at that time living in Adrian, Michigan, accepted the first appointment as senior veterinary surgeon of the Seventh Cavalry. Tom took an immediate liking to Dr. Honsinger, and he was destined to play a fateful part in Tom's future.

The regiment's year had been just the opposite of most—instead of campaigning in warm weather and holing up in the winter, Custer's men had suffered and fought through an unusually long, severe cold season. Now the Seventh returned to Kansas to camp just north of Fort Hays and, according to Libbie's cousin Florence Bingham, "to draw a six months' pay. The poor fellows had been out all winter with scarcely enough clothing and on half rations." She continued,

After tents were pitched and camp made, Custer, for their loyalty and faithfulness, gave them two weeks off duty to do as they pleased. What they "pleased" was to come to town and eat and drink; they cleared the town of food and almost of drink. Every evening Custer would send up two dozen or more six-mule teams hitched to big army wagons and have all the drunks put in, two or three deep, and hauled back to camp to sober up and let them do the same thing next day, if they wanted to.[15]

The Seventh had arrived at its camp on April 8, 1869. The regiment stayed together there for almost a month, but it was broken up in May to be assigned in detachments to protect the frontier at various places. Colonel William S. Moorhouse, the state adjutant general of Kansas, reported that there were fewer troops in the state than in the previous year. But there were still "enough Indians on the war-path to make serious trouble" and pioneers on the plains acted "imprudently in pushing too far west." The African-American Tenth Cavalry that had paralleled the Seventh into Indian Territory had been sent to Texas. To supply extra troops in case they were needed, the new governor of Kansas, James M. Harvey, a Manhattan resident who replaced Samuel J. Crawford, ordered the enrollment of the state militia. Only fifty men were left near Fort Hays, and of those, one company of the Seventh had been sent to Ogallah some twenty miles west where there had recently been an Indian "disturbance."[16]

The Indian troubles, however, did not prevent the summer from being a leisurely season. Tom, at a mere twenty-four years of age, settled back to enjoy himself, reveling in his status as a member of the best Indian-fighting regiment in the West and the brother of the most notable victor over the hostiles. Frost has described him thus: "Like the rest of the Custer family he took things in stride. Not burdened with too much responsibility, and still single, he enjoyed a good time with the boys."[17] When not on duty, he could be found sometimes playing cards in Honsinger's quarters, sometimes swilling liquor at the bar of Tommy Drumm's saloon in Hays City, sometimes whiling away his spare time in his tent fiddling with his Indian trophies.

Once, Tom insisted that Elizabeth visit his quarters to examine his extraordinary collection. Libbie later recalled that that visit was always a vivid memory thereafter. She viewed canvas walls littered with Indian paraphernalia—weapons and war bonnets, painted buffalo hide shields, Berkeley necklaces and scalp locks, including a Cheyenne warrior's leather shirt trimmed with the grisly memorials. Yet these were the least of the surprises.[18]

On the floor of his tent Tom kept his valued collection of seven rattlesnakes in emptied wooden hardtack boxes. After presenting to her his captured Indian memorabilia, he said, "Well, old lady, I have some beauties to show you this time, captured them on purpose for you." Libbie was not a squeamish sort, but she shivered as her brother-in-law stretched every one of them to its full length and urged it to shake its rattles. Tom was surprised, too. Upon lifting the lid of one box, he counted one too few reptiles. A large rattler had gobbled up his smaller boxmate.[19]

Libbie exercised her wry sense of humor by telling Tom that he should house all the snakes in the same box, explaining patiently that all animals sought and craved companionship. Tom was not fooled by the impish lady. "If you think, old lady, that after all the trouble I have been to, to catch these snakes to show you, I am going to make it easy for them to eat each other up, you are mightily mistaken."[20]

The rest of the regiment was not far behind Tom in the matter of pets. The camp contained specimens of most of the wild fauna of the prairie kept by one or another of the outfit—Libbie said that there were wolves, prairie dogs, raccoons, porcupines, wild cats, badgers, fawns, young antelopes, and even a buffalo calf. Autie possessed a wolf that he raised with his hounds, and Tom kept his snakes. To liven up a dull evening, Tom was fond of inviting an unsuspecting guest to take a seat upon one of the boxes and watching the shocked expression on his face when the rattlers started their ominous buzzing.

The Custers did not simply capture wild beasts, either. There was somewhat of a rivalry between Tom and the colonel in the matter of hunting, Custer family biographer Minnie Dubbs Millbrook has noted, "and in some ways Tom rather had the edge on the general. Elk for instance were not to be found near a town or traveled route. Hence they were taken usually by the small units on scouts out along the more remote creeks and valleys."[21]

Elizabeth Bacon Custer wrote about one hunting excursion in her book, *Following the Guidon*:

Of all the scouting parties that summer, our brother Tom and another officer had the best shooting score. . . . They had deer, antelope, elk, and wild turkey every day, while we had been blessed with little besides buffalo meat. . . . They saw two different herds of elks which numbered about a hundred each. . . . The elks, like the deer and antelopes, occasionally make themselves easy prey for the hunter . . . Colonel Tom let the elks he shot approach, gazing at him, till within seventy yards before he took aim.[22]

On occasion when a big party hunted buffalo a long distance from civilization, elk could be found. Once George tried valiantly to bag one. "The huge animal was lying down very near the place selected for our camp," wrote Libbie, "and hearing our voices . . . he leaped into the air, and bounded off like a gazelle instead of a beast of such proportions . . . Colonel Tom said it was as large as a large-sized mule. With almost as quick a leap as the game, General Custer sprang for his rifle, flung himself on an unsaddled horse, and sped over the ground after the splendid game, but it had too much the start of him and we lost the elk steak."[23]

Then, too, tourists poured in to visit them, and just about every prominent person coming west expected to be introduced to them. If he was a hunter, his greatest hope was to be invited on a buffalo hunt by the colonel. British Lord Paget went with George and Tom after woolies, accompanied by a hundred mounted troopers pulled together from their assorted stations especially for the occasion. Lord Paget was so grateful for the royal treatment that he presented Autie with a case containing a Galand and Somerville revolver that fired a .44-caliber Webly cartridge. Much to his delight, Tom received a similar weapon, which he carried with him for most of the rest of his life.[24]

Companions of the opposite sex and matchmaking also kept the Custer gang busy. It seems Tom corresponded regularly with Lulie Burgess throughout the course of the summer, and Libbie encouraged the relationship; but Tom was acquainted with the "soiled doves" that lurked around Hays City. He may, too, have had an intimate involvement with an Indian girl, about which more will be said later.

The principal love affair of the summer, however, was that between Libbie's friend Anna Darrah and Tom's friend Myles Moylan. By the end of the summer, Diana had accepted—at Libbie's and Tom's urging—the proposal of marriage from Moylan. That officer of Company A had tagged along at Miss Darrah's skirts like a lovesick puppy during the hot months, so everyone but Lieutenant Cooke, who had designs on the young lady himself, were excited for the engaged couple.

After the hard winter campaign, the spring and summer of 1869 came as a welcome relief. For a time, Tom had a chance to dwell upon his relationship with the most celebrated officer of the Indian-fighting army with pleasure, and he took advantage of the situation despite the differences between the two. George Custer was five years older. He had immediate charm; he was articulate; when he wanted to be, he was intellectual. On the other hand, Tom Custer was a younger brother, slightly smaller, less immediately charming, less urbane, less articulate. It seemed that everything came easily to George; things did not come so easily for Tom. Autie was a man of passion, a romantic, while Tom was a man of action and physical display of emotion. Yet they were joined by the closest of bonds. If myth and legend can be accepted as historical sources, other happenings of 1869 will cause one to wonder how that could be the case.

Fig. 1: Thomas Ward Custer, winner of two Medals of Honor, subject of Western lore, career soldier who always seemed to be present where there was action, yet lived and died in his brother's shadow. *Western Historical Collection, Denver Public Library*

Fig. 2: George Armstrong Custer, brother of Tom. *Kansas State Historical Society*

Fig. 3: Some of the Seventh Cavalry's officers in camp on Big Creek, near Fort Hays, following the campaign of 1867. The campaign was less than fruitful. Autie lies on the ground at left, reading a newspaper. Tom is seated on the right foreground at Libbie's right elbow.

Fig. 4: The Custers in camp near Fort Hays, 1869. Armstrong was fond of posing in this style. Tom is seated at far left, Armstrong leans against the tent pole, and Libbie appears at the extreme right. *Kansas State Historical Society*

Fig. 5: A game of charades relieved the boredom of garrison life at Fort Hays during the winter. In costume at center is Tom, somber despite his boyish nature. On the left is Maggie Custer, Tom's younger sister who later married Lieutenant James Calhoun. On the right is Elizabeth, looking as impish as she was. *Kansas State Historical Society*

Fig.6: Tom posed with fellow officers and friends at Fort Abraham Lincoln shortly after the arrival of the Seventh Cavalry in 1873. He is seen wearing a forage cap, high on the stairs leaning lightly on the banister, directly below another officer by the porch post. *Western Historical Collection, Denver Public Library*

Fig. 7: The interment of victims of the Little Bighorn in the National Cemetery at Fort Leavenworth in 1877. Tom was one of those buried there, as were his brother-in-law and close friend James Calhoun, brother Boston Custer, and nephew Henry Armstrong ("Autie") Reed. As always, Autie outshone Tom, even in death—he is buried at West Point, where he started his military career at the bottom of his class. *Kansas State Historical Society*

Fig. 8: In 1913, thirty-seven years after the battle, Rodman Wanamaker photographed four of the Crow scouts on Last Stand Hill paying tribute to those who fell with Custer. The cross marks the spot where George fell. Tom died not far from here, so badly mutilated that he was identified only with difficulty. *National Archives and Record Service*

8

IS IT TRUE WHAT THEY SAY?

Men in the East and the West found George Armstrong Custer a fascinating personality, and it is a matter of course that women did, too. As noted, Tom was popular with the ladies as well. At this point, the years 1868 and 1869, it seems a good time to explore the myriad confusing legends and the few solid facts about the Custers and women.

It is well-known that Tom was something of a hedonist, but a majority of historical writers assert that Lulie Burgess was his one and only sweetheart. Apparently, he corresponded regularly with her. If he ever made a proposal, it no longer seems to exist in written form. What *is* known is that he prepared a last will and testament, filed on June 19, 1873, in the Monroe, Michigan, county courthouse. His property was to be shared equally through this instrument between his mother and Lulie. The document further stated that in the event that Lulie was no longer living, all of Tom's estate was to go to Mother Custer. After the Battle of the Little Bighorn, his mother became the sole heir to his estate. The implication of Lulie's inclusion in Tom's last will leaves the impression that Tom was indeed in love with Miss Burgess and that she was his intended.[1]

Little is known about Lulie Burgess. The most that has been recorded are a few references in Tom's letters written to third parties. According to researchers, no letters between the couple have yet been found. Lulie was apparently in poor health for some years, and she may have died between the time Tom made out his will and his own demise. He may well have known this, since his will was written in such a way that if she died before he did, all of his estate was to be delivered to his mother. Still, no reference to Lulie's fate is recorded in any of the existing correspondence, nor has a noted authority's examination of New Jersey state records revealed anything about her fate.[2]

Tom's relationship with Lulie did not prevent him from engaging in other romantic interludes. That he had a thing for a skirt is sure. Also, the existence of photographic and printed pornography in nineteenth-century America is an undeniable fact, particularly from the Civil War years forward. Considering Tom's predilection toward that sort of entertainment common among bachelor soldiers, he undoubtedly came into contact with it. How much interaction he had with such non-Victorian materials remains unknown.

Derogatory portrayals of the Custers have become commonplace in popular media since the 1950s. Contributions to the myth showing them as vain, ambitious, and foolish include alleged affairs with women. In the society of ladies, with whom their deeds made them favorites, both brothers manifested few of the gallantries that typically arise from vanity.[3]

Novelist Douglas C. Jones took note of Autie's good-natured joshing in his best-selling book, *The Court-Martial of George Armstrong Custer*. In this fanciful fiction, which speculated on what might have been had the brothers survived the Little Bighorn, Jones used Lieutenant Luther R. Hare of Company K, Seventh Cavalry, as his spokesman: "'General Custer was always what I would call a close-mouthed commander about his plans. Yet he was vocal in all other ways. He was always talking with his officers, teasing and joking—he teased his brother Tom about women—' Hare stops and flushes, glancing toward the Custers."[4]

More substantially, Indian records comment on Armstrong's fondness for Indian girls. The Cheyenne even joked about it. According to John Stands in Timber, one Cheyenne named Beaver Heart claimed that when the scouts warned Custer about the size of the village before Little Bighorn he snickered and said, "When we get to that village I'm going to find the Sioux girl with the most elk teeth on her dress and take her along with me." Cheyenne and to a lesser extent Sioux were generally distrustful of sex, so when Custer supposedly said he intended to find the girl with the most elk teeth on her dress he, in effect, implied that he was going to locate the least chaste Sioux woman to carry back with him.

Too many sources mention the army's custom of exercising the rights of victors in the matter of feminine spoils of war to deny the existence of the practice. True, military records attempt to overlook the practice or justify it, but the numerous stories about the abuse of one Indian girl by the Custer cadre tend to demonstrate otherwise.

Monasetah, the Cheyenne prisoner Armstrong kept as guide and interpreter during the latter part of the winter campaign, was the beautiful daughter of Chief Little Rock, who died trying to save the rest of his family at the fight along the Washita. Alternately spelled Monaseta, Monaseetah, Monahseetah, and Meyotzi, the name probably means "Young Grass that Shoots in Spring." Autie convinced General Phil Sheridan to allow him to keep her around, ostensibly as an interpreter even though she neither spoke nor understood word one of the English language. Stephen Longstreet, author of *War Cries on Horseback,* asserts that Custer "lived with her as his concubine (mistress would be too respectful a word) for four months, leaving her behind only to rejoin his wife at Fort Hays."[6]

Longstreet is unduly harsh in this comment, for he repeats only scandalous myths spouted by other historical writers. The truth of the matter is that no one knows for certain exactly what Monasetah's place was in the lives of the Custers. She was constantly accompanied by an older Cheyenne woman by the name of Marissa. Autie believed that Marissa married him to Monasetah, so that she could claim the rest of the Cheyenne nation as relation, and Custer would have to make peace and to care and provide for them.

Marissa and Monasetah were taken along with the string of nearly fifty other captive women and children led in triumph across a hundred miles of snow-encrusted prairie to Camp Supply. Western writer Mari Sandoz wrote in *Cheyenne Autumn:* "When the young girls were selected for the officers' tents on that cold march, she was sent to Custer."[8] To be on the safe side, the army regularly, and often with bleak laughter, searched Indian women down to the skin to assure that they concealed no weapons, making great play with their hands beneath the skirts of their frightened victims. The troops sometimes discharged their carbines as though by accident between the feet of any warriors who looked as though they might protest. The common assumption was that Indians were sexually permissive or too uncivilized to care or both. Plenty of enlisted personnel and a few officers wound up as squawmen, in some cases going native. So the possibility is great that some Indian women were taken to warm soldiers' blankets.

In his memoirs, *My Life on the Plains,* George Custer took great pains to describe his involvement with Monasetah. Some Custer critics feel that this is a case of "Methinks he doth protest too much." George wrote that fifty-three squaws and papooses were brought before him and Tom—"Strong Arm" and "Buffalo Calf" as the two brothers were called by the Cheyenne. Marissa placed seventeen-year-old Monasetah's hand in Custer's and "began to mumble a singsong of Cheyenne formulas." He also went to great lengths to describe the girl: "An exceedingly comely squaw possessing a bright cheery face, a countenance beaming with intelligence, and a disposition more inclined to be merry than one usually finds among the Indians. . . . Added to bright laughing eyes, a set of pearly teeth, and a rich complexion, her well-shaped head was crowned with a luxuriant growth of the most beautiful silken tresses rivaling in color the blackness of the raven and extending, when allowed to fall loosely over her shoulders, to below her waist."[9]

Monasetah went along on the winter campaign that pursued her own people far south in freezing cold. Speculation runs rife as to whether George ever consummated what he supposed to be a marriage to the girl. At the same time, some critics support the claim that if George did not, Tom did. To "Buffalo Calf"—so called on account of his short curly locks—Monasetah was "Sally Ann." Kinsley has callously remarked that for Tom she was "just another convenient and compliant wench." He goes on to explain, "She submitted to him because he was Yellowhair's brother, and that was the proper thing to do. But Tom abused his fraternal rights, and everyone knew it. It was a standing joke among the senior officers. As Fred Benteen put it, 'Custer winks at being cuckolded by his kid-brother. That relieves him of his own blanket duty.'"[10]

What Kinsley noted is an anthropological fact. Cheyenne tradition placed great emphasis on kindred relationships. Ethnologically speaking, a Cheyenne woman's husband had every right to allow his brother to share his wife—by the same token, a Cheyenne husband might be expected by his wife to service her unmarried sisters, as E. Adamson Hoebel pointed out in *The Cheyenne* and Thomas Berger illustrated well in his novel *Little Big Man*.[11] If Monasetah did indeed view her relationship with George as a marriage, she would not have considered it untoward to enter into a romantic encounter with Tom. Not only that, cultural shock and her position as a foreigner to white customs would have led her to assume that if anyone, including Tom, told her that it was a white custom for a brother to share his woman, she would likely have gone along with the explanation for fear of what might happen to her if she did not.

That Tom enjoyed some form of romantic tryst during that interminable expedition is highly possible. He was still unattached at that time, and only twenty-four years old. Some Custer authorities claim that while at Fort Sill in Indian Territory, Tom and several other members of the notorious Custer clan took the mercurial cure for venereal disease. The source of this knowledge—the Fort Sill medical records for January and February, 1869—have mysteriously vanished, but they evidently listed numerous officers of the Seventh Cavalry as treated for a social disease. Those noted had all entertained sexual contact with infected Indian women. It is alleged that those same missing reports included G. A. Custer's name, as Kinsley wrote, "by virtue of the curse of Venus, which poses several possibilities." Unfortunately, this cannot be verified.[12]

About the same time, Armstrong observed that Tom was "becoming more profane and a little vulgar." That comment, in light of the misplaced medical records, becomes more meaningful. And his careless remark that Monasetah "had become a great favorite with the entire Command" would tend to give credence to Benteen's claim that Strong Arm had been cuckolded by Lieutenant Tom, if not by any number of the rest of the Custer gang.[13]

The implied sexual affairs between Monasetah on one side and Tom and George on the other raises another interesting question. Did one or the other of the brothers father a child by her? Many Southern Cheyenne, with a half-hearted sort of pride, allege that George did, wryly pointing out Custer's way with women.[14] John Stands in Timber, however, discounts this tale in his memoirs, *Cheyenne Memories.* Yet it is a fact that toward the end of the campaign, Monasetah bore a son.[15]

Mari Sandoz wrote, "When Custer's wife was coming to him, the Cheyenne girl was sent back to the Indians, where his son was born toward the autumn moon." It is significant to note that Sandoz does not refer to the pair's relationship as a marriage. Frost ardently denies this statement, placing the birth of the baby in January 1869, and saying, "Historical writers, more inclined to accept gossip rather than facts, have tried to link the child to Custer. One respected writer—Mari Sandoz—accepted the gossip without question. Describing the baby as light skinned and light haired, a genetic rarity under the circumstances, she repeatedly calls it Custer's child. . . . Libbie, who saw the baby that spring, described it as dark skinned and dark eyed."[17]

Still another set of facts and another interpretation comes from

Kinsley: "Late August, 1869. According to medical records, a fair-haired boy was born to Meyotzi in the stockade at Fort Hays. She named him Yellow-Bird. It has been assumed by many Cheyennes and anti-Custerites, that the child was sired by Yellowhair; but the weight of evidence seems to rest on Brother Tom. Autie and Libbie certainly wanted a child, and their disappointment in this desire raises a significant question."[18]

A question to be considered is whether the Cheyenne confused Autie with Tom. It has been seen in an earlier chapter that Tom borrowed clothes from Armstrong after the incident with the polecat and, being brothers, they resembled one another in some physical ways. Tom rarely let his hair grow long and usually sported only a pencil-thin mustache, unlike Autie's goatee. But references to the name Custer could have referred to either George or Tom, causing confusion to the Cheyenne understanding of sibling relationships. Moreover, had Tom taken advantage of his fraternal rights with Monasetah, the child of their matching would probably still have been considered George's in the eyes of the Cheyenne.

Brave Bear, a minor Cheyenne chieftain with a faulty memory, recalled his reaction to Monasetah's story this way: "When my mind darkened with thoughts of Meyotzi's disgrace, I spilled dead ashes from the peacepipe on Yellowhair's boots, thus cursing him into eternity."[19] He was undoubtedly describing the truthtelling ceremony conducted by Medicine Arrow when the white women were returned to Custer during the late campaign, but Indians were noted for telling white interviewers what they thought the white folks wanted to hear. Still, Brave Bear believed that the child was the son of one or the other of the Custer gang, for he said of the girl, "She was a proud woman; she kept silence as the child of the soldier-chief grew in her womb. Finally, when the soldier-chief was talking peace with us, Meyotzi told him she was happy to bear his child. After that, he shunned her like a plague."[20]

It was curious yet probably better for her that Monasetah kept silence concerning the whole affair. On that fact everyone agrees. Had she stated that the child was definitely the son of Custer, or of Tom, or that of any of the other officers of the Seventh, some would point to that as proof, others as mere Indian boasting. She may have kept quiet in deference to her own dignity as she belonged, as Autie pointed out, "to the cream of the [Cheyenne] aristocracy, if not to royalty itself."[21]

More likely, she held her tongue out of embarrassment. From all the evidence available, Monasetah was in her teens. Cheyenne courtship was a long, bashful, drawn-out affair, so it is safe to assume that she was unmarried. So her bearing of anyone's child, whether the father was white or Indian, dictated that she was an unchaste woman, as she apparently had sexual relations before marriage. This caused her acute embarrassment. George Bird Grinnell has accurately described the Cheyenne social dictums regarding fallen women in *The Fighting Cheyennes:* "The women of the Cheyennes are famous among all western tribes for their chastity. In old times it was most unusual for a girl to be seduced, and she who had yielded was disgraced forever. The matter at once became known, and she was taunted with it wherever she went. It was never forgotten. No young man would marry her."[22]

It was only years afterward that traders told Monasetah that Autie included her in a book, praising her charms, beauty, and grace.

The child Monasetah bore was named Yellow Bird or Yellow Swallow. This causes even more confusion. Those who claim the child was Custer's say that his mother named him after George, which may be the case whether or not it was his spawn. Monasetah and Yellow Swallow were ignored or abused by the Cheyenne. After years of degradation, mother and son and the old woman Marissa took their leave of their own band to join the Sioux, perhaps to be with a people not so prejudiced in their pride. It was only after she knew that the Custers were dead that she took a husband, and then not a Cheyenne.[23]

From all this jumble of allegations and reputed facts, nothing but questions crop up. If, however, all this information could be proved legitimate, then an interesting and thus far unexplored possibility also lives. To give way to speculation for the moment, a combination of all the previously mentioned data indicates the chance that there may have been two girls who bore children at Fort Hays in 1869. The several variations of the spelling of Monasetah's name might be construed to refer to two different girls; the different dates of the birth of Yellow Swallow—one in January and one in August—could mean that there were actually two babies born; and the documented statements of Elizabeth and a letter from Benteen to an acquaintance that the child was dark-haired and dark-skinned refer definitely to the child born in January, while most of the comments about the papoose born in August depict him as light-skinned and fair-haired. The truth will probably never be known, but, as Kinsley concluded, "such is the stuff of which legends are made."[24]

The rumors about Autie's bedding of Monasetah met him at Fort Hays in the spring of 1869. They had Libbie upset, too. She was anxious to meet Monasetah and her baby birthed during captivity. Tom did not ease her anxieties with his teasing. Once at the fort he told her, according to Margaret Leighton: "You'd better go along with Autie, next time," to see the Indian captives. "He walks right into the stockade, and you should see how all the squaws come crowding around him, petting him and stroking his hair and rubbing their cheeks against his!"[25]

It took a while, but at her request her husband at last consented to take her to see Monasetah and the other Cheyenne prisoners. Allowing Libbie to go along with him to see Monasetah and her baby was something Custer would never have done to his wife had Yellow Swallow been his son. Also, if Monasetah's papoose was born in January, as Mrs. Custer's memoirs indicate, the time element crumbles the half-breed son theory. Since Custer had never laid eyes on the girl prior to the November 27 fight at the Washita, she could in no way have borne his baby. The assumption that Custer took Libbie to see mother and son to disprove the nasty rumors carries considerable weight.[26]

When Colonel and Mrs. Custer entered the stockade, the Cheyenne women closed around Libbie to touch her and to brush their cheeks against hers in the same form of affectionate, respectful caress that they used with George. Elizabeth visited the stockade frequently after that initial trip, and although the captive squaws never showed her any but the utmost respect, she had been told stories—largely by Tom and his fellow officers—of the craftiness of the cunning Indian women. Tom told her why the enlisted men searched them inside and outside their clothing and about their willingness to plunge a blade into an enemy—the thought never left her mind.[27]

Fear was something that came through the kinship of the Custers in vigorous undertones. Armstrong, it was felt by many, ruled the Seventh Cavalry by intimidation. Shooting an enlisted man in Texas, ordering Tom and Cooke to shoot deserters, broad arrests of officers and enlisted men alike, even arresting his own brother on several occasions, all point to Custer's fear for his position in the regiment and his attempt to instill a similar fear in his underlings. Douglas C. Jones illustrates this fear in his novel, *The Court-Martial of George Armstrong Custer*, during his fictional prosecutor's examination of Major Marcus Reno.

"Major Reno, are you afraid of Custer?"

For the first time since he took the stand, Reno looks squarely at Custer for an extended moment. He shakes his head. "I am not personally afraid of him—or any man, sir. But as my commanding officer I was. Anyone who has ever served under him is frightened of what he might do. He is a cruel and unjust—"

"I object!" screams Jacobson [the fictional defense attorney]. "Sustained!"

"Even his own brother, who served under him? Was he frightened of Custer too?"

"Mr. President, I object," Jacobson fairly screams. Reno shouts, "Yes, he was afraid!"[28]

In regard to Thomas Ward Custer, the colonel's fear may have been prompted by jealousy. In more than one way, Tom excelled in areas that Armstrong considered his fields of expertise. It has been demonstrated that a rivalry existed between the brothers in the realm of hunting. Custer, the career soldier and most famous Indian-fighter in the West, never received the Medal of Honor, although Tom delighted in wearing the two he won in the War Between the States. The colonel occasionally allowed his jealousy to emerge—in a letter to Elizabeth he wrote that "Tom appeared at formal mess last evening wearing both of his baubles."[29]

Here again we witness the sibling rivalry out of which the two brothers never grew. George was the most popular, most urbane, most skillful; he had the rank and position to which Tom aspired, he had a wife of the sort Tom wanted, he was recognized as an authority in the same circles in which Tom traveled. Tom had the proof of his own successes, physical evidence like his medals, his Indian souvenirs, and his big game trophies. Since he was not as free to travel as Autie, since he was not close personal friends with the big shots as was Autie, he was frustrated by his ambition and the realization that his success and advancement thus far would not have been possible without his brother. George could have been jealous of Tom because, having been a hell-raiser in his own youth, his station and his wife kept him in line according to the Victorian moral attitudes of the nineteenth century. And Tom's flaunting of his material reminders of his accomplishments could not have helped soothe any ruffled feathers.

Popular as George and Tom were in Hays City in 1869, there was someone else there who attracted an equal amount of attention. Several contemporary writers have described how Wild Bill Hickok, the Seventh Cavalry's former Great Plains scout, was eagerly sought out by visitors. Mrs. Custer and others specified that ladies were particularly interested in seeing the famous frontiersman. Joseph G. Rosa's biography of Hickok, *They Called Him Wild Bill,* reports that "it has been alleged that trains made special or extended stops for this purpose."[30]

Libbie went into perfect ecstasies describing Hickok—"Wild Bill reminded me of a thoroughbred horse." Like the other female persons she mentioned, Elizabeth was thoroughly taken by the man:

Physically, he was a delight to look upon. Tall, lithe, and free in every motion, he rode and walked as if every muscle was perfection, and the careless swing of his body as he moved seemed perfectly in keeping with the man, the country, the time in which he lived. I do not recall anything finer in the way of physical perfection than Wild Bill when he swung himself lightly from his saddle, and with graceful, swaying step, squarely set shoulders and well poised head, approached our tent for orders. He was rather fantastically clad, of course, but all that seemed perfectly in keeping with the time and place. He did not make an armory of his waist, but carried two pistols. He wore top-boots, riding breeches, and dark blue flannel shirt, with scarlet set in front. A loose neck-handkerchief left his fine firm throat free. I do not at all remember his features, but the frank, manly, expression of his fearless eyes and his courteous manner gave one the feeling of confidence in his word and in his undaunted courage.[31]

Mrs. Custer's literary fascination with Hickok's physical characteristics has led some writers in recent years to suggest that Libbie and Wild Bill conducted a love affair of several year's duration. Private sources indicate that although barren, Elizabeth Bacon Custer was a high-spirited young lady fond of costuming herself, and suffered great loneliness and deprivation during the long absences of her husband. Custer experts categorically refute the innuendo of assignations between the lady-killing Hickok and the colonel's wife. The love affair between George and Libbie is one of the famous romantic instances in the history of the American West. Rosa mentions the suggestion that Hickok and Mrs. Custer corresponded but admits that the evidence is not conclusive.[32]

At Hays, the three Custers were almost inseparable. If Tom and Autie were not campaigning and if Tom was not carousing and George not entertaining his many admirers, the brothers could normally be found in Libbie's company. Rumor has it that some

Hickok letters exist which link Tom and Libbie romantically. Of course, this would mean that brother Tom not only cuckolded the colonel with Monasetah (if he really did) but also with Custer's own wife. The rumored letters have never been made public, if they exist at all.

Given the staunch Victorian morals of the time, Tom dealt with Libbie in a far from flattering manner both personally and in correspondence. The few letters available from the lieutenant to his brother's wife are somewhat frank. One in particular was at one time comical and intimate. Libbie had learned basic sewing skills from her mother in Monroe, and when she evidenced an urge to save some money for her new clothes by staying at home while George went to Louisville, Kentucky, on a horse-buying trip, he returned home with a newfangled sewing machine, of which his little wife was very proud. Although the New England textile factories turned out manufactured clothes, lingerie, and underclothing, she delighted in making her own dresses, becoming so deeply involved in it that she made brother Tom some underdrawers and nightgowns. Tom's very personal letter thanking her showed that he was a perfectionist and that Elizabeth still had much to learn about men's clothes:

"The drawers are better than the first pair, but you didn't make the strap so it wouldn't twist the leg halfway round. The nighties are very nice, but don't put so much lace on them. Ruffles are better. Make the buttonholes run up and down instead of crosswise. Don't think I'm finding fault. I showed them to Doc [Dr. Honsinger] and Lt. [Thomas] French and they think they are grand." He wound up his hints with this conclusion: "I wish you would keep your eye on that old hag that is doing my sewing and make her more careful and write oftener to your devoted brother Tom!"[33]

What was George doing while he was away from his little wife and she and Tom were intimated to be intimate? Well, those who allege that Libbie and Tom had an affair also claim that Autie possessed wandering eyes. For instance, he is often reputed to have had a thing for Eliza, the young, married black woman who was the Custer family's cook and maid. They point to Armstrong's complaining letter to Libbie, which expressed his desire to have Eliza and her biscuits along with him on the Washita campaign, stating that he wanted more than her culinary talents and turned to Indian girls when the black woman failed to show up. There are other suggestions about Custer's supposed intimacies with another black woman who replaced Eliza in later years and also plenty of stories about him and his involvement with white women in the East. Rumor and gossip are again the basis for such fables; solid evidence indicates that Custer never expressed an interest in eliciting extramarital experiences, in spite of opportunity. Whittaker, his first biographer, said that he manifested none of the exaggerated chivalrous actions which develop from personal vanity, but in the company of women he was always gallant and courteous.

Yellow Swallow, the young Indian lad whom Cheyenne say was fathered either by Armstrong or Tom, and his mother Monasetah, were released from the stockade at Fort Hays and sent back to the Indian Territory. Years later, when some of the Southern Cheyenne tried unsuccessfully to join their relatives on the northern plains, mother and son traveled with them. Some of the Cheyenne believed that all their troubles happened because their women had lost their virtue, giving themselves to the white men that their ancient leader Sweet Medicine had warned against. Monasetah was among those blamed for the disappearance of the buffalo, the hard life on the reservations, and the enforced idleness because they gave themselves to those who killed their people. Mari Sandoz said, "To those who said that she was a helpless captive, they replied that a good woman knows how to avoid marrying the man who has killed her father." Sandoz also recorded the fate of Monasetah's son: "Some of the Cheyennes thought that Yellow Swallow died in the Last Hole beyond Hat Creek bluffs, but the boy lived out his sickly way to seventeen at home [in Indian Territory]."[34]

A final footnote to this chapter occurred in December 1869. Colonel Custer took a leave of absence to go home to Monroe that year, arriving there on December 13 accompanied by his brother and their friend, Lieutenant Cooke. It seemed that Cooke, frustrated because Myles Moylan's proposal to Anna Darrah had been accepted, could barely wait to see that femme fatale. The trio had hardly arrived before Autie showed him the street to her house where she had been since leaving Libbie at Fort Hays in the early fall. Tom and Autie slapped him on the back and told him to stay as long as he liked—Cooke took them at their word and visited with Miss Darrah until 3:00 A.M.

The three comrades took an early breakfast, wandered to Monroe's downtown area to play a few rounds of billiards, then went on rounds of visiting. Their last stop was at the Darrah house, where Cooke remained again, for dinner this time. Tom, according to Armstrong's letter to the match-making Elizabeth, thought the vivacious Diana would have Lieutenant Cooke "on the string" before the officers left Monroe. When Cooke came back from the Darrahs he told the Custer boys that Anna had told him "that her engagement with Mr. Moylan had been broken off and that she had not written to him for over a month." Autie concluded that "if Cooke is goose enough to bite, at the bait that is held out I'll tell him something that will make him think twice."[35]

George evidently knew something about Libbie's friend that might have changed Cooke's mind about her. If he did know something and told Lieutenant Cooke, the fact never came out. Strangely enough, at this point Anna Darrah drops out of the lives of the Custers and the Seventh.

Questions are more evident than answers about George, Tom, and Libbie and their private lives. In summary, Autie is supposed to have had eyes for other women, especially Indian girls. Some say that he fathered a child by one of those Indian girls, others that it was not George but Tom who made her pregnant. Tom may have undergone treatment for venereal disease, perhaps George did so as well. Tom's true sweetheart was Lulie Burgess. Libbie might have had eyes for Wild Bill Hickok, but it is doubtful that she ever made a pass at him. Tom's relationship with Libbie was very close, and some say that it was entirely too close for respectability.

Unfortunately for readers and students of Western history, these stories will remain no more than stories unless new, undeniable evidence enters the public domain.

9
A SHOOTOUT IN HAYS CITY

One of the most popular stories related about Tom Custer involves the New Year's Eve in Hays City, Kansas, that the handsome young lieutenant and some of the Seventh Cavalry's soldiers chased the famous Wild Bill Hickok, the acting sheriff, from his own bailiwick. The veracity of this legend has been disputed back and forth by writers of Old West history, but it was at this time that Tom had a falling out with his old friend Hickok and, to a lesser extent, with brother George.

Wild Bill's friendship with the General and Mrs. Custer is legendary. Although they did not associate so frequently, Tom nonetheless formed a reverence for the lanky, long-haired, and mustachioed plainsman during his years in Kansas that ranked second only to that in which he held big bub Aut. Hickok's allure lay in his melodramatic appearance and his past laurels, a charisma that fascinated an entire generation of youngsters through the pages of Ned Buntline's dime novels. It was only natural that the impressionable Tom might lionize and idolize him.

However, Tom had a reputation of sorts which he felt obligated to uphold, although it was neither as glamorous nor as widespread as Hickok's. In his book, *Triggernometry,* Eugene Cunningham has implied that Tom's independent nature concerning everything but his brother's military commands made him assume that his position in the Seventh Cavalry rendered him immune to any authority other than that of the army, including civilian law enforcement officers. He discovered that he was not above civil law when he rode into Hays City, said Cunningham, and there ran afoul of Bill Hickok.[1]

Hickok by this time possessed a reputation calculated to swell the head of even a soberer man, and with an ego that could barely withstand a rude remark and a life already packed aplenty with legend-making experiences, his exploits threatened to turn him into a self-proclaimed god. He surrounded himself with poker-playing, hard-drinking associates and did not deign to contradict any fabricated tales of his feats—even though those actually assignable to him were more than enough to fill a good-sized book. After serving in 1867 as a scout during the Hancock campaign, he served the army again from the first of September to the end of December, 1868. Beginning at the end of the year, he traveled from Leavenworth in eastern Kansas to Colorado until August 1869, plying several of his various trades, which included professional gambling and hiring out his guns.

Ever since the two Custer boys met Wild Bill they had been favorably impressed. In his memoirs the colonel discussed all of the military scouts who served with him, both white plainsmen and Delaware and Osage Indians, and he dwelt upon James B. Hickok, whose awe-inspiring appearance, flamboyant nature, and gregarious disposition absolutely captivated the cavalry officers. Wild Bill was apparently used as a scout for the Seventh only after Custer's detachment arrived on the scene at Fort Hays back in the spring of 1867. As soon as he reported for duty he was immediately sent to Fort Harker with a request that more fodder be sent to Fort Hays at once.

Among Hickok's final army assignments was as escort for Senator Henry S. Wilson and a party of politicians over the plains. In gratitude for the fine adventure that Hickok provided, Wilson presented the scout with a fateful gift. He gave Hickok a pair of ivory-handled New Model Army Colt .44 revolvers, which the frontiersman carried for the rest of his life, butts turned forward for the backhand draw that he eventually made the most deadly in the West. The tour ended in Hays City. Even though this was not Hickok's first visit to Hays City, it was the first time that he really noticed the little burg and examined its possibilities.

Hays City, Kansas, with its wicked reputation, was an indomitable tourist attraction. It was just developing as a town. It was sited along the Kansas Pacific Railroad whose tracks were then stretching westward toward Denver. Every tourist wanted to visit the saloons, gaming houses, and brothels or spend their time hunting buffalo and enjoying the variety of tamer entertainments that the frontier village had to offer.[2] Fort Hays had originally been established to protect the railroad construction crews, but it eventually became a supply point for military posts to the south. The nearby city that blossomed on the prairie around the fort and the railroad overflowed with ox-teams, horses, wagons, bull-whackers, and colorful men—including Wild Bill Hickok and the Custers.[3]

In 1869, Fort Hays was garrisoned by only about fifty men,

while one company was stationed at Ogallah about twenty miles to the west where there had been recent Indian disturbances. Units of the Tenth Cavalry, the African-American regiment previously camped near the fort, had been sent south to Texas and were replaced by companies of the Seventh Cavalry. At that time Tom lived in a tent shared with other single officers of the Seventh. The tent was along "officers' row" in the regimental camp on Big Creek north of the fort but south of the town.

By 1869, the little frontier town also swarmed with hundreds of cowboys and trail hands—thanks to the final arrival of the Kansas Pacific railhead and of the trail herds of cantankerous longhorn steers from Texas destined for the dining tables of the prosperous East—who rode into the town bent on having a good time. In fact, the Manhattan, Kansas, *Standard* of May 8, 1869, reported that "officers, soldiers, citizens, blacklegs, gamblers, pimps, nymphs do pave, and all mingle here."[4] Desperados rode into town seemingly from nowhere to take advantage of the free-flowing volume of money in the gambling dens and saloons.

Violence was an everyday occurrence in Hays City. Sudden death was common enough to have decent citizens alarmed. They needed a courageous, quick-drawing, experienced lawman to establish some semblance of order in a town desperately in need of civilizing. Wild Bill Hickok was in the right place at the right time.

The exact date that Hickok became acting sheriff around Hays City has escaped the pages of history, but it was evidently sometime in August 1869. He was already famous as an Indian fighter and plainsman; he had also served as a lawman in eastern Kansas during its troublesome, formative years when proslavery proponents and free-state men were at each others' throats. Now he became a lawman again, and he immediately settled down to keeping the peace in Hays City—in a fashion all his own.

Owing to his reputation as a gunfighter, every aspiring gun-slinger who hit town had to feel him out. One of the most famous costumes when he patrolled the streets included a shotgun under his arm, a bowie knife sticking out of his boot top, and the twin ivory-handled Colts backward at his waist. Once while dressed this way, according to an undocumented story, a daring fellow named Sullivan leaped from a Hays City alley with his pistol drawn. Snig-gering over how he got the drop on Hickok, he called bystanders over to observe the end of the gunfighter. While Sullivan's atten-tion was on the gathering crowd, Hickok made a lightning draw and slew him. Once the sheriff had the drop on someone he sel-dom showed any mercy, and he was contemptuous of Sullivan's mistake. "He talked his life away," said the gunman.[5] At least this is the description by writer Bern Keating in *The Flamboyant Mr. Colt and His Deadly Six-Shooter.* Hickok authorities such as Joe Rosa, Nyle Miller, and Joe Snell fail to mention this particular incident.

Other shooting incidents took place while Hickok was sheriff around Hays—the most notable of which was when he shot a man who he saw draw a revolver on him in a barroom mirror. In his official capacity as sheriff, he strolled up and down the dusty main street, tall and erect in his dark broadcloth suits and fancy ruffled and laced shirts, sporting the pair of expensive ivory-handled six-shooters backward in his belt. Generally, he ruled the town from a card table in Tommy Drumm's saloon.[6]

Although Wild Bill genuinely liked Autie Custer and adored the voluptuous Libbie from afar, his friendship toward Tom was lukewarm. He and Tom were one of a kind, men chipped from the same block. He held a grudging respect for the colonel's younger brother, not so much because Tom was related to George as because Hickok recognized in Tom the same libertinism and streak of deviltry that he owned himself. Over a period of six months, during which time the pair were necessarily thrown together, Tom realized that his personal esteem for Wild Bill was not returned, and it hurt his feelings that the man whom he wanted so badly to impress remained adamantly cool toward him.[7]

It was probably this state of frustration in combination with his natural proclivity for rowdyism that got Tom into trouble with the lawman in Hays City. Ever since the post sutlers were replaced by franchised traders who set up permanent stores at army posts in 1867, it had been difficult to obtain liquor at Kansas military establishments. Therefore, most of the men in the Seventh's camp lit out for town to buy whiskey, beer, tobacco, canned fruit—to satisfy their craving for relief from staid army rations—and canned meat or other food when they were simply hungry for a break from hardtack and salt pork. Tom made frequent jaunts into Hays City, and was a regular customer at Drumm's drinking emporium. As officer of the day, he also often had drunken soldiers carted back to camp.

Sometimes at the saloon, Tom supposedly expressed his candid, embittered opinion of Wild Bill in an attempt to relieve his frustration and demonstrate his disdain for his former hero. According to several popular authors, anxious to glorify Hickok and criticize Tom, on one particular, unknown day, Tom had one of his periodic bouts with the bottle and got carried away. Not only did he voice his contempt for Hickok, he also rode up and down several streets shooting up the town, as noted by those writers. Hickok quietly took him into custody to preserve the peace and at the same time the well-being of Tom himself.[8] Although the arrest (if arrest it was—there is no evidence one way or the other that

Tom was arrested) took place as an orderly affair, and the sheriff hustled Tom out of Hays, the incident rankled with the lieutenant.

What passed between Lieutenant Custer and his brother as a result of the incident is unknown to this day, but if detractors are to be believed it would have been the cause of a disruption of amicable family relations in the Custer clan. George never relented in his staunch support and praise of his friend Hickok. Predictably, this hurt Tom even further. He adored and emulated George, and now the latter turned his back on his little brother in favor of his friend, whom Tom had insulted and who in turn insulted him. Always a strict disciplinarian even with his brother, of course, Autie only saw the facts as they stood—Tom had disrupted the peace, and the civil authority; Hickok had dealt with the situation handily and diplomatically. He supported the sheriff as the man who represented the law and who was in the right. There is no army record of an official reprimand of Tom for such an offense.

Tom's pride and the sibling rivalry between him and Autie would not allow him to back down in the face of Armstrong's obstreperous if somewhat muted and only implied reprimand. He faunched around camp. He failed to appear at the usual family conclaves. He exhibited distaste when the colonel received honored guests. But most of all, according to his detractors, his bitterness against Hickok for publicly humiliating him became an obsession.[9]

The writers of popular Western gunfighter history—Eugene Cunningham and Harry Sinclair Drago—state that Tom enlisted the aid of a conflicting number of troopers and rode into town to kill Hickok. The truth is that Tom Custer's name cannot be directly connected with the subsequent attack on the vainglorious sheriff. The desire to even the score for disgracing him in front of the town remained; and, given Tom's known association with some of the rough characters of the Seventh, the likelihood of his involvement in the ensuing incident is possible if not probable. But the question remains unanswered.[10]

History also fails to record whether or not the little group who showed up in the village almost six months after Tom was allegedly thrown out of town had murder in their hearts or simply intended to work Hickok over to teach him a lesson. Obviously, a sheriff, even if his name was Wild Bill Hickok, needed a lesson in manners when he demonstrated the audacity of humiliating a member of the Custer family.

There were three identified members of the band of intrepids who jumped Hickok—Privates Jeremiah Lonergan and John Kelly, each of Company M, and Private John Kile, of Company I. Kile had earlier won a Medal of Honor with the Fifth Cavalry fighting Indians on the plains. It should be noted that none of the soldiers were from Tom's company. It is at this point, on Sunday, July 17, 1870, that documented accounts begin to differ concerning who was to blame, the physical condition of the participants involved in the row, how the townspeople reacted, and even the day of the event. It is not hard to mentally reconstruct the scene of the drama unfolding.

The troopers from the camp of the Seventh found Hickok at Paddy Welche's place instead of Tommy Drumm's saloon, his favorite haunt from which he ruled Hays City with an iron hand—the extra hand provided him by the manufacturers of his two Colt revolvers. They moved toward the saloon with a great rambunctious display. They went to great lengths to be considered soldiers free on a pass in town to rest and relax. They kissed the girls who habitually haunted Paddy's bar, tossed back glasses of rotgut whiskey, laughed those gay reckless laughs, and snapped their fingers to show what they thought of the authority that Hickok had held over the town—for he had been replaced as defender of law and order in Hays City, probably in January 1870.[11]

Some newspaper men were partial to Hickok as is evident from reading this article in Topeka's *Kansas Daily Commonwealth:* "On Monday last 'Wild Bill' killed a soldier and seriously wounded another, at Hays City. Five soldiers attacked Bill, and two got used up as mentioned above. The sentiment of the community is with 'Bill' as it is claimed he but acted in self-defense."[12]

Other correspondents saw only disgruntlement on the part of Hays citizens. Such was the case with a reporter to the Junction City *Union:* "Two soldiers of the Seventh cavalry were shot at Hays City last Tuesday night by Wild Bill. The names of the men were Lanagan and Kelly. The greatest excitement prevails in the town owing to the outrage. After the shooting was over Wild Bill made for the prairie and has not been heard of since. The citizens were out *en masse* looking for Bill, so that he might be summarily dealt with. The parties were all under the influence of liquor at the time."[13]

A few newspaper editors were simply noncommittal, among them the editor of the Clyde, Kansas, *Republican Valley Empire:* "Wild Bill, of Harper and plains notoriety, got into a friendly scuffle with a soldier at Hays City on the 20th, which ended in a row. Bill shot and mortally wounded another soldier who had a hand in the mess and left for parts unknown."[14]

It can be seen in these accounts that no date for the affair is agreed upon. The three papers each cite different dates—July 18, 19, and 20. It is apparent, however, that there was a shootout between Hickok and a superior number of soldiers from the Seventh's camp along Big Creek. Evidently, they caught the former lawman playing cards in the saloon, as was his wont. From details supplied by onlookers, even though these are not the most reliable sources, Hickok seems to have been provoked regardless of the play-acted peaceful demonstrations of the cavalrymen. Even a gunfighter the ilk of Hickok would not voluntarily go up against that many fully armed men.[15]

As nearly as can be ascertained from the accounts, one of the troopers plunged upon Wild Bill from his front while another pinioned his arms from behind. Hickok managed to get an arm free and, assuming that the soldiers figured to do him serious bodily harm, pulled one of his pistols, poked it over his shoulder, and shot the private still holding his arm behind him. By now some of the bystanders in the bar had reached their feet, leaped in, and squeezed themselves between Hickok and his antagonists. They pulled the soldiers and Wild Bill apart and then drove the troopers out of town. Custer's cohorts beat a hasty retreat away from Hays, carrying their casualties with them.[16]

The spark that set off this veritable powder keg was supposedly a remark about Hickok's personal appearance. In 1904, Alfred Henry Lewis wrote in the *Saturday Evening Post,* in his unparalleled fashion, that "in an evil hour a trio of soldiers . . . led by one Lanigan (Lonergan) . . . took drunken umbrage at Mr. Hickok's hair." Lewis's comment excludes Tom Custer, and it is fairly safe to say that Tom was absent during the shootout. But Lonergan and his boys got just retribution for any snide remarks about the gunfighter's hair style.[17]

Privates Lonergan and Kelly were admitted to the post hospital at Fort Hays for treatment of gunshot wounds, according to the "Register of Sick and Wounded at Fort Hays, Kansas, During the Month of July, 1870." Private Lonergan, allegedly the leader of the attackers, was returned to duty with the regiment on August 25, 1870, but John Kelly died of his wounds on July 18, the day after the fight took place. The muster role of the Seventh Cavalry for July 1870 listed Private John Kile, of Company I, dead of a "pistol shot wound received July 17th, 1870, at Hays City, Kansas, in a drunken row and not in the line of duty." At least the army doctor faithfully recorded what he saw of the action—namely the casualties.

The actual fight took only a moment. When the gunsmoke cleared, three of the men who accosted Hickok at Paddy Welche's looking for trouble were lying on the boards—one was dead, one mortally wounded, and the third hurt seriously enough to require more than a month of hospitalization. After being separated from his attackers, Hickok realized the tremendous amount of damage he had accomplished. He then had a serious decision to make— should he remain in Hays and face the consequences or should he make his escape and let the guilt fall where it might?

If he remained, he could not be certain of the reaction of the citizens of Hays City. After all, they had recently replaced him with a new sheriff less inclined to shoot first and ask questions later. And, as already shown, contemporary sources did not agree on the mood of the good people of Kansas, some saying Wild Bill should be summarily dealt with, some that he was guilty of no more than defending himself against superior foes who, for all he knew, were intent on his undoing. So according to all the accounts available, both defenders and detractors, Wild Bill Hickok lit out for the high plains.[18]

It took no persuasion—and none was offered—to convince Hickok of the wisdom of a hasty departure from Hays. Whether he was guilty of anything or not, he was no longer lawman in the rowdy little town, but he was a well-known personality, a gunfighter, and a regular customer of the bars, casinos, and bordellos of Hays. As such, he represented the epitome of the evils that the decent citizens of the fledgling city feared. His critics from all over Kansas had for some time been besmirching his name in an effort to force him either to alter his popular image or depart from the state, which was in haste to become civilized in the eyes of her Eastern counterparts. On top of all this, Hickok stood a fair chance of suffering further injury at the hands of some of the Seventh Cavalry troopers who held members of the Custer family in high regard or were friends of the shootout victims. If there is any veracity in the tales of Tom's involvement, he had now twice been humiliated by Wild Bill. Without further ado, the plainsman took his leave, to turn up sometime later in Abilene. There he was asked why he had fled, since most of the folks around that town thought him guilty only of self-defense. He laconically replied, "I couldn't fight the whole Seventh Cavalry."[19] Whether he left Hays voluntarily or was coerced to leave by public sentiment, his decision to leave was entirely in his own best interests.

About the aftermath of the imputed Tom Custer–Wild Bill Hickok feud, Joseph G. Rosa—the foremost authority on Hickok— has written: "It has been alleged that General Phil Sheridan issued a 'dead or alive' order for Hickok. But this is unlikely, for such brawls were common in frontier towns between soldiers and civilians."[20] Actually, the fracas had little or no repercussions so far as the army was concerned. The character of the frontier regulars was such that no one was surprised at the shootout. And if his brother was deeply involved, it can be assumed that Autie worded his report to General Sheridan in such a way that Tom's name was excluded. Being so tailored, it left the impression that no detailed investigation was required.[21]

Yet another indicator that Tom was not involved is the fact that there is no correspondence nor record of the incident in any of the Custers' memoirs or voluminous correspondence. Tom could not have gotten out of this predicament lightly, nor without mention by a family member. Armstrong might not have had anything to say about Tom in his report to the departmental commander, but he surely would have had a few words to say privately. The Company A lieutenant often received a stern reprimand from George not as his brother but as his colonel. Autie would have recognized the seriousness of Tom's escapade, even if Tom did not put Lonergan, Kelly, and Kile up to the attack; Tom should have left the colonel's tent not a little disgruntled, if not under arrest, under the impression that Armstrong's stinging rebuke was the result of his friendship with and admiration for Hickok. The fact that he apparently did not speaks loudly that he was not involved.

The only remaining unanswered question concerning the incident is that although Fort Hays post returns, located in the National Archives, supposedly record the name of each commissioned officer stationed at or attached to the fort, no officer named Custer appears for July 1870. Some historians have impugned that this famous shootout is complete fabrication using this fact as their major supporting element. This can easily be explained. Throughout its career in Kansas, the Seventh Cavalry regiment was stationed at Fort Riley, more than 100 miles east of Hays City. All the while the regiment was absent from Fort Riley—which was a majority of its time in Kansas—it was listed as "in the field." Thus both Tom and George Custer were stationed at Fort Riley and were never stationed at nor attached to Fort Hays and therefore would not be mentioned in its post returns. The Seventh's commander normally reported directly to General Sheridan.

Nyle Miller and Joseph Snell, in their book *Great Gunfighters of the Kansas Cowtowns, 1867-1886,* have written that "sometimes legends are indeed based on a bit of fact. The fight occurred, but long after Hickok had shed his star. Variations in contemporary reporting might have been the cause for some of the discrepancies of the legend." The gunfight at a Hays City saloon on a hot Sunday afternoon is shadowed in controversy to this day, but it definitely left two troopers of the Seventh dead and one seriously wounded.[22]

It also marked a point of jarring dissension between the Custer brothers. For once, Autie and Tom disagreed on something. Thereafter, Tom held little but contempt for Wild Bill, while Armstrong went on in the near future to write glowing accounts of Hickok in his memoirs of his service on the plains. Although the discord never reached the point of a quarrel, the topic was seldom broached when the Custer clan congregated, and when it was someone always quickly changed the subject. For Tom, it was another grievance in the lopsided rivalry with his brother. Ironically, even though no shootout took place between them, both Tom and Wild Bill died violently only a few hundred miles and several months apart—Custer at the Little Bighorn and Hickok in Deadwood, in the Black Hills—both in 1876.

10
RECONSTRUCTING ERRING SISTERS

The year 1871 saw the disruption of the Custer entourage. The inseparable family and friends in Kansas were physically separated when the Seventh Cavalry was withdrawn from the plains to serve on Reconstruction duty in the defeated Southern states.

Lieutenant Thomas Custer found himself reassigned from his old company to Troop M, Seventh Cavalry. This small unit was sent to South Carolina, just as the other units of the regiment were distributed piecemeal throughout the deep South.

Although most Southerners accepted the result of the war and were eager to rejoin the Union, they were not over-endowed with goodwill toward their Northern conquerors. Of the eleven states that seceded from the Union, some were not inclined to admit even the most obvious results of the war. For example, Tom discovered that rather than repudiating secession or a sovereign state's right to leave the Union, South Carolina simply repealed its ordinance of secession that the state government had passed in 1861. Moreover, although the federal government had offered amnesties and pardons to former Confederates, a minority of Southerners would have nothing to do with them. John Garraty has quoted a bit of doggerel that expressed their sympathies in his massive history, *The American Nation:*

Oh, I'm a good old rebel,
Now that's just what I am;
For the "fair land of freedom,"
I do not care a dam.
I'm glad I fit against it—

I only wish we'd won
And I don't want no pardon
For anything I done.[1]

Several dozen men who served in the Confederate Congress during the war years were elected to the reunited United States Congress after the surrender, along with four generals and numerous other officials of the old Confederate administration. Southerners naturally elected locally respected and politically experienced leaders to represent them in the rejuvenated House of Representatives and Senate. But it was reasonable to assume that these selections upset Yankees.[2]

Back in 1866, just as the Seventh Cavalry was being activated, Congress passed the Fourteenth Amendment to the United States Constitution and submitted it to the states for ratification. This amendment supplied a broad new definition of American citizenship, which included blacks; it provided that no state could deprive any citizen of life, liberty, or property without due process of law;

it attempted to force the defeated Southern states to permit black voting; and finally, former Federal officials who had served the rebel government were prevented from holding either federal or state offices unless they were first specifically pardoned by a two-thirds vote of the Congress. The South failed to accept the amendment. With the exception of Tennessee, all of the former rebellious states refused to ratify it, and without their formal ratification, the majority of the states that were needed to make the amendment an official part of the Constitution could not be obtained.[3]

Had the Southern states been willing to accept the Fourteenth Amendment, forceful measures by the Union might have been avoided. However, their refusal to ratify and continuing persecution of blacks at the local level led to the passage of the First Reconstruction Act on March 2, 1867.[4]

This law was the reason Tom was separated from George, Libbie, and the rest of his friends of the Seventh. The act divided the former Confederacy—except Tennessee, the sole state of the South that had ratified the Fourteenth Amendment—into five military districts, each commanded by a major general of the federal army. The Seventh was divided up as well, various companies being sent to various localities.

Before the regiment was dispersed there had been rumors of the Seventh being transferred because a regiment on the Pacific Coast requested assignment to the Department of the Missouri. Although it caused some excitement among the officers, no changes were made. But during 1870, Autie heard that his Seventh Cavalry might be parceled out for garrison duty in the states being reconstructed. Armstrong made formal application to accompany its headquarters with the expectation that Tom, Cooke, Moylan, and others of the Custer gang would serve in that unit. "The request was warmly endorsed by General Sturgis, who had succeeded the retiring General A. J. Smith as colonel of the regiment," wrote Libbie's literary executor. "Nothing came of this, either. [George] Custer accordingly took stock of his prospects."[5]

Tom had little chance to explore any prospects. In his fifth year as a career officer in the cavalry he could look forward only to a short leave in Monroe before his transfer. Not only was the regiment broken up—so were some of the companies, as enlistments expired, new officers and recruits showed up, and experienced officers were placed in charge of companies while new ones assumed the day-to-day activities of the units. Tom was reassigned to Troop M while remaining a lieutenant. For the veteran officers, company command meant only more responsibilities but generally not promotions.

The commanding general of each of the five military districts possessed almost dictatorial powers to protect the rights of all citizens, black or white, under his control, maintain order, and supervise the administration of justice. To lift themselves from under the thumb of military control, the Southern states had to adopt new constitutions allowing African-Americans to vote and disfranchising those ex-Confederates who refused to accept a pardon. If these new constitutions satisfied Congress and the new state governments then ratified the Fourteenth Amendment, their elected representatives would be admitted to Congress and martial law rescinded.[6]

Although it looked good on paper, the First Reconstruction Act was so vague that it ultimately failed. Military rule was already established, because units like the Seventh had *de facto* control all over the South. But the law did not specifically state the process by which the new state constitutions were to be written. Southerners preferred keeping their governments the way they were, even under the bayonets of the army, to giving freed slaves the right to vote and excluding their own experienced leaders from holding office.[7]

Therefore, a second law was passed by Congress that made the military responsible for registering voters and supervising elections, and a third law further clarified procedures. Nevertheless, white Southerners continued to resist. The laws required that the new constitutions be approved by a majority of voters. The Southerners got around those laws by registering to vote, then simply staying away from the polls in droves on voting days. In this way they defeated ratification in state after state.

Finally, a full year after the passing of the First Reconstruction Act, Congress saw the light. The rules were changed yet again, this time so that they read that the constitutions be ratified by a majority of the voters, not merely a majority of those registered to vote. By July 1870, the last Southern state qualified to the satisfaction of Congress.[8]

But military rule continued, because even after the former Confederate states were readmitted to the Union, troubles continued. Already inflamed by the freeing of the slaves who had worked their farms and plantations, and by enfranchising the freed slaves with the right to vote, anti-black sentiments intensified as many African-American troops of the conquering Union army patrolled the states. All Southerners acquired their full share of that smoldering anger.[9] Tom and Company M were sent to South Carolina to serve two purposes.

The first was to track down whiskey distillers who sold bootleg moonshine by the thousands of gallons, regardless of the regular sale of bottled liquor. The temperance movement had been important since the age of Andrew Jackson, and by the 1870s many reformers were eager to prohibit drinking entirely. Although the cause stood in direct opposition to Tom's own personal opinion, his duty with the Seventh came first. It is no wonder that Whittaker wrote in *A Complete Life of Gen. George A. Custer* that Tom was "heartily sick of the nauseous business."[10]

Reformers of the temperance movement opposed drinking on moral and religious instead of medical grounds. They demanded prohibition of all alcohol instead of mere restraint. Their methods and their objectives roused bitter opposition, especially in the West and the South. Just as converts at religious camp meetings, many in attendance at lectures and rallies were overwhelmed by the eloquence of the reformers and "signed the pledge," only to backslide as soon as they passed the nearest bar or tavern. Tom's distasteful details hunting down moonshiners were made even more difficult by the attitude of the reconstructed rebels. Southerners were generally opposed to any sort of temperance, and they detested Yankee occupation troops. Hence, when they saw Tom and his troopers approaching, they spirited young bootleggers out of sight.[11]

The other reason the Seventh was sent to the South was to help control the Ku Klux Klan. Originating in Tennessee in 1866, it was at first only a social club for former rebel soldiers, but by 1868 it had been taken over by vigilantes wanting to drive African-Americans out of political office and voting booths. It spread rapidly.

Soon sheet-clad Klansmen roamed the countryside by night, intimidating freedmen with rumors, boldly printed broadsides, and claims that they were ghosts of dead Confederate soldiers—all these things carefully planned to prey on the superstitious minds of the recently freed blacks.

The intimidation campaigns failed, so the Klansmen turned

instead to outright violence, beating or murdering their victims, often in the most gruesome manners. The situation became so bad that Congress passed three Force Acts during 1870 and 1871. The Force Acts were designed to protect black voters. They put all elections under federal control and imposed fines and prison terms on anyone convicted of preventing any citizens from exercising their voting rights.[12] Troops were dispatched to parts of the South where the Klan was powerful. The Seventh's record of active Indian fighting on the Great Plains made that outfit seem to be an apt candidate for stopping the nightriders.

When Tom arrived in South Carolina, he found the Klan particularly strong. That state had been well endowed with wealthy plantation owners during the antebellum years. These planters were among the first to espouse secession, they were among the most prominent slaveholders in the South, and they were not pleased to suddenly have their state government run by former slaves. African-Americans composed the majority of the population of South Carolina, so they naturally elected their own candidates. One African-American in the state rose to be a justice of the state supreme court, and for a brief period freedmen controlled the lower house of the state's legislature.[13]

During 1871 and part of 1872, Company M was stationed at the cities of Darlington, Spartanburg, Yorkville, and Unionville, South Carolina. Detachments from Tom's new troop were frequently furnished to the United States marshals to assist in serving federal warrants against members of the Ku Klux Klan in the state. In 1872, the company was posted to Oxford, Mississippi, to perform the same duties. Finally, by late 1872, the federal authorities had arrested enough Klansmen to break up the secret societies. Otherwise, the soldiers performed no more than the usual garrison duties.[14]

George Custer was not idle during these years. He and part of the Seventh were stationed at Elizabethtown, Kentucky, and he took Libbie there with him. There, Autie had the time and convenience to indulge his love of high-spirited, thoroughbred racing horses. Previously, the regimental light colonel now without a regiment had invested in three city lots in Council Grove, Kansas, and a house in Topeka. He also invested in several racing horses. His horses won very few races, and the house in Topeka remained vacant. Thus, any new opportunity to make big bucks that came his way would probably be grabbed up.[15]

His chance at that opportunity came in June 1871, while he was in New York. Ostensibly, he was dissatisfied with his role in the army and was in the city looking for different employment. However, he had an ulterior reason. Ever since his regiment was activated, the Seventh had lost men due to altogether too frequent desertions. As mentioned, a good many men enlisted in the regiment merely for the free transportation to the Western gold fields. The fabulous tales of rich strikes in Colorado Territory had been the topic of the day around mess tables the entire length of the Seventh's tour of duty in Kansas, and such talk influenced some men who had enlisted only for soldiering to desert.[16]

In New York, the dream of investing in one of those mines with the tremendous returns he had heard about seemed attractive. Armstrong had already investigated several such wealthy lodes in the vicinity of Clear Creek, Colorado Territory. One that especially caught his eye was called the Stevens Lode, situated some ten miles out of Georgetown. The original lode was about 1,400 feet in length.

The western half of the mine belonged to the Crescent Silver

Mining Company of Cincinnati, Ohio. The eastern half was up for sale, even though almost sixty feet of it had previously been opened. Custer bought a $35,000 interest in the lode, although the notes left after his death fail to record whether this was in cash, which was unlikely on a lieutenant colonel's salary in that era, or as a promoter's share. Probably it was the latter, for if Autie did not have cash, he did possess a highly marketable name.[17]

One of the men Custer tried to interest in his mine was Charles Osburn. At first, Osburn was leery of the deal, but when Autie showed him that he had sold interest to John Jacob Astor, Osburn relented. By mid-1871, Custer and Osburn were fast friends.[18]

In fact, Osburn and some companions once drove Armstrong from New York City to the training ground of Joe Coburn to visit the prizefighter and watch his workout. Coburn was then touted by many to be the best bare-knuckled boxer in the United States, and, at the time Autie saw him, he was preparing for a fight with the English champion, Tim Mace. At the training camp it was learned that the heavyweight championship fight between Coburn and Mace was to take place in Canada just across the border from Buffalo. It was rumored that upwards of 10,000 people would be in attendance. Custer wanted to go along because he wanted to "witness one and only one prize fight" in his lifetime, yet no one can say for sure whether he attended. He did tell Libbie, however, that he was sure that Tom and his friend Cooke would have liked to see the bout.[19]

Autie had decided to go with the Osburn party if his business would permit him. Word had just arrived from the silver mine. The purchase of the east half had been completed for $100,000. Business looked good for the older of the Custer brothers.[20]

Still a soldier, Armstrong also worked for his regiment. From his station at Elizabethtown, Kentucky, he wrote to his younger sister Margaret about the results of a horse-buying trip. "We sent Tom's troop 24 very handsome black horses. 'M' [Troop] is to be mounted like 'D' on black. Mr. My [Moylan] went in charge, his wife with him. The horses reached the troops with manes and tails cut off. Tom is awfully put out about it. Col. [Cooke] thinks Mr My cut the hair off to make 'waterfalls' for his wife."[21]

Tom may have been separated from his brother and commanding officer by four states, hundreds of miles, and the Appalachian Mountains, but he remained in contact, sometimes through letters to sister-in-law Libbie. From Oxford, Mississippi, he sent advice of an upcoming inspection. "We received a telegram yesterday, saying that Genl. McDowell would be here in the afternoon to inspect the Fort. [Captain] French and I were at the depot to meet him. After looking at us dismounted we had to saddle up and come out mounted. By that time it was dark. He intends to inspect all the Kentucky Posts. Tell Armstrong."[22]

Tom was not selfless at this time—he still thought about himself. He was equally interested in Kentucky thoroughbreds, so he wrote Libbie also to "tell Armstrong that when the sale comes up to buy a fine horse for me and one for French. I have a stable all fixed up for them."[23]

Late in March 1873, Tom Custer went to Memphis, Tennessee. It would be his last post in the South, for the Seventh was assembling there for a new assignment. The reunion that spring was a jubilant one. Tom again met George and Libbie, but also Cooke, Keogh, Yates, and Moylan. Tom and the other officers were in Memphis to greet the light colonel and his lady. With them came Lieutenant James Calhoun, a youthful officer recently wed to Tom's and Autie's younger sister, Margaret. The young couple were accompanying the regiment, with which Calhoun was assigned, to its new post. Elizabeth was overjoyed to have Maggie's companionship on the long trip.[24]

Calhoun was a handsome, well-built fellow, a slim six feet one inch tall. Like his two brothers-in-law in the regiment, he had flaxen hair and a blond mustache, which contrasted brightly with his dark hazel eyes. He was also reserved and very much the gentleman in his manners—he seemed to fit in well with the Custer gang anyway.[25]

There was also another new addition to the Seventh. After three years, Dr. John Tempany, a native of New York state, enlisted as the first junior veterinarian on March 19, 1872. He was a quiet, well-mannered man, who did not fall into the clan as well as Dr. Honsinger had, but he was a competent veterinarian, probably the best the regiment had until after the battle at the Little Bighorn.[26]

Orders had come in February 1873, transferring the Seventh from its tour of duty in the South to the Department of Dakota. The Sioux and treaties with them stood in the way of American progress—specifically, the progress of the Northern Pacific Railroad. Although chartered in 1864, the Northern Pacific did not begin to build west until February 1870. By 1871, however, it had only reached Fargo, in Dakota Territory. The construction crews pressed on slowly, under the protection of the military, across the Sioux hunting grounds. They reached as far as Jamestown, Dakota Territory, by the summer of 1872. When the snows melted enough for the crews to continue, they reached only to Bismarck on the Missouri River, by summer. There progress stopped, and that was where the railhead lay when the Seventh got there.

Certainly, the regiment's new assignment was not to be an easy one. Its two-year term of Reconstruction duty was over, and the Seventh was to go again into the field. The regiment had been split up, divided among small posts in the South, mainly to suppress moonshining and to deal with the KKK. "Now it was to be reintegrated, reunited, prepared for active operation in Dakota Territory, 'outside the States.'"[27]

The troopers and officers and horses all packed into steamboats at Memphis for the trip up the Mississippi River to St. Louis, then up the Missouri to Fort Abraham Lincoln across the river from Bismarck.

The two-year separation of Tom Custer from Autie was, without their knowing it, a welcome respite. Tensions had been building between them as it often does between any siblings when they are thrown together day in and day out. The Hickok affair in Hays City had brought the problem to a head. Tom's rivalry with George in many fields of endeavor had not set well with the colonel. George's obvious popularity and fame did not set well with Tom, either, because while he desperately wanted to be near his older brother he was just as desperately trying to establish his own identity.

To do this, Tom went after glory and fame himself. When a stern reprimand was his reply, Tom became despondent. Thus, although there was little action and no chance for notoriety in the Reconstruction duty for Tom, and George was dissatisfied with his lot in the army and looked for outside employment, the years 1871 and 1872 presented a twenty-four-month cooling-off period. The return to the plains, in March 1873, would bring the Custer family together once more and bring more than enough action to the Seventh.

11
RETURN TO THE PLAINS

A blizzard of immense proportions struck Bismarck as soon as the regiment reached Fort Abraham Lincoln. It was the next-to-last gasp of a hard winter, smothering the post with sheets and layers of white snow. Colonel Custer and aides Tom and Jim Calhoun went ahead with the laying out of the Seventh's camp despite the deep drifts and biting cold. George took sick as a result, along with many troopers of the outfit. Tom took advantage of Autie's illness to enjoy himself as much as possible before the summer campaign started.

Fort Abraham Lincoln was built on the west bank of the Missouri River across from Bismarck in 1872. It was established principally for the protection of surveyors and construction crews of the railroad. The compound encompassed a smaller post called Fort McKean, after Colonel Henry Boyd McKean, who was killed during the Civil War, and constructed the same year. The location of the latter fort was situated on the site of the "Slant Village," a fortified encampment of the Mandan Indians occupied nearly two centuries earlier.

Shortly after Fort McKean was completed on the bluffs overlooking the Missouri, the name was changed to Fort Abraham Lincoln, and an addition to the fort appeared on the river shore below, nearer the mouth of the Heart River. The summer of 1872 saw a flurry of activity in building. After the cavalrymen of the Seventh crossed the ferry across the river from town, they saw neat lines of structures built by the army engineers—the post trader's stores, civilian quarters, officers' club, post bakery, the barracks for regimental noncoms, and band quarters, post hospital, gardens, and parade grounds.[1]

In spite of the snow, the troopers erected a crude structure of cottonwood logs and canvas, covered by a large tarpaulin, in their spare time. This they called the "Opera House," a spacious building that appeared everywhere the Seventh camped for any length of time. Practically, it served as a quaint sort of recreation hall for the soldiers' leisure time, housing such things as minstrel shows, band concerts, special entertainment performances, and dances. The officer cadre of the regiment gave a weekly "hop" in the Opera House, with carriages chock-full of young ladies from the infantry encampment in old Fort McKean and from the town across the river showing up to lighten the load of the enlisted men and unmarried officers alike. Once Armstrong recovered from his illness, no man at the hoedowns danced more lightly, and no lady danced more often than Elizabeth.[2]

It was almost two months before the regiment left for the summer campaigns, and Autie spent the daylight hours whipping his cavalrymen into fighting trim. The evenings were dull when dances were not scheduled. Card games were the most common method of killing time. The only other recreation was at "the Point," an area of houses of ill repute, shanty saloons, and card parlors that was just outside the limits of the military reservation. It was definitely a bad place, and troopers were advised, when they had money to spend, to avoid the Point.[3]

By June 1873, Little Phil Sheridan ordered Custer's regiment into the field and up the Heart River to the Yellowstone, land that the government had set aside for the Sioux Indians. The western terminus of the Northern Pacific was still near Bismarck, and the Seventh was dispatched to scout out the Yellowstone River country.[4] No one could deny that the army was invading Sioux land. The Sioux had been taking the boot for more than twenty years, and sooner or later they were bound to balk. They had already tried in 1866 at Fort Phil Kearny, at which time the great chieftain, Red Cloud, forced the government to back down and abandon the fort.[5]

The Indians were readying themselves for their next balk. Before, when they fought they carried ancient trade muskets or bows and arrows arrayed against the repeating rifles and carbines carried by the regular army. But just before the Seventh left Fort Abraham Lincoln, repeating rifles were recalled by the ordnance department and replaced with single-shot .45-caliber rifles and carbines made at the Springfield Armory.[6]

The official reason for recalling repeating weapons was that no suitable guns were available for military use. Skeptics snorted that Sam Colt had been selling repeating firearms to the army for years and that the year the recall was made was the same that the famous twelve-shot Winchester '73 was made available to civilians, not to mention to the red warriors "for hunting purposes" by reservation agents. Most officers armed themselves with the new Winchester carbines, but enlisted men had to save their pay for months or be lucky at poker to afford such a weapon. For all intents and purposes, the Sioux were better armed than the army sent out to contend with them.[7]

The first major of the Seventh, Marcus A. Reno, took Company I—Myles Keogh's troop—and Company D to St. Paul, Minnesota, to escort the International Northern Boundary Survey along the Canadian border that summer. Three companies were still stationed in Louisiana waiting to rejoin the regiment. Colonel Custer and the other eight companies went first to Yankton, from where they marched up the Missouri River to meet General David S. Stanley's expedition to escort railroad surveyors.[8]

The procession was a large one, and among those Armstrong met in the retinue was an old West Point classmate and antagonist, Thomas L. Rosser. Late in June, Autie wrote his wife of his meeting with the former Confederate general on the Yellowstone River and of the long hours spent recounting their various engagements during the War Between the States. While that pair reminisced, the other officers spent their own evenings in Dr. Honsinger's tent playing poker.[9]

"The officers have been sitting night and day, playing, since we left Fort Rice," Armstrong wrote from the Seventh's camp on the Heart River, Dakota Territory. "They are now in Dr. H's tent, next mine. I carry Tom's funds now. Mr. C[alhoun] began playing as soon as we left Rice, and only stopped, night before last, from lack of funds. He'd borrowed $20 from me, but cannot get any more from me, nor any from Tom, since Tom has to borrow in order to play."[10]

George was fortunate that in the same letter he could write Libbie, "I congratulate myself daily—as often as the subject enters my mind—that I have told Satan to get behind me so far as poker is concerned. You often said I could never give it up. But I have always said I could give up anything—except you."[11]

Tom was almost as lucky—Armstrong held most of his money for him at his request so that he would not be able to play cards and lose it. Lieutenant James Calhoun, who kept his money in his pocket, played and lost consistently. He was anxious to impress Tom—which gratified Tom—with whom he shared a tent. Calhoun's luck continued poor. He was too young and inexperienced to hold his own with the regular card players among the Custer gang. Calhoun's brother Fred, who accompanied the expedition, and Tom tried to reason with him, but he still lost his whole bankroll. "Tom and Fred tried to dissuade him from playing," Autie wrote Libbie, "but he refuses."[12] When Calhoun attempted to borrow money from Tom, his brother-in-law refused: "Relationship don't count in poker," Tom said. "Bunkey or no bunkey, keep your hand out of my haversack."[13]

Even though Autie was holding most of his money, the poker evidently paid off for Tom, if not for young Calhoun. By the middle of the summer Armstrong could write to Libbie, "I enclose $100 which Tom asks you to add to his deposit. I am to tell you it is money some of the officers owed him."[14]

Dr. John Honsinger, the German veterinarian whose tent was so popular, was fated not to return from the 1873 campaign. In spite of the difference in their ages, Tom had become quite fond of the old gentleman. Expedition correspondent Samuel J. Barrows, reporting to the New York *Tribune,* described Honsinger as "a fine-looking, portly man, about 55 years of age, dressed in a blue coat and buckskin pantaloons, mounted on his fine blooded horse. . . . No man of the regiment took more care of his horse than Honsinger. It was extra-professional care—a love of the horse for his own sake. . . . He had taken the horse at Yankton, in the Spring, from one of the cavalry troops—a gaunt-looking steed then, but under his fostering care he had grown fat and sleek." Barrows also noted that the good doctor had served throughout the Civil War and was "greatly esteemed by officers and men for his personal and professional qualities." Tom was one of his great admirers.[15]

The course of march was up the Yellowstone River. The country being surveyed, however, became rough and broken, so that the command met serious delays in making camp at the end of each day. Autie commiserated with General Stanley, suggesting that he should take some troops of the Seventh and a few Indian guides to prepare camps in advance of the Seventh and a few Indian guides to prepare camps in advance of the main column. Stanley agreed to the idea. Custer and his troopers rode out early in the mornings, marking the trail and locating suitable campsites early in the afternoons.[16]

Along the Yellowstone, a steamer with supplies was to rendezvous with the expedition. The meeting site was at the place Glendive Creek emptied into the Yellowstone. The problem was that no one with the expedition knew where that was. So with tongue in cheek, George wrote to Libbie, "When we arrived within, as was supposed, about fifteen miles of where the steamer would be found, I volunteered to go on a steamboat hunt, as I had secured almost every other kind of game." The hunt turned into a merry sightseeing cavalcade quickly.[17]

"Everybody wanted to go along, first Tom, then Mr. Calhoun." Before long the steamboat hunting party consisted of a doctor, General Rosser, two of his assistants from the surveying crew, several more officers, and two troops of the Seventh. After a long trek through breathtaking scenery, they finally found themselves a dozen miles above the rendezvous point. After some backtracking, the column located the steamboat *Far West*. The steamer captain's wife spread a "well-stocked table" of which the officers partook. Then Armstrong ordered the horses and men aboard the steamer and the boat to proceed up the Yellowstone until it was too dark to go farther.[18] That night Tom and Jim Calhoun slept on the boat, while everyone else slept in their clothes on deck or on the ground. "It rained during the night," wrote Autie, "but that did not disturb us, so fatigued were we with our exertions of the preceding day." Nevertheless, Tom and Calhoun were the only ones comfortable that night.[19]

Armstrong's system of locating campsites ahead of the column worked well through most of the month of July, but the surveyors were moving deeper and deeper into Sioux country. On the morning of August 4, two companies of the regiment, commanded by Myles Moylan and Tom, accompanied Autie, Jim Calhoun, and the Arikara scout Bloody Knife when they left camp at 5:00 A.M. Bloody Knife immediately discovered fresh Indian signs. Since the party numbered eighty-six men and five officers, Armstrong felt safe, even when Bloody Knife reported that a band of Sioux warriors had been snooping around the main encampment the night before. The officers were so sure of their superiority over any red enemies in the area, though, that no change was made in routine or plans. Most officers used to fighting Indians would have promptly put their command on alert.[20]

Dr. Honsinger and a friend, sutler Augustus Baliran, were in the habit of straying away from the main body of Custer's column, prowling for souvenirs and natural oddities. On that fateful day, the pair of older men forged ahead to water their thirsty horses at a stream in a grove of trees. Moments later Tom heard the loud reports of rifle fire and the spine-tingling Sioux war cry "Hoka hey! Hoka Hey!" and the shouts typical of warriors in combat, "It's a good day to die!" Dr. Honsinger and Baliran had run smack into an ambush laid by Rain-in-the-Face for the Custer party.[21]

Instantly, the troopers spurred their mounts to the rescue. The Sioux chieftain had planned the trap to catch the entire command, but when over-anxious braves sprang the ambush too soon, the Sioux dispersed. All the column found when they got to the scene of the incident were the bodies of the veterinarian and the sutler. Dr. Honsinger's skull was fractured as with some blunt weapon. Baliran's body was riddled with arrows. Because the Sioux fled in haste at the approach of the cavalrymen, neither corpse was mutilated.[22]

The same day, another soldier of Company F was also found dead. He, too, had been surprised at a spring. The discovery of these bodies and the reports of white scouts and Indian guides induced General Stanley to send help to Custer, which arrived in time to completely scare any remaining Sioux out of the vicinity but too late to help.

For the next three days after this incident, stealthy shadows and strange sounds were observed. The Arikaras explained that Sioux were hovering all around the expedition. On August 8, the reason was uncovered. A trail of pony tracks and the dragging ends of lodge poles, indicating a very large village, crossed the route of the command. General Stanley sent Armstrong with all the cavalry and scouts to follow the trail which led up the Yellowstone valley. They followed the track for thirty-six grueling hours. On August 10, they found that the Sioux had crossed the deep Yellowstone in "bull boats," the old mountain men's name for wicker coracles covered with buffalo hide used by the Indians of the northern plains.

Custer made repeated attempts to ford the river, but fruitlessly. The cavalry horses refused to swim the stream so heavily laden.

After that, the column was repeatedly attacked by the Sioux in guerrilla-style raids, stealing horses and keeping the nerves of soldiers tense. As the season drew to a close, the weary command turned back toward Fort Abraham Lincoln. The soldiers were only too glad to get back, away from almost a month of sleepless nights. Besides, they had allowed the railroad employees to survey as far as construction gangs could build in the following year.

To replace the dead veterinarian, Dr. Tempany was promoted to senior horse doctor. He and Reno's two companies returned to the fort on October 29. The day before, Dr. John Bretherton, an English vet from Minnesota, was assigned to the junior position, but he fell ill and resigned in August 1874. Dr. Tempany was the sole veterinarian for the regiment, and the card games in the veterinarian's quarters abruptly ceased. Tom was obviously affected by the loss of so companiable an old gentleman as Honsinger, not only because they had become fast friends but also because he and his poker-playing crowd had to find another place to deal out their cards.

Life went on for Tom without much change without the kindly fun-loving veterinarian. The days were spent drilling as long as the weather stayed good. But by November the long Dakota winter moved in around the fort. After that, garrison duty was pretty much the same as it had been at the other posts where he had been stationed. At night when it grew late, Tom was invariably impatient to be free. He might join the inevitable poker game at the unmarried officers' quarters, or cross the river to the Point, or read, or write letters to his sweetheart Lulie Burgess. Sometimes he rested beside the fireplace in his own quarters; at other times he merely sat idle and reveled in the comfort and the freedom that his position in life permitted him to enjoy. Occasionally, he wandered down "Suds Row," the string of small houses occupied by the married noncoms. He would start out walking rapidly, but when one of the sergeants' marriageable daughters emerged he dropped into a casual saunter and began to whistle. Then small talk and flirtation would fill his time.

Of course, he spent many long winter evenings with his family. He was back on cordial terms with George and Libbie, and he honestly liked his brother-in-law James Calhoun and loved the company of his sister, Maggie. On nights when there were no visitors at the Custer house on the grounds of Fort Abraham Lincoln, a game of charades provided a great deal of entertainment while snowflakes drifted through the darkness and a fire danced gaily on the hearth.[23] At other times, the Custers put on balls for the regimental officers stationed at the fort. The company captains and lieutenants showed up in full dress uniforms complete with gold epaulets, sashes, and the Seventh's regimental cords lashed over their shoulders. The bright blues and yellows sparkled and gleamed in contrast to the beautiful long gowns of the ladies. Ernest Haycox, in his novel *Bugles in the Afternoon,* said "there was a sharp exuberance in all of them, a health and a happiness and a childlike response to one night's freedom."[24]

Companies H and M, under the overall command of Captain Fred Benteen and led by Lieutenant DeRudio and Lieutenant Gibson respectively, were stationed at Fort Rice farther south. Captain Keogh's I Company and Captain Ilsley's Company E were at Fort Totten. B, G, and K Companies were still serving on Reconstruction duty at a far-away station in distant Louisiana. The able and careful research done by Haycox for his novel about the Seventh Cavalry resulted in this comment: "The regiment was a clannish thing even though it had not been together as a complete unit for many years; in spite of its jealousies and cliques and animosities, the Seventh was tied together by its traditions, its decade of service."[25]

One thing that strengthened those traditions was a lively Irish jig that Armstrong had once heard in New York and liked. He brought the lyrics and sheet music back to the Seventh's camp with him, introducing it into the outfit as the regimental aire. Its title was "Garryowen." Autie was pleased to find that most of the officers and enlisted men were as excited by the tune as he himself had been. The bright melody seemed to make the men ride more upright and proud, made their horses prance more smartly whenever the Seventh's band struck it up. If the parade ground was cleared enough for mounted drill, the lieutenant colonel could typically be found astride one of his thoroughbred chargers acquired during his sojourn in Kentucky, nodding his head in time as a squadron or two of troopers and steeds rode by in formation, guidons snapping sharply in the crisp, cold air.

George and Tom were still boisterous boys at heart, and one of their favorite pastimes was dreaming up practical jokes to play on each other or scheming together to pull a gag on one of their comrades. Ever since they had come together in the same unit in Texas they had been collaborating in practical jokes. Their father had played tricks on them as children, so it came naturally. On the trip to Texas, Tom shared a room on the steamboat with old Emmanuel. Their father had sewn some money into his vest. Tom pilfered the piece of clothing after Emmanuel laid it aside to pull off his boots, then pitched it over the transom above the door to Autie. The old man ran down the hall to Autie's cabin and pounded on the door—only to find one of Libbie's friends in the room at the time, who, offended, threw a glass of water through the transom onto his embarrassed, balding head. The teasing the next morning was merciless.[26]

To even the score, Emmanuel snitched Autie's cash purse. He stayed away from his sons for a couple of days, but they finally cornered him. Tom held him from behind while Autie rifled his pockets, taking all his money. To add insult to injured pride, they had asked the boat's purser to request their father's passage ticket while he was penniless. His excuse that it had been stolen failed to suffice—he had to ask Armstrong to float him a loan until he got back to Monroe.[27]

Whenever the boys got together with their father, one of their favorite tricks was to engage him in a political argument—which was easily begun either by smearing the Democratic Party or praising Republicans—during a meal. Tom would slip his father's dinner away, gobble down the food, and sneak the empty plate back under his father's nose. Armstrong would pretend to be tired of arguing and say, "Well, come, come, come, Father, why don't you eat your dinner?" The foul expression that covered Emmanuel's face was more than worth the cost of the second dinner the brothers later bought him.[28]

On the Yellowstone expedition, James Calhoun, the Custers' new brother-in-law, became the butt of many jokes. "How the boys do tease and devil Mr. Calhoun!" wrote Autie. "When a poor old horse died they accused him of starving the animal that a mare might have double portion of oats. When the theatrical ventures of Buffalo Bill and Texas Jack were discussed Tom said it might be a good speculation to back our own 'Antelope Jim'—on which Mr. C[alhoun] rushed out indignantly from the tent."[29]

During one formal officers' ball at Fort Abraham Lincoln,

George could not resist the temptation to humiliate Tom, who had leaned a straight-backed chair against a wall and fallen asleep during a lull in the activities. George tied a piece of string to the heels of his brother's dress boots and had a bugler summoned. While all the guests at the ball watched, stifling sniggers and snorts, the bugler blew "Boots and Saddles" in his instrument. Instinctively, Tom bounded from his chair and fell flat on his face before the whole gathering. Everyone doubled up with laughter over the joke at the young officer's expense.[30]

Not everything was fun and games during the long winter. One night, Armstrong and Elizabeth awoke, to their great consternation, to the sounds of a blazing fire. Suddenly, a boom like a cannon's roar shook the house. The fire was caused by sparks in a faulty chimney, and the blaze utterly destroyed the couple's house. Most of the personal possessions Libbie had brought with her to Dakota Territory were lost as a result.[31]

The ladies of the fort quickly rallied in support. Clothes and furniture to replace those consumed by the fire appeared as if from nowhere. The commissioned officers and their wives kept the Custers company for many nights until the shock of their loss gradually wore off. The fire caused a lot of commotion when it happened, and it was the topic of conversation for most of the rest of the winter among ladies and officers at the post.[32]

A new residence was built in the spring of 1874. Elizabeth described it in her diary: "We now have new quarters, next to brother Tom's, with archways cut in the dividing wall, so that we have the use of his as well as our own."[33]

The commissioned officers with wives numbered about forty altogether. So far from the East, their primary source of recreation was themselves. Therefore, when the commanding officer and his wife were not giving parties, the other officers spent their evenings together.

Everyday life at Fort Abraham Lincoln during those long, wintry months was very quiet after the exciting activity of the summer campaign. Tom, Armstrong, and Calhoun left the fort occasionally to hunt, using the hounds that Autie had with him, the Winchester rifles they purchased, and the best horses they could lay their hands on. But the weather was generally so severe that the three cavalrymen stayed close to home. Autie seldom left the house, where he occupied his time writing or studying Indian sign language, field maps of the Yellowstone country, and learning as much as he could about the northern plains.[34]

Tom's fellow unmarried officers discovered a new place to convene their disrupted card games. They congregated in the sutler's store near the main gate at the fort. There they continued the poker sessions so sorrowfully halted after Dr. Honsinger's death. They also played billiards on a table the sutler owned. They rarely saw Autie there since the sutler had lent him a billiards table, which he put in an upstairs room in his house so that he and Libbie could enjoy a quiet, private game of pool together. All in all, the peaceful solemnity of the snow-covered fort caused many of the officers and men to incur a severe case of cabin fever, while they listened to the wind whipping out of the north as much as fifty miles per hour.

The first break in the weather freed them to get back out-of-doors. And it also brought fresh military activity. Plans were being laid by the war department for the continued surveying and construction of the Northern Pacific—to the Sioux, a fire road—up the Yellowstone River valley, the last of the great buffalo grounds, and an additional branch line through the Black Hills where by treaty no white man was to go. The high brass wanted Custer's advice because he was the most experienced cavalry commander on the plains. He had encountered the Sioux during the summer of 1873, so he knew the score.[35]

Tom's return to the plains meant several things: for one, the Seventh regiment was partially reunited, which meant that he was reunited with his family and friends; it also meant that after a couple years apart from his brother, they came together again on their former amicable terms, a fact which really pleased Tom; finally, it meant a return to the action and glamor that the young Custer craved. The upcoming years would bring more of the same, along with a few events that would lead to a final, fateful meeting with the Sioux.

12
A Warrior Angered

The first long, snowy winter drew to a close. Autie returned to find the roofs of buildings at Fort Abraham Lincoln still peeking out of drifts, marked only by the dark silhouettes of chimneys breaking the hoary surface. The wind, which often made the buildings shudder with its velocity during the height of storms, would calm so that the compound was wrapped in an unearthly stillness in which the voices of men carried with ringing clarity. Nevertheless, as soon as he arrived at the fort, preparations for the campaign into the Black Hills commenced.

By this time almost half the officers of the regiment were either comrades of long standing or relations of the Custers. Of course, George and Jim Calhoun were Tom's brother and brother-in-law. Captain George W. Yates had been with the Custers since the days of the Civil War, while others like Myles Moylan, Myles Keogh, Algernon E. Smith, and William W. Cooke had served with them since the formation of the Seventh.[1]

Additionally, the Custers' rather sickly younger brother, Boston, in his mid-twenties, had come west partly to be with his famous older siblings and partly to receive the benefits of the rigors of outdoor life much like Theodore Roosevelt did a decade later. He signed on as a civilian forage master with the Seventh, possibly because he was not healthy enough to enlist.

The troopers may have had some difficulty drilling. The Seventh's encampment seemed to be overrun with dogs. One report has it that Armstrong alone had forty hounds with him, some of which he used for hunting, which were always getting under Libbie's feet. And besides the countless dogs, the men had acquired a veritable zoo—wolf cubs, antelope, raccoons, prairie dogs, and even a skunk. Most of these creatures were collected during the trip up the Yellowstone. It isn't known, but Tom may also have gathered up another bunch of rattlers.

The spring evenings renewed the love between Libbie and George. Lawrence Frost implied that there was no place for anyone else between the couple with the possible exception of Tom. Tom had his two Congressional Medals of Honor to console him—Armstrong had Libbie to make up for physical military honors. The colonel might spend long days training his troops, but when darkness settled over Fort Abraham Lincoln the love-struck couple had time for no one but each other.[2]

Spring also brought an increase in Indian activities. Bands representing a variety of Indian nations raided settlements and once drove off a herd of mules used to pull army wagons and kept not far from Fort Abraham Lincoln. After the expedition of 1873, Phil Sheridan recommended that a military base similar to Camp Supply erected by Custer in Indian Territory be established at the base of the Black Hills, for he considered the Sioux, who called the hills

"Paha Sappa," to be the villains at whose hands the depredations were made.

Autie had long had a desire to explore the Paha Sappa and to lead his command. Considering his investment in the silver mine at Georgetown, Colorado, he may also have been interested in determining for himself what sort of wealth might lay beneath the hills. He reported through army channels that "it would open up a rich vein of wealth calculated to increase the commercial prosperity of this country."[3]

By late April, the Seventh's leader had provided Sheridan with the estimated cost of an exploratory expedition, and Sheridan and General Alfred Terry had appointed Custer the commander of a body of troops to enter Sioux holy land.

Terry made it clear that this was strictly a military operation. If necessary, civilians following Custer's force would be forcibly ejected. The regiment awaited new revolvers and the .45-caliber Springfield carbines and the rest of the contingent—one company of the Twentieth Infantry, one of the Seventeenth Infantry, a large group of scouts, interpreters, and civilian employees, three Gatling guns, and a three-inch howitzer. Terry did not expect George to take any chances.[4]

The cavalcade, about one thousand horses, six hundred mules, three hundred head of cattle and about a thousand men, set out early in July 1874. Included among the men was N. H. Winchell, a geologist. The Black Hills lay a few hundred miles south and west of Fort Abraham Lincoln. The lengthy caravan snaked across the plains with an almost casual attitude.[5]

On this trip, big bub Aut enjoyed himself. He had a large following of friends and family along for what he considered a pleasure excursion, in spite of the fears that Elizabeth, other ladies at the fort, and General Terry harbored. The commander especially enjoyed the members of his family surrounding him. His nepotism increased as time went by. Tom, Boston, and Calhoun brightened his days during the march. The month it took for the column to string into the central portion of the Black Hills passed swiftly.[6]

To Tom's chagrin, the colonel banned poker and alcohol on the march. At first, Tom believed he would have nothing to do in camp, but his disgruntled mood dissipated. He and Autie began playing more and more of their practical jokes on the new low man on the family totem pole. For instance, in the rolling terrain of the hills, Armstrong rode alongside Boston, the former on a thorough-bred named Vic, the latter on an army mule. Whenever the colonel reached the crest of a hill, he raced Vic down the opposite side, while Bos—as he was affectionately called—plodded along on the mule. Thinking his older brother rode at a uniform pace, Boston could not understand how Autie was continually far ahead of him and his mule. Finally, Armstrong confessed the prank, thereafter tempering Vic's pace to that of Boston's pokey mount.[7]

About the same time, Tom gathered up a pocketful of stones. As they sat around the campfire with steaming mugs of coffee, Tom handed Bos the rocks, informing his victim that they were "sponge stones." He said they would soften and sop up water if soaked for a while. It took Boston several nights of intent watching before he realized that he had been duped.[8]

The expedition moved methodically through the Paha Sappa. William Illingsworth took innumerable photographs; Dr. J. W. Williams, the chief medical officer, collected botanical specimens; two mining engineers explored the possibilities of ore mining; and George Bird Grinnell and his assistant, Luther North, took notes on the natural history of the region. Professor Winchell's findings were kept under Autie's hat, although he made frequent reports to General Terry, which were carried to the telegraph station at Fort Laramie by Charley Reynolds, a scout about Tom's age.[9]

Sixty days after leaving, the command returned to Fort Abraham Lincoln without incident. But just in the nick of time—a paleontologist and his expedition searching for dinosaur bones in the Badlands a hundred miles or so east of the Black Hills were set upon by a Sioux war party. Fortunately, the leader, Professor Othniel C. Marsh of Yale University, managed to talk his party's way out of the tight spot. But Custer's intrusion infuriated the Sioux.[10]

As it turned out, that was the least of the Indians' worries. For what Professor Winchell discovered during his geological investigations would mean that in a few short years Custer's thousand men would be a drop in the proverbial bucket compared with the thousands of miners who invaded the sacred hills of the Sioux.

Gold was the most valuable mineral Winchell found. Custer kept mum about the discovery, but the news soon leaked out anyway. It was said that nuggets could be found "among the roots of the grass and, from that point to the lowest point reached, gold was found in paying quantities.[11] The government tried to buy the Black Hills from the Sioux, but negotiations broke down. Nothing the army could do stopped the gold seekers from swarming into the Black Hills, defying Indians, the government, and soldiers alike. By 1876, the gold rush would be in full swing and the Indians, already at the boiling point in 1874, would be ready to explode.[12]

In a roundabout sort of way, Custer's discovery of gold in the Black Hills was the reason for the demise of himself, his family, and a battalion of his regiment. His reports certainly brought on the gold rush, and they brought other profit-seekers as well. Unscrupulous traders who gave unwary red warriors whiskey and guns for buffalo hides came. Sod-busting pioneers flooded onto the plains to tear farms from the virgin soil. Bribed officials in Washington, including President Grant's own brother, sent two-timing agents and traders to forts and reservations where they made exorbitant profits off of soldiers, farmers, and Indians alike.

Immediately after the regiment returned from the Black Hills, Tom had time to reflect briefly on these groups of humanity pouring onto the prairie. One or more of them often came up in discussions around the dinner table at the new Custer house. The entire family—Autie, Libbie, Maggie, and Jim Calhoun, Boston, Libbie's friend Agnes Bates from Monroe, and Tom—met often and the discussions grew vehement when the subject turned to traders and agents. Armstrong particularly despised them.

Sometimes, reclining on his bunk alone, Tom stared into the brass lamp lighting his quarters and considered the intrigues with which those political appointees and private entrepreneurs filled their lives. He somehow could not believe that they would ever leave the plains and pass into the old East he had known as a boy to reach the land of business and politics on the shores of the Atlantic. He thought that Washington, with its capitol and other buildings housing the War Department, the Indian Affairs Office, even the White House with the president, Ulysses S. Grant, were all part of a mirage in their minds. The open spaces of the prairies were reality. He could understand why the nomadic Indians wanted to preserve it.

Of all the newcomers to the northern plains, Tom best identified with the farmers. They were simple, hard-working folk, trying to eke a living from the stubborn soil. Having come from a poor farm background himself, Tom could sympathize with them.

On excursions outside the fort he could see them work from dawn when it was still icy cold and pitch black outdoors until hours after their supper, breaking the sod. They no more wanted to leave the land than the Sioux and Cheyenne. Now, if Americans decided they wanted the gold in the Black Hills, the red nations might come together—something they had never done before—and teach the intruders a sorrowful lesson. There was no need to deny future troubles. Why else was the Seventh—still thought to be the best Indian-fighting regiment in the army—stationed at the hottest spot on the Great Plains?

Armstrong was incensed over the traders and Indian agents in the Dakota Territory, whom he blamed for much of the unrest among the Sioux and Cheyenne. He informed Tom that a delegation of fair-minded Indians from the Standing Rock Agency had gone to report to Major James McLaughlin that the traders were robbing them of their furs and hides. McLaughlin believed their story because his suspicions, like those of Colonel Custer, had been aroused by rumors from other quarters. The major had sent a message to Fort Abraham Lincoln the year before saying that no one could trade on the reservation without first obtaining a permit bearing his signature. Back then, one report has it, Dr. Honsinger stole one of the permit papers, forged McLaughlin's name on it, then began trading with the Sioux. There is no evidence that this accusation is true, but the source claims that Honsinger worked with three other men.[13]

It is doubtful that Honsinger was consciously involved in the shady deal, but one day a Sioux named Eagle Shield, a friend of Rain-in-the-Face, attempted to force the three traders to pay for some buffalo hides he had brought them. It is possible that Mr. Baliran was among those three traders. One of the trio of desperados shot and killed the brave. As the story goes, a niece of Rain-in-the-Face witnessed the murder and hurried to the chieftain's lodge in the camp of the Buffalo Clan of the Hunkpapa Sioux. It was then that the chieftain laid the ambush that Honsinger unexpectedly sprang.[14]

Tom and Calhoun were sent to the Standing Rock Agency to investigate the matter, but the Sioux kept their mouths closed. They saw no justice in surrendering the warriors who had killed men they thought were cheating them and murdered one of their band. From then until 1875, the mystery remained unsolved.[15]

It was still unresolved when George and Elizabeth departed for a trip to the East to witness the marriage of President Grant's son and to visit friends in Monroe. Tom heard that the wedding, while impressive, was unexciting. After the initial welcome of the couple to their hometown, prospects improved. Offers of all kinds began to pour in to Custer. Businesses large and small, and major financial institutions seemed eager to the point of flattery to obtain Armstrong—or more precisely, Armstrong's prestigious name—to enhance their business standings. He was told that the reputation he had earned during the war and on the Great Plains meant there was no limit to how far he could go in politics. Some omniscient political hack influential in the national government even thought it wise to suggest a diplomatic post for Custer to remove complaints from military circles.[16] Tom's absence was conspicuous, and nothing at all was offered to him.

George quickly perceived the reason he was wanted out of the army. In a moment of pique against Secretary of War W. W. Belknap, he offered to appear as a witness for the prosecution in the impeachment proceedings being brought against the cabinet member. He wrote a letter making this offer. He hoped it would lead to an opportunity to come before the American public on an important issue.[17] It provided him with an opening, a rare opportunity for an officer stationed on the distant frontier. He required action to survive, but triumph and public acclaim on any level, political or military, were for Custer the same as to any other public men who desired them. Haycox has written in his own inimitable style, "Fame was a jungle in which predatory beasts roamed; there were no rules in that jungle, only the bitterest kind of fighting. And at fighting he had considerable skill."[18]

Autie had seized the opening provided him by Tom's comments about the post trader, who by chance was one of those who bribed Belknap to appoint him to the fort. After several months of wily consideration, Armstrong reported to the Secretary of War, as Judson Walker said in *Campaigns of General Custer*, "that the trader in question was a man of intemperate and profligate habits, which fact had a demoralizing tendency among the young officers and private soldiers of the garrison."[19] Custer referred to the drinking and gambling the trader conducted in his store and upon which Tom frequently availed himself.

Belknap could not pigeon-hole such an accusation. Personally, George had no interest in who traded at Fort Abraham Lincoln. He wrote his letter outwardly for the sake of the younger officers, including his own brother, but he knew Belknap had to preserve the dignity of the cabinet of President Grant. Grant's administration had purposely ignored Custer's political chances, which, because Custer was a Democrat, posed a threat to the Republican president. Custer had a record and enough influence in the northern states that he hoped to force the removal of the trader by having his letter on record, thereby embarrassing Grant's cabinet.[20]

With the trader's store under pressure, things became quiet for

Tom. Little of importance requiring Autie's presence was happening at Fort Lincoln, and he, too, was becoming wary of the relative inactivity. One day late in September 1875, the restless Custer took his wife east for the duration of the winter. With them went Tom and his close friend William Cooke. They took with them the energy that pushed the Seventh into peak condition, so without their presence the outfit relaxed into a calmer routine. On the way, Libbie stopped off in Monroe to find some new prospective brides for unmarried officers of the regiment.[21]

The three men proceeded to New York for a fling of theaters, operas, and concerts. This was tame entertainment for Tom and Cooke, so while Autie enjoyed the big city in his own businesslike way, they enjoyed most of its more ribald attractions. Autie tried to drum up more financial deals and felt out some politicians he knew about the effect of his letters to Belknap. The furor had temporarily died down, and as Tom and Cooke, single and uninhibited, made the most of their time away from Fort Abraham Lincoln, Autie decided on more forward measures to confront the secretary of war and claim a place in the public media.[22]

George was granted several extensions to his leave, but Tom and Cooke returned to Dakota Territory early in 1876. Tom learned of his official promotion to captain as of December 2, 1875. With his promotion he received an increase in pay, and since Autie had not yet eliminated liquor and gambling on the post, he had a place to spend it. But unlike his brother, still busy trying to find new investments in New York, Tom saved part and sent part to his mother in Michigan. He apparently took Libbie's advice to heart, even though the old lady held no influence over him other than that of their mutual affection. Always the matchmaker, she wrote to him, "Don't spend more money than you can help at the Sutler's, drinking and card playing. Don't be influenced by the badness around you. Oh, Tom, if I find that the boy I have loved, and prayed over, has gone downhill. Oh, if only you had a companionable wife."[23]

It was February before Armstrong and Elizabeth journeyed back to Dakota Territory. Between St. Paul and Bismarck another blizzard moved in and buried Fort Abraham Lincoln in snow. The whole world seemed to turn white. The wind, howling down from the north at sixty miles per hour, packed all exposed walls in the Seventh's cantonment eave-high with drifts and laid a two-foot-deep carpet over the parade ground.[24]

Tom had been expecting the larking couple to return soon. He was worried after the storm lulled somewhat, because there was no word from them. He personally supervised a squad that went out in cutter sleighs—they found that the fierce wind had blown down telegraph lines not far from Bismarck. By tapping into the wires, contact was made between Fort Abraham Lincoln and Fargo.

The news he heard frightened him. The train carrying Autie and Libbie had stalled in deep drifts over forty miles east of Bismarck.[25] They had been trapped for several days. Tom answered Autie's message to that effect with a question: "Shall I come out? You say nothing about the old lady [Libbie]; is she with you?"[26]

Elizabeth was definitely with George, because she sent a reply ordering Tom not to come get them in such frigid weather. Disregarding his sister-in-law's command, Tom hired the best stagecoach driver he could find in Bismarck. He pulled on his heavy, buffalo-skin, army-issue overcoat and Berlin mittens and moved into the white outside world with the driver in a cutter drawn by sturdy army mules. The storm swept around them again, but the dauntless pair made their slow way to the helpless, stranded train. Tom thoughtfully packed straw, extra coats, mittens, mufflers, and blankets into the bobsled for his rescue mission to pick up not only his family but also three new stag hounds the colonel had purchased in the East. The extra clothing kept George and Libbie warm on the dangerous trip back to the fort.[27]

The happy homecoming was brief. The family had warmed themselves at Fort Abraham Lincoln for no more than a week when Autie received a summons from Washington ordering him to return to the East to tell a House of Representatives committee about traders' questionable activities on the frontier posts. Libbie hoped to go to Washington with the colonel, but Autie put his foot down. The last thing he wanted was to have his wife along on another harrowing journey across the snow-covered, windswept landscape. From the moment he left Bismarck's depot, there was no way Tom could make her relax until they heard by telegram that Armstrong had traveled the entire 250 miles of bleak, treacherous country to civilization in safety.[28]

A short time after Autie left, Tom and Calhoun got the first inkling of who had planted the ambush that killed Dr. Honsinger and Baliran. While Tom was in New York, the Sioux gathered one morning at the Standing Rock Agency to draw their monthly supplies from the government. For the occasion, the warriors held a dance. In the course of the dance, in which individual Sioux boasted of their prowess, Rain-in-the-Face allegedly told another brave in sign language that he had killed the veterinarian and the sutler, and in proof he produced some of Dr. Honsinger's personal effects taken from the body.[29]

There were a few white men and half-bloods present at the distribution of rations, among them Custer's scout, Charley Reynolds. "Lonesome Charley," the half-breed frontiersman, reported what he had seen to Tom and Calhoun, since he knew they had been the officers in charge of the investigation many months before.[30]

George's sojourn in Washington was embarrassing. In a few short sessions, it became apparent that he actually held little, if any, valuable information for the impeachment trial of Belknap. This fact annoyed the Congressional investigating committee and angered President Grant, who saw Custer's active testimony as a direct attack on his administration. The Seventh's colonel was kept cooling his heels in Washington for a long spell.

When he returned, he was not in a good mood. He had been made to look foolish in Washington. Worse, General Terry had been ordered to take over the command of the upcoming summer campaign. He had to plead with Phil Sheridan at Chicago to let him at least assume command of his own regiment.

He found a mess when he got to Fort Abraham Lincoln. Tom and a detachment of one hundred men from the post had ridden seventy-five miles to the Standing Rock Agency, as per his brother's telegraphed orders, on the next day that rations were distributed to the Sioux. Amid hundreds of armed braves, women, and children, Tom arrested Rain-in-the-Face. The arrest caused great excitement, but Tom pulled it off without a hitch.[31]

Tom's nature allowed him to hold a grudge, and because his dear old chum Honsinger was the victim of Rain-in-the-Face's trap, he was not very cordial to the chieftain. One writer even accused the new captain of beating and spurring the prisoner.[32] Although it has never been proved, many historians claim that as they arrived at the stockade, Rain-in-the-Face told Tom that, should he ever have the chance, he would cut out Tom's heart on account of the way he was treated after his arrest.[33] The Sioux was deposited unceremoniously in the Fort Abraham Lincoln stockade with a few other prisoners. Reportedly, he confessed his crime once incarcerated.[34]

Before he left for Capitol Hill, Armstrong had appointed a new lieutenant to investigate a ring of grain and horse thieves troubling the cavalry contingent at Bismarck. The young officer, fresh to the frontier and the regiment, fell in with Tom's cronies and, instead of carrying out his orders, he took up with "a damsel of African extraction and chocolate complexion, who had long been a sort of silent partner in his household joys and sorrows, and who added to his responsibilities and contributed an infinitesimal unit to the roll of the census-taker of the village" and also with some of Tom's acquaintances, "the miscreants and low flung gamblers of the town."[35]

Of the gang, the lax lieutenant arrested a small number, a few of whom were brought to trial and two who were convicted and given sentences in the Fort Abraham Lincoln stockade. They were the other prisoners there when Rain-in-the-Face was jailed.[36]

Their presence evidently amounted to little at the time, but the Sioux's entrance into the guardhouse had far-reaching consequences. For one thing, Rain-in-the-Face learned from them that President Grant had ordered the government agents to halt the hunting of buffalo by Indians, the order to be enforced by the army. The chief knew that this meant that the Sioux would be infuriated. The rations of beef from the agencies were hardly enough to feed the many bands on the reservations, so the Indians depended upon the buffalo they killed for the hides they needed for clothing, robes, and lodges and a good share of the meat they got for food.[37] What's more, the corrupt traders stole the meager rations issued by the government from the Indians for whom it was intended.

More concretely, however, the two grain thieves planned to break out of the stockade. With the help of a couple disgruntled Seventh Cavalry troopers implicated in the gang, they cut a hole in the outside wall of the guardhouse and escaped. Rain-in-the-Face was not stupid. He knew the fate awaiting him if he stayed locked up. He escaped through the same route and high-tailed it to the Hunkpapa Sioux camp of Sitting Bull, the ringleader of the hostiles who refused to settle peacefully on the reservations. Rain-in-the-Face was violently angered. He raved and ranted against both Custers. He called on the agency Sioux to join him, Sitting Bull and other resisters—Crazy Horse, Two Moons, and Gall, among others. He ardently awaited the opportunity to carry out his alleged threat on Tom's life.[38]

Tom made a dangerous enemy when he arrested Rain-in-the-Face. The red warrior held grievances of long standing against soldiers. He had helped Red Cloud drive the white men away from Fort Phil Kearny in 1866. He had seen the vicious attack on Hot Springs. He had spent some time in prison thanks to Tom Custer. Now he longed to sing his victory song over the dead bodies of the Seventh Cavalry's troopers.[39] The death of Dr. Honsinger at the hands of the Sioux chieftain in 1873 was the first in a chain of events that would bring Tom, George, and the rest of the Custer clan to their own deaths within the next few months.

13
THE LAST CAMPAIGN

Preparations for the summer campaign of 1876 began, even with Armstrong and Elizabeth away in the East. Major Marcus Reno and Tom Custer took charge of the Seventh in Autie's absence. Processions of wagons with supplies poured into Fort Abraham Lincoln, caravans of equipment to restock the cavalry unit rolled up to the quartermaster's facilities, fresh recruits to fill vacancies in the troops arrived by train, and officers came in on stagecoaches. The companies at Fort Totten and Fort Rice moved to Fort Abraham Lincoln to bring the outfit up to its full strength on the plains.

George had hoped for a promotion because of his trip to the East but learned instead of army reduction and the summer campaign. He wrote Tom, "The latest in regard to Army reduction is that the House will not interfere with the Cavalry, but will cut off 5 regiments of Infantry, and one of Artillery.

"I have no idea of obtaining my promotion this spring or summer. On the contrary. I expect to be in the field, in the summer, with the 7th, and think there will be lively work before us. I think the 7th Cavalry may have its greatest campaign ahead."[1]

It had been March 1876, when the simmering scandal which sent its harbinger out from Grant's White House a year before erupted. A broker in New York brought forth incriminating evidence that Secretary of War Belknap—or possibly his wife—had accepted a cash bribe for assisting certain individual businessmen to obtain the highly profitable post traderships. Custer's less-than-helpful testimony came a bit too late, because Belknap resigned on the eve of the Congressional investigation.[2]

Armstrong was retained in the capital in the hopes that he might yet be able to give some kind of important testimony. He was wined and dined in many quarters, but he was anxious to be back with the Seventh. Using some of his numerous contacts in Washington to help Tom improve the regiment, he secured the release of Companies B, G, and K from Reconstruction duty in Louisiana. They were ordered to move out from Shreveport to Fort Abraham Lincoln to join the regiment.

With them came Dr. Charles A. Stein, the German who had accepted the appointment of junior veterinarian in July 1875. He became senior veterinarian when the Englishman, Dr. Tempany, resigned on October 1. In late March, he and the companies left Shreveport with a herd of mules for delivery to the snowbound station. They arrived in the middle of April, augmenting the Seventh at last to its total strength for the first time in five years.

Dr. Stein's first duty was the inspection of the mounts in preparation for the campaign. He reconditioned those not up to snuff and removed those that were useless. According to regimental returns, the Seventh Cavalry held over 700 horses, of which 39 were unable to perform. Within two weeks after his arrival, Stein had lowered the number of mounts to 683, with only ten unserviceable. To the veterinarian's dismay, 64 new recruits to the companies from Louisiana brought the total of troopers to 718, and, given the use of army horses by officers who could just as well have purchased their own steeds, the shortage of mounts ranged between fifty and seventy-five.

Had Autie not been involved in the administration scandal in the nation's capital, he would have done all that was humanly possible to rectify the shortage. Grant, however, had demoted him, humiliating him publicly and leaving Reno and Tom to deal with the situation. Tom kept up a steady flow of telegraph messages to his brother requesting advice and orders regarding the expedition. He was now in Armstrong's boots, and he soon realized that as much as he wanted his brother to trust and respect him, he had never obtained the experience needed to command the Seventh. He relied on Autie's recommendations. His telegrams displayed great anxiety. While he wiled away the years basking in the light of his family name, he knew George had learned all he could about the art of leading cavalry. Tom realized his mistake too late in life— he would never lead more than a troop in the army.[3]

Compared with Autie's anxieties, Tom's worries were negligible—at least to the colonel's way of thinking. He wanted to be freed by the Congressional investigating committee in time to meet the tribes of the northern plains before the various bands combined into a single major force. Charley Reynolds, Bloody Knife, and many other knowledgeable scouts had been reporting such a formidable gathering for the better part of the winter. Rain-in-the-Face, when he joined Sitting Bull, added impetus to the possibility of the bands' collective resistance. Custer assumed that it would be midsummer before the reservation Indians could get their spring hunting done and meet Sitting Bull, but the longer the committee detained him the greater the number of warriors the Sioux medicine man enlisted.

Armstrong grew anxious as the spring wore away and still he was not released. He wrote Elizabeth in April 1876, from Washington, "I calculate on one week more here. Should I be detained longer I should give up all thought of a summer campaign and send for my Bunkey. Many would rejoice at a summer in the east . . . but not I." Referring to the inspection tour in Kentucky before much of the regiment moved out for reunification in Dakota, Custer railed against Secretary Belknap's attempts to defame him. "I paid General Belknap every official courtesy on his tour of inspection, of course. It was Tom, not I, who drove him through the precincts." At the end of the letter he noted, "I telegraphed Tom in regard to papers he is sending me on Government account. Every dispatch is overhauled by the Paymaster-General. All unimportant matters will be charged to Tom. My pay has been stopped several times on this account."[4]

In a letter as his leave to the East was about to expire, Autie was more confident and even light-hearted. "I send you a newspaper describing my dress as I sat with Representatives Clymer, Blackburn, and Robbins of the Impeachment Board," he wrote Libbie on April 25, 1876. "It states that 'Genl. Custer wore black coat and light pants'—both Tom's—and 'white vest.' Tell Tom I intend to charge him for having his clothes advertised."[5]

At last, at the very end of April, Custer's leave expired. He immediately took a train west through Chicago to St. Paul. At Chicago he got Sheridan's permission to join the campaign. In St. Paul he reported directly to General Alfred Terry, who would assume the command Custer had expected.[6] By the first of May, the reunification of the Seventh was completed by the arrival of its lieutenant colonel.

The crisp notes of the stockade bugle split the afternoon of May 10. Its sharp flourish announced the arrival of a general officer. Accompanied by Armstrong, General Terry and his staff rode through the main gate and down the regimental street. All the soldiers who witnessed the entrance stiffened as though electrified. The arrival of Terry indicated the start of the campaign, and Custer's presence meant that the hard work of preparation was as nothing compared with the future weeks of marches and battles.[7]

A week later, on the misty morning of May 17, another tune split the air:

The hour was sad I left the maid,
A ling'ring farewell taking;
Her sighs and tears my steps delay'd
I thought her heart was breaking.
In hurried words her name I bless'd;
I breathed the vows that bind me,
And to my heart in anguish pass'd
The girl I left behind me.

The song was "The Girl I Left Behind Me," which has been traced back to the eighteenth century. By the early nineteenth century it was popular in Civil War music halls before it found its way west to be sung by cowboys and soldiers.[8] The occasion was the departure of the Seventh Cavalry from Fort Abraham Lincoln. Sometime between midnight and dawn it had rained tentatively, leaving the fresh blades of grass heavy with pearls of moisture. The early morning rays of sunlight lifted the tinge of fog hanging over the regiment. The company guidons fluttered at the head of each troop. At a command from Armstrong, married officers and private soldiers swung down from their saddles to the parade ground to kiss wives and sweethearts goodbye.[9]

The Custer family believed itself above this military tradition. Mrs. Custer and Maggie Calhoun rode alongside their husbands, Libbie dressed in a lavishly simple buckskin riding habit and a royally scarlet hunting cap. Directly behind the colonel and his consort trotted Captain Tom Custer, senior officer of the five-company Custer battalion. He, too, wore buckskin and a broad-brimmed white slouch hat for the occasion. For once, with trim sideburns and a newly grown sandy goatee, he cut a more dashing figure than Armstrong. Beside him were civilian forage master Boston Custer and a personal guest of the colonel, his favorite nephew, eighteen-year-old Henry Armstrong (Autie) Reed. He completed the cloister of family sides with the colonel.[10]

Custer led the Seventh in a rippling circle past the new boardwalks in front of both Officers' Row and Suds Row while women and children waved goodbye.

Weeping mothers held little ones on their shoulders for a glimpse of their proudly mounted fathers. Young boys aped the guidon-bearers by carrying handkerchiefs bound to bits of wood and marching haphazardly as near to the horsemen as possible. The fort's Indian quarters, where Custer's Arikara and Crow scouts camped in buffalo hide tepees, was filled with the raucous sounds of squaws keening, children wailing, dogs howling, and warriors alternately crying out their war whoops and singing their death songs. Kinsley has implied that it was a bloodcurdling racket, and the troops breathed a little easier when they had passed. Libbie herself commented, "The most despairing hour seemed to have come." Of course, she wrote those words in retrospect.[11]

The last parade of the Seventh Cavalry was its finest. In the face of the days of anguish and dread that everyone connected with the regiment expected, the hearts of men, women, and children participating and looking on swelled with pride when the "Garryowen" was struck up.[12]

Libbie Custer and Maggie Calhoun accompanied their respective husbands on the first day out of Fort Abraham Lincoln. They brightened the officer cadre with their forced laughter and cheering banter on the trail. Libbie recalled that Armstrong often swiveled in his saddle to look over his shoulder and proudly observe the two-mile-long cavalcade wend its way among the short grass and gently rolling hills. He admired his men. "Just look at them, Libbie," he once exclaimed. "Did you ever see a grander sight in your life?"[13]

Libbie wrote of the first day's march in one of her books, "The soldiers, inured to many years of hardship, were the perfection of physical manhood. Their brawny limbs and lithe, well-poised bodies gave proof of the training their outdoor life had given. Their resolute faces, brave and confident, inspired one with a feeling that they were going out aware of the momentous hours awaiting them, but inwardly assured of their capacity to meet them."[14]

Libbie expressed her fears for her beloved Armstrong to brother Tom. The captain laughed at her worried countenance, waving his hand in a gesture of disdain and calling, "A single company of [our troops] can lick the whole Sioux nation!"[15]

Tom's confidence had been restored when Autie came back to Fort Abraham Lincoln from Washington. His brother had overcome the political machinations of the Grant administration. What worse fate could Sitting Bull, Crazy Horse, Gall, Rain-in-the-Face, and the others devise than that of Washington politicos?

The Seventh that left Fort Abraham Lincoln was made up of many raw recruits, some of whom were recent immigrants from Europe who barely spoke English. Enlistments to the regiment in 1866 and reenlistments in 1871 had expired, requiring new recruits to fill the empty ranks. Even some of the older soldiers had little practical Indian-fighting experience. Regardless of the training and preparation Marcus Reno and Captain Tom had done with the outfit, the Seventh was deficient in a few areas. For instance, at the tail of the procession with the pack train marched the sixty-four new recruits for B, G, and K companies. They never got their horses. Private Jacob Homer, one of the dismounted cavalrymen, left a bitter account describing the pain and degradation of proceeding on shank's mare the three hundred miles from the expedition's launching point to the mouth of the Powder River in spanking new cavalry boots, not yet broken in, choking on the dust raised by the horses of those who were mounted.

The entire contingent commanded by General Terry consisted of not only the Seventh Cavalry but also two companies of the Seventeenth Infantry, one of the Sixth Infantry and a complement of three Gatling guns in charge of two infantry officers and thirty-two men. The Gatling guns were an innovation which the Custers looked upon with mixed emotions. It will be remembered that those issued to the regiment at Fort Riley in 1867 were never used—as far as the cavalry was concerned, these would not be of service, either. In addition to the soldiers, there was a wagon train of 150 vehicles containing the commissary and quartermaster supplies and driven by 175 hired civilian mule skinners who stayed in a close-knit group. Heading the column was the party of Crow and Ankara scouts, including Charley Reynolds, a young half-breed named Mitch Bouyer, and two interpreters, Fred Girard and a black called Isaiah Dorman, and commanded by Lieutenant Charles Varnum of the Seventh.[16]

The column and its scouts would move rapidly to the mouth of the Powder River. The infantry companies and the Gatling guns would go with General Terry on a steamboat—the *Far West*—up the Yellowstone. The wagons would keep up as best they could. The plan Terry set forth called for a junction with a column commanded by General George Crook coming up the valley of the Rosebud Creek from the south and one moving down from Montana led by General John Gibbon. The meeting was to occur on June 26. Combined operations by the three commands would then subjugate the hostiles.[17]

The march of the Seventh, which had been somewhat altered, made good time after Libbie and Maggie Calhoun turned back after the first day. The companies were full of enlisted men, but they were under-officered. Armstrong made some changes of assignment. Myles Moylan retained A Company, and Tom was shifted to the command of Company C in addition to his duties as his brother's aid and leader of the Custer battalion. Among Tom's friends and acquaintances, Algernon Smith was taken from A to E; Yates had F; Donald McIntosh, an officer with Indian blood, led G; stodgy old Captain Benteen commanded H; Keogh, as always rode at the head of Company I; Godfrey, the lieutenant who never fired his Gatling guns, now had K Company; Tom's brother-in-law, Calhoun, was given command of L.[18] There was some shuffling of other officers to ensure that each troop had plenty of leaders. Boston and Armstrong Reed, although nominally civilians attached to the supply train, usually rode either with the colonel or with Tom.[19]

Several years before, to make the regiment look sharper and to instill *esprit de corps* in the Seventh, Armstrong switched horses from company to company until each unit rode horses all of the same color. Tom's C Company was mounted on sorrels—horses of light reddish-brown coloring with a white blaze on the forehead and white forelegs. Keogh's I Company rode horses that matched the captain's own spirited mustang, Comanche, the same one that Tom had brought back to Fort Riley eight years before, who would find itself a celebrity in a short while.[20]

Many private soldiers gave up animal friends of long-standing when the mounts were reallocated. The sixty-four, foot-sore cavalrymen without mounts complained with at least as much justification. The scattering of officers meant that some troops lost trusted captains and lieutenants for Custer's family and favored officers. The proud troopers who left Fort Abraham Lincoln were not as jovial or high-spirited as Libbie pictured them, either. Custer withheld the entire regimental payroll so that the typical drunken revelries of payday would not dissipate the Seventh's enthusiasm for the expedition. The payroll was carried along on the march for distribution during the campaign. By doing so, Armstrong also hoped to again eliminate booze and gambling from the rank and file while in the field. The regiment of which Autie was so proud was not so fond of its colonel as they approached the Powder River.[21]

Heedless of an order from Terry to have no civilians with the column other than those in the employ of the army, Armstrong invited a newspaper correspondent, Mark H. Kellogg representing the New York *Herald,* to accompany him. Kellogg's personal conveyance was an army mule thoughtfully provided by the colonel. Custer planned to keep his name before the public in one way or another. Glowing reports like those he received after the Washita fight would enhance any future political or business ambitions the colonel held.[22]

Kellogg's diary revealed more about the march than about Custer's accomplishments. He may have been planning to write a book about Custer much as Frederick Whittaker did within six months of the Little Bighorn expedition. Whatever was the case, Kellogg's diary mentions that on May 21 a mule, diseased with glanders, was shot, but Dr. Stein, the vet, took special care to keep the cavalry mounts and draft animals in top physical condition. He conducted a daily animal inspection during the march. Kellogg also fell into Tom's circle of gaming comrades.[23]

During this part of the march, George and Tom played more of their practical jokes on Boston. Once when the three brothers went for a ride, Boston's mule again fell behind. "Let's slip round the hill behind Bos," Autie suggested to Tom, "where he can't find us, and when he starts we'll fire in the air near him." The older brothers hid, Boston came over the hill, and a bullet whizzed over his head. The youngest Custer spurred his mule back to the column with his joking brothers shooting over his head. "Tom and I mounted our horses and soon overhauled him," George wrote Libbie. "He will not hear the last of it for some time."

Tom, Boston, George, and their oldest sister's son, Autie Reed, slept in the open around a campfire. "Tom pelted 'Bos' with sticks and clods of earth after we had retired," Custer wrote to Libbie. "I don't know what we would do without 'Bos' to tease."[24]

Boston took the teasing good-naturedly, even returning the humor on occasion. He wrote his mother from a camp about twenty miles from the Powder River, "I am feeling first-rate and joke Tom and Mr. Cook [Cooke] about their being tired by the ride to camp, for, as soon as a fire was built, they both stretched out for a sleep."

He added that he was not the only family member to participate in the fun, although he refers to their time at the fort and there appears to be yet another female authority figure in the Custer clan. Boston wrote an unintentional farewell while describing the participation of his sister:

Good-bye. I will take good care of myself, and not fail to write to you and Maggie—to you, even if Maggie goes without, for you come first with me in everything, and Maggie next. Sometimes she cuffs my ears, saying that if you did so when I was a child it is perfectly right for her to do so now. And sometimes she starts in on Tom and Jim and I with some good thumps of her fists, and warns us if she repeats it we shall all be sorry.[25]

The column camped near the Little Missouri River on May 31. Dr. Stein took a horse count there for the monthly regimental returns. After two weeks and 177 miles, only seven horses were reported unserviceable. However, although General Terry ordered no more than half forage for all animals after May 21 and the Seventh marched only twelve miles a day, Dr. John S. Gray implied in his article about veterinary care on the last campaign that neglect or accident—not overwork—brought on these animal casualties.[26]

George led the column constantly, usually several miles ahead of the main column. With him much of the time was Tom, Boston, and Cooke. A small escort commanded by Lieutenant W. S. Edgerly accompanied them. When this advance party first viewed the Powder River, the colonel told Edgerly, "This is just such a place, and the circumstances are almost identically the same as when we had that fight [on the Yellowstone expedition] in '73." Edgerly recalled that George and Tom then compared and pointed out similarities in the terrain. "We then built some fire," Edgerly wrote, "took off boots and neckties, and went to sleep, the General, Tom, Cook, Bos, and myself."[27]

Most of the regiment rested a few days at the end of the initial leg of their journey, the mouth of the Powder River, early in June. On June 10, Major Reno passed up the river on a reconnaissance. He rode for ten days and covered over 240 miles. Upon his return he reported to General Terry that his horses were "leg weary and in need of shoes."[28] The horses were keeping up nobly, but instances such as this one should have indicated that the pace being set should remain constant if they were to stay in shape for the remainder of the campaign. It has been suggested that because it did not, the horses were not ready for swift action when the regiment met the hostiles.[29]

At a council of war with Gibbon, Terry, and Major James S. Brisbin, commander of the detachment of Gatling guns, meeting on the *Far West*, his superiors offered Custer the use of the battery of guns in support of the regiment, at Brisbin's suggestion. Custer formally and politely refused. Meeting Tom on the shore, Armstrong told his brother about the council and haughtily added, "That was very clever of Brisbin to offer to go with me. But you know, this is to be a 7th Cavalry battle; and I want all the glory for the 7th there is in it."[30]

That Autie was supremely confident there is no doubt. As the march moved along briskly the colonel wrote to his wife regularly, as was his custom. He reported from the Powder River that Charley Reynolds, the column's chief scout, was confused and lost—in country Lonesome Charley knew intimately—and that Armstrong himself had guided the column to their camp. On June 11, he wrote that he was again leading the command through badlands. As an afterthought, he wrote, "P.S.—We are living delightfully. *You* might as well be here as not!"[31]

Hoping to make better time, Armstrong called a council of his own. He informed the Seventh's officers that the unmounted men, unnecessary equipment, and the baggage train would be left behind. Needed supplies would be placed on pack mules in the method George Crook had proved so effective. Dr. Stein and another officer were attached with those staying behind, displaying a remarkable disregard for the animals that would carry Custer's proposed search-and-destroy mission.

The meeting left the officers split. On one hand, Tom led a faction of glory-hunters who supported the colonel—Calhoun, Boston, and Autie Reed, Cooke, Keogh, Weir, and Yates. Among them also was a Lieutenant Harrington, who was certain that he would be captured by the Sioux and tortured to death and who went so far as to draw a sketch of himself dismembered. He would be a controversial figure after the fight on the Little Bighorn. Major Reno, who may very well have been intimidated by the Custer gang, equivocated, against his better military judgment. On the other hand, Benteen headed up a group of commissioned men who saw a danger in Custer's proposal—the plan might very well put the 597 officers and men who would continue the campaign on the Little Bighorn before the junction with Crook and Gibbon for which Terry's plan called. Benteen had been a thorn in Custer's side since the colonel's court-martial in 1867. He and Tom had never seen eye to eye, so now Tom sneered to himself over the older man's military opinions. It was obvious to Benteen that Custer wanted only the Seventh to win the victory, and it went against his grain to waste human lives for one man's self-seeking purpose. The Seventh had left reinforcements behind at the battle on the Washita, neglecting to meet the Nineteenth Kansas Volunteers, and had come out of it luckily. He did not think it would happen again.

All the older campaigners agreed that Custer seemed less enthusiastic than usual when scouts discovered an Indian trail. Mari Sandoz has written in her history, *The Battle of the Little Bighorn*, that he was surely less assured and self-sufficient than on his attack against the Cheyenne village in Indian Territory. He seemed uneasy about something, as though troubled by a premonition.[32] It was not that he feared the meeting with the Sioux and Cheyenne— no, more likely, he feared that he would miss the chance of meeting them or that Crook and Gibbon would defeat them before he could strike a blow. Custer's entire future hinged on his performance this summer, and even Tom's presence could not allay his worry.

Tom had no such troubles. True to their sibling rivalry, while Autie's life became more complicated, Tom's flowed along smoothly. Safe under his brother's over-protective wing, Tom had been having the time of his life for the past few years. Back on the campaign trail, he was light-hearted and free-spirited. The disquiet that lasted among the officers long after they left Custer's tent had little impact on Tom. He had the same confidence in the Seventh that George did. Several little groups of officers talked quietly, seriously, throughout the night. But Tom Custer and Jim Calhoun were little concerned with military matters.

They, too, lost a lot of sleep that night, but their insomnia took them to the *Far West*, the shallow draft, stern-wheeler steamboat which carried Terry's headquarters staff and Major Brisbin's Gatling guns, anchored in the Yellowstone. A game of poker had started with Captain Grant Marsh, the steamer's chief officer, Tom, Calhoun, and others, although at Autie's instructions the regimental paymaster had accompanied the command to the first camp out of Fort Abraham Lincoln.[33]

It rained again and grew colder while Tom and Calhoun played cards. The bleary-eyed officers stepped off the steamboat into light fog and three inches of new-fallen snow. Troopers in C and L companies tried to light wet buffalo chips for fires, but the fuel only smoldered without burning. Horses on short rations grew hungry because they could not forage for grass.[34]

Nevertheless, on June 22, the noonday sun high overhead, Autie led the regiment out in pursuit of the hostile band Major Reno ran across on his reconnaissance. The mule train carried rations for fifteen days for the troopers, and again one-sixth rations—about two pounds of grain per animal—for the horses. Terry's plan called for marches of thirty miles a day, so no one expected any serious danger for the horses. The strike force would overtake the hostiles in only a few days.

Custer's riding pace up the course of Rosebud Creek followed the prescribed rate closely—twelve miles the first afternoon, thirty-three were covered the next day, and twenty-eight on the third day. The marches included a few rest breaks and a three-hour halt in the early afternoons. The old nicknames for George reappeared, however—"Iron-Ass" and "Horse-Killer" used in Kansas eight and nine years before.

The landscape the regiment crossed seemed like a parched, lifeless desert, even though precipitation had fallen several times during the march. Most of the grass was short and brown, and the few draws and coulees which ran across the trail were barren of water or turned to alkali. The terrain was difficult—eroded and rasped by ages of sterile wind into ragged hills, arroyos, and stretches of greenish-gray, treeless steppe. The result was a stark land of weird beauty. The horses struggled over hard-packed ground, and yet it sent up thick dust as if the soil underfoot were nothing but powder.

The pace was hard on the horses, already on short rations and with little time to graze, but it served Custer's purpose. On the evening of June 24, the hostile trail suddenly became remarkably fresh and turned undoubtedly west over the wide ridge separating Rosebud Creek from the valley of the Little Bighorn River.

All minds in the Seventh's encampment that night swiftly shifted to the business of Indian fighting. Some of the old campaigners followed Tom's example of slipping the McClellan saddle from his mount's sweat-scorched back, but most of the stock remained under saddle, ready for instant use. The Crow and Arikara scouts rubbed their ponies down with wads of grass. The many new recruits tried to ease the burning of their galled thighs and made gray coffee from the alkali water found near the camp. Suspecting that a fight was slated for the next day or so, they collapsed on their blankets to catch forty winks to refresh themselves.[35]

Colonel Custer was anxious for news from the detachment of scouts ahead of the main command. Tom and Lieutenant Cooke waited up with him. His excitement affected both of them. Another sleepless night passed while Boston and Autie Reed, the youngest members of the Custer family, slept.[36] The tension mounted, midnight approached, and the expectation of the coming battle with the able-bodied warriors of the recalcitrant hostiles with Sitting Bull and the runaways from the Standing Rock Agency under the leadership of Rain-in-the-Face. The red warriors outnumbered the Seventh—a fact as yet unknown to the colonel—and were almost as well armed. George, considered by Tom and the rest of the Custer clan to be an unsung military genius, had made one mistake in the name of personal ambition. He would soon make several tactical blunders through ignorance and pressure in the classic confrontation.

Tom felt concern for the campaign of 1876 until his brother joined the regiment at Fort Abraham Lincoln. Once Armstrong arrived, however, his entire attitude had done an about-face. He still worked hard to whip his new company and the rest of the Seventh into fighting condition, but he took the expedition less than seriously. He did not have the chance to carouse in the joints of the Point because he did not get his pay, but he made up for that by losing a sum of money to Grant Marsh on the *Far West* and playing pranks on Boston. The hard-riding of the next three days exhausted him just as it did all the Seventh, but the physical stamina he shared with Autie and the pre-battle excitement his older brother infused in him kept him from sleeping. Instead, he conferred with George and Cooke and finally braced himself for what would be the most terrible battle of his thirty-two years.

14
THE LAST BATTLE

Shortly after midnight, June 25, 1876, Tom Custer led Company C of the Seventh Cavalry out at the point of the regiment. The troop headed the five companies of the Custer battalion, then those men under Reno, followed by Benteen, who protected the pack train. The sleepless night seemed to have had no effect on Tom—he felt buoyant, refreshed. He moved his troop out briskly toward the longest and last day most of them ever faced.[1]

Tom may impulsively have glanced at the tattoo he received years before. His initials, the goddess of liberty, and the stars and stripes were embossed on his right arm above the elbow. The tattoo reminded him that he was going out to fight hostile savages to clear the way for the civilization of his country.

C Company led the entire regiment up the eight-mile ascent of the divide between the Rosebud and the Little Bighorn. The outfit rested at the crest for six hours. Armstrong and the scouts joined Tom at the head of the column for another five-mile climb in the late morning. The crest of the ridge was used like the crow's nest of a ship, and it was so named by Tom. The scouts had reported a large village of hostiles on the Little Bighorn, and under normal circumstances this would have been the last stop for the day. As he had done at the Washita, Autie hoped to plan a surprise dawn attack.

By this time, however, Sioux braves had been snooping near the approaching cavalrymen. A couple packs had fallen off of a mule, spilling hardtack all over the ground. Several Indians were discovered swarming over the packs by soldiers returning to pick up the missing hardtack. Reports like these convinced Armstrong that an alarm would warn the village, causing it to disband and flee. Conferring briefly with his officers, he announced that he planned to attack that very afternoon.

What Custer did not know was that Crazy Horse with a large force of Sioux and Cheyenne had defeated George Crook's column farther down the Rosebud in late May. After the battle, the warriors moved their tepees and families down to the Little Bighorn and pitched their lodges beside Sitting Bull's encampment.[2]

Additionally, no one with Custer knew the mood of the Indians. They were cornered. This was the last chance for their freedom, and the Seventh posed a direct threat to their women and children. This temper would unleash a desperate, fierce resistance to any assault.

The impetuous colonel was rash in striking at the huge village without more intensive scouting. Many historians contend that his concern over the presidential rebuke and his own political ambitions clouded his judgment. These were probably not uppermost in his mind, in spite of what these historians say. Custer was a military man, and his thoughts most likely dwelled on defeating the enemy. His information—which he trusted more than that his scouts provided—did not indicate that the Indians would be numerous or well armed, and only Crook knew that they figured to stand and fight. Custer expected another Washita and planned accordingly.[3]

A cardinal rule of military tactics is that the commander should never divide his forces and never deploy them piecemeal. Custer successfully did both during the Indian Wars and tried to do so again at the Little Bighorn.

After Mitch Bouyer, Fred Girard, Lonesome Charley Reynolds, and the Arikara told Autie that there were more Sioux and Cheyenne in the Little Bighorn village than the Seventh could ever handle—adding ominously that if the regiment descended into the valley it would not come back—Custer remained confident. He hefted a lanky leg over his sorrel without bothering to saddle the horse. He rode down the ridge to where Tom had established a temporary bivouac of sorts to brew coffee for the Custer battalion. Kinsley wrote that he called out, "Hey, Tom! Move 'em out at eight o'clock sharp. I'm heading up the divide to have a look. Follow my trail at a fast walk. We'll meet yonder and cross over the ridge before noon."[4] Even though he had two officers who were Tom's senior, Armstrong relied on his loyal brother to follow his instructions. Tom did what his colonel told him; Reno or Benteen might use their own discretions concerning his orders.

Faithful to his brother's trust, Tom pushed the troopers after the colonel and the scout detachment. About ten-thirty in the morning, a hollow rumble signaled their approach into the valley. Custer galloped down from the Crow's Nest, reining up beside Tom. The saddle-sore cavalrymen were thankful when he called a halt. They had covered ten painful, twisting miles up the ridge since moving out two and a half hours before.

Again according to Kinsley, Tom leaped from his sorrel shouting, "We've been spotted!" He explained about the dropped box of hardtack and the sightings of hostiles along the trail. Custer sent a messenger to recall Myles Keogh, who had his Company I scouting in the rear with a couple of the Crows, and another summons to Reno. He turned to his orderly bugler of the day—an immigrant Italian, Giovanni Martini, who had Americanized his name to John Martin—ordering him to blow "officers' call."[5]

Having reluctantly abandoned the dawn attack for an afternoon surprise approach, at noon the colonel flagged his men forward in a steady, fourteen-mile ride down the opposite side of the divide. The command moved out at a faster pace on already wearied steeds.

Custer and Tom took the lead with the Custer battalion; Reno and three companies followed closely; Benteen, three companies, and the pack train moved to a high ridge two miles to the left to see whether the village attempted to escape. Benteen received instructions to hurry to rejoin the regiment, but he lagged behind. To complicate matters, the civilian mule skinners allowed their caravan to fall even farther behind, siphoning off manpower equal to Benteen's battalion.

As the rapidly moving column neared the village, Custer split off from his own detachment to ride back and confer with Marcus Reno. He ordered Reno to take the advance to attack the village from upstream, while he turned right to deliver a supporting blow from downstream. Armstrong hopefully lifted the onus of the fighting from his own battalion, preserving the safety of his personal command, his family, and himself while gaining a victory to bring to his own name. Not that he was afraid to face the enemy—his courage had been proven time and again—he had too much to live for to die at the Little Bighorn. Unbeknownst to Autie, however, the wick of his lifetime burned perilously low.

Shortly after his right turn, Armstrong waved forward one of the sergeants of Tom's C Company. He dispatched the noncom, a Sergeant Kanipe, with an order for the commanding officer of the baggage train. Kanipe rode hard to instruct the officer to "hurry up the packs." The sergeant delivered the message to Captain Benteen, who sent Kanipe on his way to find the train.[6]

Meanwhile, the Custer battalion proceeded north at a gallop for over a mile, following Mitch Bouyer and four Crows to a spot in the shade of the ridge they had lately crossed. Custer halted the command there. Tom whistled Lieutenant Cooke and Autie Reed over to meet him and Armstrong, and the four rode to the summit to get their first glimpse of the village. At least one enlisted man, the orderly bugler John Martin from H Company, went with them.[7]

The sun was moving west rapidly—it was then almost three o'clock in the afternoon. Custer was impatient to get on with his assault. Still, there appeared to be no out-of-the-ordinary activity in the Indian camp. He handed the binoculars to Tom and murmured something about catching the Sioux napping. When Tom took a look he saw nothing happening. Soon Reno's run at the upstream end of the village would commence. Custer informed Tom and Cooke that he would cut off any retreating redskins. He then ordered John Martin back to Benteen to urge the old captain up with reinforcements and the ammunition in the packs. Cooke took out a pencil and pad, hurriedly scribbled down the colonel's order, tore off the page, and handed it to the excitable young Italian. The officers on the knoll did not think Martin could repeat the instructions orally and still understandably.[8]

Sometime between the moment Sergeant Kanipe left the command and when Martin turned back for Benteen in the rear, the Custer battalion moved forward in columns of fours. The terrible pace was beginning to tell on the horses of the whole detachment. At one point, four troopers dropped out, their animals exhausted. Two of these men—Privates Thompson and Watson—were members of Tom's company. These two joined Reno and Benteen very late that day. The other two men were never heard from again— W. A. Graham, one of the most careful Custer researchers, has remarked that they were probably killed by the enemy.[9]

Several miles behind, Sergeant Kanipe, arrived from C Company with the first order for Benteen to hurry up the packs. At the same time, Reno struck at the upstream side of the camp. Firing of army carbines and Indian Winchesters could be heard in the distance. Reno was handily repulsed by the Sioux and Cheyenne.[10]

Trumpeter Martin, the last messenger from the Custer battalion, hurried on to Benteen and the lagging pack train. During his ride he met Boston Custer, the youngest of the brothers, who had left his siblings for some reason and returned to the slow-moving train.[11] He was riding furiously to overtake the other members of his family. They were turning toward the village at that very moment.[12]

Benteen heard the firing from the river and knew that Reno would need help. He did not plan to let the senior major wind up like Joel Elliott after the Washita. Kanipe was sent on back to the train commander with Custer's order to rush while Benteen led his three companies toward the sound of the firing—the valley where Reno fought.[13]

The hands of the clock hovered around 3:30 P.M. as Custer's five companies positioned themselves for their part of the attack on the village. It was a tremendous village, the largest any of the scouts had ever seen. The Crows said that they could not even count the number of lodges. Along the eastern edge of the encampment flowed the Little Bighorn, with some timber growing sparsely on its banks. The stream ran full from the melting snow in the Bighorn Mountains off to the south and east.[14]

On Tom's side of the river there were bluffs and beyond those the hills they had crossed on the trek to their last Indian fight. Some gullies—called coulees—came through the bluffs. On the far side of the village Tom could see a pony herd grazing, guarded by teenage Indian boys. A Sioux named Black Elk later told historian John G. Neihardt, "There were so many they could not be counted."[15]

Not until Armstrong heard the firing from Reno's attack did he order the battalion to the fore. The weary troopers and exhausted horses pushed down into the fateful valley through a washed-out arroyo called Medicine Tail Coulee as though they were poured out through a funnel. Tom instantly grasped the colonel's idea—the Custer battalion would cross the river to hit the center of the village while the warriors were diverted by fighting with Reno. With any of the celebrated "Custer luck," his troop would spearhead the drive to seize the pony herd, cutting off the Indians' transportation for escape. The effect would be similar to Autie's triumph at the Washita.

To maintain the columns of fours, Custer marched the troops on the far side of the ravine. The late afternoon sunlight glinted off weapons and clearly defined the varying colors of the troop horses—Tom's favorite sorrels of C in the lead, the bays of F Company, the grays of E—then a gap which Keogh's I Company and Calhoun's L Company tried to close up.[16]

Minutes ticked by as the horses alternately cantered and walked over the broken ground, trying to maintain some amount of military precision. The column entered the center of the basin of the Little Bighorn, heading for the ford that would take it across the river and into the midst of the tepees.

Tom followed on Autie's heels when their horses hit level ground at the mouth of Medicine Tail Coulee. They pounded toward the ford just ahead of the soldiers of C Company. Suddenly, a handful of Cheyenne warriors—some accounts say four, some six—rode out to meet the white soldiers. At first they roweled their ponies up into the river and gestured fiercely. Sporadic fire from troopers' pistols sent them plunging into the brush, riding in a zigzag course up a ridge and shooting so that the cavalrymen assumed that there were more of them than there really were—an old Indian trick which should not have fooled either the colonel or Tom.[17]

All three companies moved off after this suicide squad. Custer may have thought that these were the refugees from Reno's action. He had no way of knowing that Reno had been soundly whipped and chased from the field. Keogh and Calhoun, moving more slowly, rode out of the coulee with carbines at the ready in preparation for their charge—and ran headlong into Gall, a Sioux leader, and forty or fifty warriors fired up by having seized a small victory over Reno. They wanted more blood.[18]

George and Tom heard the firing erupt in their rear. Circling to look, they saw the Indians fall upon Calhoun's company. The colonel sent Cooke down to George Yates of F Company and Algernon Smith of E with orders to deploy their men at the foot of the ridge, thereby giving support to Keogh and Calhoun. He and Tom took C and spurred after the fugitive Cheyenne at the brow of the hill.[19]

The Cheyenne believed that Custer was struck blind and made foolish because he broke the promise of peace he had made many years before when Monasetah led him to their fleeing tribesmen and he seized them until they turned over the white women. Monasetah and her son, Yellow Swallow, were among the old men, women, and children in the village that day, and although some Indians thought that the mother and son would bring bad medicine, they watched the tragic events unfold from among the lodges.[20]

Gall's party rode parallel with the gray horse troop, E, successfully cutting I and L off from the rest of the battalion. Keogh prepared to fight his way through to Custer, but Yates and Smith were already dismounting their troops to begin a heavy firefight. Keogh pressed on until he nearly reached the river.[21] Mark Kellogg, the newspaper correspondent, had been near the head of the column when it entered the ravine, but his slow-gaited mule could not keep up with the cavalry mounts. He kicked and spurred to get more speed out of the lumbering beast as the regular firing increased to a steady beating. As he reached the mouth of the dry wash he saw the valley spread out before him. Smith's troop was nearest the river, its mounts forming an oval around the horse holders—every fourth man in the unit. Tom's troop was also dismounted by this time, troopers clinging desperately to the reins of frightened, plunging animals. F Company was still mounted on its bays in a thin line, supporting C with fire over the heads of Tom's men. Farther north, Kellogg saw Keogh leading two troops to their aid, having trouble maintaining formation across the formidable terrain.[22]

That was evidently the last Kellogg ever saw. He was shot in the back with arrows—perhaps the first intimation that anyone in the command had that the Custer battalion's retreat was cut off.

A Cheyenne named Lame White Man now led the attack from

the village. Many of the Cheyenne had not gone upstream to fight Reno. As luck would have it, the ford Autie chose to use was right across from the lodges of the Cheyenne. More and more red men moved through the water to shoot bluecoats. Meanwhile, a large party of Sioux under Crazy Horse returned from the Reno encounter and, circling around the west side of the village, came up the ridge smack in front of Custer.[23]

If there had not been so many Sioux on the ridge above him, Custer might have retreated that way, either then or later when the fighting really got bad. Instead, according to Indian reminiscences, he turned back in the direction he had come. Seeing this route blocked, too, he stopped. Apparently, he called a short council of war, likely with Tom and Cooke since all the other officers had their hands full. He wasted twenty valuable minutes trying to figure a way out of the hopeless trap into which he had led his battalion.

But it was too late. The firing became progressively heavy as increasing numbers of Sioux and Cheyenne entered the fray. Between the river and the foot of the hill, dying and wounded men of E and C companies slumped to the ground. Many Indians were swimming the river while noncombatants fled west of the village. And Indian criers spread the word the length of the valley that the soldiers had come and were falling from the sky—dying.

George, Cooke, and Tom returned to the top of the knoll with a few men to see if there was any chance of clearing the enemy from it. Myles Keogh, seated on his spirited Comanche, directed the fight at the river. He held the rearguard because Smith had fallen. All around him, horses and troopers were cut down, but he rallied his and Tom's men into a tight circle, and they poured a blistering fire into the red braves, forcing the Cheyenne back for a moment.[24]

When they charged again, ponies and warriors went down as though a scythe swept through their ranks. Gradually, they drove Keogh's men up the slope. The Irishman instructed the men to hold steady on the firing line, kneeling until the Cheyenne—this time joined by hundreds of Sioux—came near. Then the cavalrymen loosed volley after volley into the massed bodies.[25]

As their numbers dwindled, the men of these companies could see the headquarters guidon fluttering at the summit of the ridge. They began a dogged fighting retreat through the storm of dust, bullets, and arrows up the slope. Indians now attacked them from both sides and their front. The withdrawing circle of soldiers grew smaller, and yet smaller. A string of dead bodies, men and horses alike, marked the retreat like pearls on a necklace.[26]

Graham accurately summed up this action from all the sources that he could muster for his book, *The Story of the Little Big Horn:*

It was apparent that the brunt of the Sioux attack came from the south, that Calhoun's troop was the first to be struck by the savage mass, and, immediately after, Keogh's. Aside from these two troops, in which officers and men died in their places, in platoon formation, there was no semblance of battle-lines anywhere on the field. All was confusion. The tide of battle had swept over Calhoun and Keogh, crushing them by sheer weight of numbers, and, rolling around, had first enveloped, then engulfed, the other three companies.[27]

The noise must have been unbearable. Women in the camp below were singing and making the tremolo. Old men cried out, "Boys, take courage! Would you see these little children taken away from us like dogs?" Sioux warriors cried, "Hoka Hey! Hoka Hey!" Cheyenne howled, "Hey, Hey, Hey!" Rifle and carbine fire all but drowned the bloodcurdling war cries, the screams of dying horses, the moans of dying men.[28]

For a few minutes, the remaining three companies held their own without direction from their officers. Yates and Smith were wounded, and Tom stood on the hill beside George. His right arm was broken by a Winchester shot. Then Lame White Man led a strong force against what was left of E and F and C. Lame White Man had had a good day that far. He even wore a bluecoat jacket he had snatched from a dead cavalryman. In the clouds of dust and smoke of the battle, the Cheyenne leader was killed by a Sioux who thought he was one of the Seventh's Crow scouts. His followers redoubled their efforts, charging *en masse* until all the soldiers were dead or running for the crest of the ridge.[29]

Indians said that at this moment a soldier on horseback bounded away from the circle. The man was not wearing a regulation uniform, and he wore his hair long. Some braves pointed and said it was Long Hair Custer. Crazy Horse, one of the witnesses, replied that no, it was not Custer. Many Sioux assumed that it was Tom, but Tom's body was found near that of his brother.[30] It may have been Lieutenant Harrington, second-in-command of C Company, trying to escape the unsettling fate he had sketched for himself. Nevertheless, the fleeing soldier died trying to escape.

Within three-quarters of an hour after the Custer battalion entered the Little Bighorn valley, the area filled darkly with dust and smoke. The air abounded with cries and hoofbeats and the pops of gunshots. The remnants of the three companies met Custer at the hilltop and readied themselves for the last stand. They would sell their lives dearly. Almost fifty men kneeled behind a crude breastwork of dead horses, wondering what had become of Reno and Benteen, fighting back the knotting fear, watching the savage horde creep up the ridge.[31]

Many of them were reduced to firing their pistols—their single-shot Springfields had become fouled with cartridges swelling in the chambers, causing the weapons' extractors to pull past the heads of empty cartridge cases, which then had to be pried out of the chambers with knife blades. That was in addition to the simple fact that the men had exhausted their supply of ammunition.[32]

Not that it made much difference. Gazing down over the field, Tom knew that the end had come. He and the ragged band of fifty soldiers and civilians clustered around Autie's personal guidon. It was tipped ever so slightly, for no one now took time to straighten it to the colonel's satisfaction. Tom's buckskin jacket had become insufferably hot, so he had stripped it off. He was covered from head to boot in stinking alkali dust. Clouds of smoke and dust floated precariously over the hilltop. Tall clumps of prairie grass and sagebrush moved where Sioux or Cheyenne warriors lurked, all around. It was a hellish way to die. Probably, the only good thing he could think of was that he would die defending his older brother—just like back home in Michigan as boys playing at war.[33]

In less than an hour, the fight was over except for the Indians' celebration. The corpses of men and horses lay at the ford and up the hillside for about three-quarters of a mile, exposed to the mutilating knives of vindictive squaws. Jim Calhoun's whole troop sprawled in an irregular line with Calhoun and Lieutenant John J. Crittenden in their proper positions behind the line. A mile beyond, Keogh's company lay in their place, their right flank on the slope of Custer Hill. Behind them were Yates' company and a few of Smith's and Tom's men. Most of E and C had fallen in a ravine near the river.[34]

In a small circle around the madly tilted headquarters flag was the Custer gang. Yates had made it to the crest of the ridge. Lieutenant William Van W. Reily lay there, too. William Cooke died beside his colonel. Autie Reed, who had come along for the ride, and sickly Boston, who had finally caught up with his brothers, were killed beside Armstrong. The ill-fated Custer was found stripped to his underwear but otherwise unmutilated. According to Captain Benteen, "There was an arc of a circle of dead horses around them." Custer died as he had lived while in the army—surrounded by friends. He would have appreciated that.

Tom's body was the most hideous sight on the gory battlefield. It was mangled almost beyond recognition. Either Rain-in-the-Face or some of his followers extracted the revenge that the Sioux chieftain had promised. Tom's corpse lay face down, its scalp removed except for a few tufts of tawny hair on the back of the neck. His skull was crushed and arrows quilled the shattered head. His body, first recovered by the long-suffering Lieutenant Godfrey, was rolled over. Pressed into the ground, the features were flattened and badly decomposed. His eyes and tongue had been gouged away. His belly was slashed and the insides spilled on the ground. His liver but not his heart had been torn out. His thighs were split open and his genitals carved off. His right arm was broken by a shot, but there was enough of it left to reveal a goddess of liberty and an American flag and the initials T. W. C. tattooed above the elbow.[36]

As sundown covered the grisly scene with darkness, the Sioux and Cheyenne went back home. Yellow Swallow had not brought bad luck that day, they agreed. They gathered all the camps scattered up and down the valley into one solid village in case any more soldiers were in the area. A few warriors surrounded the survivors of the battle, taking pot shots when they ventured out for water.[37]

Benteen and the pack train had finally joined Reno on another hilltop several miles from the site of the Custer fight. They stayed there, besieged by the enemy, until General Terry, with John Gibbon's column from Montana, relieved them on June 27. By then, the Indians had departed. It was a fleeting victory for the Sioux and Cheyenne—the last gasp of a primitive society.

Reno took charge of collecting the bodies of his dead comrades. For a few days, burial details made trips through the valley, identifying and interring corpses. Reno recorded in his journal, "The harrowing sight of those mutilated and decomposed bodies crowning the heights on which poor Custer fell will linger in my memory till death."[38]

Lieutenant Harrington's body was never recovered. The officers of the Seventh recalled the man's premonition that he would be captured and tortured, but thorough examinations of the deserted village revealed no sign of captives and none of torture, especially not the horrid burning at the stake that Harrington had pictured. He may have escaped, but if he did he was never heard from again. Dr. Charles Kuhlman, the late expert on the Custer battle, believed that another trooper of Tom's C Company, Frank Finkel, also somehow escaped from the battlefield.[39] It is curious to note that of about a half-dozen men of the Custer battalion known or supposed to have survived the fight, four were from Tom's C Company—Kanipe, Thompson, Watson, and possibly Harrington and Finkel.

The toll was high—more than 250 men were dead, along with 319 killed horses and 15 more unserviceable. Twenty-nine of the cavalrymen with Reno and Benteen were wounded. Remarkably, burial details found one horse—Keogh's Comanche, whom Tom Custer had acquired so long before and brought to Fort Riley—

alive, but suffering from many wounds. Comanche became the Seventh's mascot in later years. He was not ridden and appeared in parade with the regiment, draped in black with his saddle cinched on backward.

Comanche was also a monument to the men and animals that descended into the Little Bighorn valley that Sunday. He alone of the Custer battalion survived the rigors of an exhausting march, the wounds of battle, and the days without treatment or succor. The plucky little mustang alone remained of five companies led out by Tom Custer on the most fateful day in the history of the U.S. Cavalry.

CONCLUSION

The terrible debacle at the Little Bighorn swept across the country, which was still celebrating its centennial festivities. The news shocked the nation. At Fort Abraham Lincoln and in Monroe, Michigan, survivors of the Custers set about the depressing business of reorganizing their lives without the most exuberant members of the family.

The shock was terrible to old Mrs. Custer upon receiving word of the utter destruction of her family. Of all their sons, only Nevin had avoided the colonel's tempting military aura. He lived a long life, a gentleman farmer until his death in 1915. Even their daughters were affected—Maggie lost her husband, James Calhoun, and Lydia Reed lost her son, Autie.

Once the initial grief passed, Elizabeth Bacon Custer took the disaster well. Of course, she was heartbroken over the loss of her long-beloved husband, but she had grown almost as fond of brother Tom. She had only a short time to grieve before she lent comfort to the widows and families of the casualties and defended Autie's reputation.

The colonel had succeeded at last in putting his name before the public and keeping it there. He had been a national hero during the Civil War; his colorful personality, his accomplishments on the plains, his articles, and his recently published book had kept him in the nation's eye. His standing in the heated political controversy a few months earlier provided his enemies the chance to accuse him of mistakes—but more important, enemies of Grant's administration pounced on the opportunity to accuse the president of the fault for Custer's demise. George Custer became a national figure beside which all others paled—including Tom. On the third of July, the whistle of the *Far West* sounded for the Fort Abraham Lincoln landing on the Missouri River. Onlookers noted that the steamboat's flag hung at half-mast and the jack-staff was draped in black. A messenger from Captain Grant Marsh immediately spread the word, and in the dark hours of the night officers at the fort reluctantly walked the length of Officers' Row notifying new widows. The wounded of Reno's and Benteen's battalions were hurried into the fort for treatment at the post hospital. Across the river in Bismarck, a telegraph operator stayed up all night pushing his key, flashing the news on the wires. Upon questions by officers about what happened to Custer and his men, Captain Marsh sadly shook his head. He then related this story: "A Crow Indian came on board, and when I asked him about Custer he kneeled down and drew a group of dots on the deck. He then made the signal for white horse-soldiers. Around the dots he drew a circle of dots and made the sign for Sioux. With a swipe of his hand he wiped out the center dots."[1] This first tale of the annihilation made marvelous newspaper copy. For weeks, other stories—many unbelievable—

appeared in print, keeping the public's interest at fever pitch.

Among the few accounts printed concerning the initial burials, most were very brief. There were reasons for this. The families of the dead were to be considered. The actual deaths were bitter enough without mentioning the fact that the burials even of most of the officers—with the exception of Armstrong, Tom, Calhoun, Yates, McIntosh and Smith—were mere gestures as far as interment of the remains was concerned.

The grounds superintendent of the Little Bighorn Battlefield reported in 1924 that there were, known and unknown, 262 dead listed on the monument set up on the battle site—five of them members of the Custer clan. J. M. Thralls prophetically added in the *Kansas Historical Quarterly* of that year, "But why call it a massacre any more than if our army were fighting an enemy other than Indians? The battle was fought in an open field, slightly hilly, covered with short sagebrush. The Indians advanced out from their camp and met General Custer's command on the ridge, outnumbering the soldiers perhaps eight or ten to one, outgeneralling our officers until they ran out of ammunition, and the rest were shot down like targets."[2] The statement rings of the sentiments expressed by many modern historians.

Of the 416 Medals of Honor awarded by the United States Army during the Indian Wars, twenty-four went to survivors of the Little Bighorn—none being awarded posthumously. More than fourteen years later, 18 more medals were awarded when the Seventh finally avenged Custer at Wounded Knee.

Many requests came for Libbie to speak at public meetings all over the country. She defended her husband and Tom and their men very well. After a few years she began writing. Three books made her a celebrity in her own right, but never in her own eyes.

She died believing that all she did was for her Autie—without admiration for him, she would be nobody—and, vicariously, she made Tom look far better than he really was.

Elizabeth was also subjected to the details, rumors, and fabrications about the last battle. Aside from the stories about survivors of the Custer battalion, some of the most interesting were about Tom.

Among the wounded of Reno's and Benteen's detachments who returned on the *Far West* were Lieutenant DeRudio, an Italian from Tom's old A Company, and Private Thomas O'Neill, a survivor of G Company. Both men survived Reno's fight but were separated from their commands. While they awaited rescue, hiding in the underbrush and dodging rampaging Indians, DeRudio spotted a procession of mounted men wearing blue blouses. The leader wore a buckskin jacket, tall boots, and a broad-brimmed white slouch hat identical to the apparel Tom wore on the day of the battle. Thinking he recognized his former A Company comrade, DeRudio helloed the riders. To the besieged white men's surprise, a war cry sounded and a volley of bullets spattered against their hideaway. The riders were all Sioux dressed in Seventh Cavalry uniforms and mounted on horses seized from Custer's battalion. The soldiers disappeared among the bushes, and the Indians rode on to shoot up Reno and Benteen farther down the river.

Sometime after the battle on the Little Bighorn, one man, W. F. Fowers, wrote to Mrs. Custer to claim that he "brought in one of [George's] stag dogs in camp I [and] bought from a Indian a gold ring for one dollar said to belong to Tom Custer made out of native gold and I sold it to the Post Trader at Fort Bufort N. Dakota. Afterwards he told me you rec'd it from him O.K. is that true?"[3] Whether Libbie received either dog or ring is not known.

Another letter written to Mrs. Custer fifty years after the Little Bighorn by a man named Willard J. Carlyle raised a favorite story about Tom. Carlyle wrote on July 4, 1926, and among other things he told her, "One red-skin cut out the heart of Col. Tom Custer and carried it around on a pole."[4] This letter is not the most reliable source available—Carlyle also claimed to be the only white to witness Autie Custer's death.

Tom's heart has been a point of contention ever since the news of the Custer battle first reached Fort Abraham Lincoln. The tale held water because Rain-in-the-Face had made his threat. Lieutenant Bradley, one of those who took care of the remains of the Custer battalion, denied the truth of Rain-in-the-Face's accounts. Libbie had plenty of other sources that she believed more reliable than Bradley. She thought the officer denied the story to ease her troubled soul. She presented the story as fact in *Boots and Saddles,* one of her subsequent books.[5]

Rain-in-the-Face was originally thrust forward as the perpetrator of George Custer's murder, rather than for Tom's death. Frederick Whittaker, who produced the original biography of George Armstrong Custer in December 1876—just six months after the colonel's death—found his villain in the newspaper reports that followed the disaster. In Whittaker's book, the Sioux held a grievance against the colonel for an imprisonment in 1874 and avenged himself by killing Custer and carving out his heart. According to Whittaker, this occurred only after Armstrong emptied his revolver and "like a tiger . . . killed or wounded three Indians with his saber."[6]

Rain-in-the-Face became a celebrity after he gave up his hostile ways and settled down to reservation life. Late in his life, he went on tours with Wild West shows. At a Coney Island performance in 1894, a couple of reporters cornered him, intoxicated him, and extracted a "confession" about his role in the battle. The old Indian drunkenly told them what they wanted to hear. It was Tom Custer, the colonel's brother, he said, that he had killed. The sensation-seeking journalists recorded his words this way:

I was mad . . . I saw Little Hair [Tom]. I remembered my vow. I was crazy; I feared nothing . . . I don't know how many I killed trying to get at him. He knew me. I laughed at him. I saw his mouth move, but there was so much noise I couldn't hear his voice. He was afraid. When I got near enough I shot him with my revolver. My gun [rifle] was gone, I don't know where. I leaped from my pony and cut out his heart and bit a piece out of it and spit it in his face.[7]

Ten years later and a lot more sober, Rain-in-the-Face informed a writer and fellow Sioux, Dr. Charles Eastman, that he had not come to believe the story by telling it so many times but realized the uselessness of denying it:

Many lies have been told of me. Some say that I killed the chief, and others say that I cut the heart out of his brother, Tom Custer, because he caused me to be imprisoned. Why, in that fight the excitement was so great that we scarcely recognized our nearest friends. Everything was done like lightning. After the battle we young men were chasing horses all over the prairie; and if any mutilating was done, it was by the old men.[8]

These were the truest words Rain-in-the-Face ever spoke. The fervent statement is consistent with what other Sioux told of the closing minutes of the fight. It is also consistent with the facts that

Armstrong's corpse was not cut up and that Tom's was badly mutilated. Paul Hutton, a modern Custer expert, wrote in the *Western
Historical Quarterly* that Rain-in-the-Face's comment, "Many lies
have been told about me," was a fitting epitaph for the old warrior.[9]

Early in April 1877, Colonel Mike Sheridan, once a member of
the Seventh, replied to an inquiry from Mrs. Custer. He wrote that
he "had already begun to make arrangements to have the remains
of the officers who fell at the Battle of the Little Big Horn brought
in to Fort Abraham Lincoln with a view of the final interment of
the bodies of all those who are not taken by their friends to their
various homes, in the National Cemetery at Fort Leavenworth,
without expense to the relatives of the deceased so far as this is
practicable."[10]

Colonel Mike had written his brother, General Phil Sheridan,
requesting full authority for his reply to Elizabeth and recommending that the remains of George Custer be interred at West Point as
his widow wanted. General Sheridan agreed with the sentiments of
the family that the bodies of Jim Calhoun, Boston, and Tom should
be buried in the National Cemetery with the graves of soldiers who
died in service to their country. Little Phil Sheridan instructed his
brother to make the appropriate arrangements.

Therefore, on the hot, windy afternoon of August 3, 1877, the
remains of George Yates, Algernon E. Smith, Donald McIntosh,
James Calhoun, and Thomas Ward Custer were buried in the National Cemetery. Captain C. S. Ilsley, the lieutenant at the time of
the Little Bighorn fight who had been promoted to fill one of the
many emptied ranks in the battered Seventh Cavalry, acted as marshal of the funeral procession through Fort Leavenworth while the
living Custers looked on sadly.

The Seventh Cavalry that Autie put together remained a functioning entity after his death. As if in revenge for the shame of its defeat at the Little Bighorn, it participated in the massacre at Wounded Knee, South Dakota, in 1890. In this last confrontation between Plains Indians and the army, troopers of the Seventh—some of whom had been present at the Custer fight—shot down almost three hundred Sioux men, women, and children. In the spring of 1895, the regiment left Fort Riley, where it had been stationed, for Fort Grant, Arizona. It had engaged in thirty-five Indian fights during its career, including the Washita, the Little Bighorn, and Wounded Knee.

The battlefield is now located on the Crow Agency, Montana, and is maintained by the National Park Service. On Thursday, June 25, 1976, some six hundred Americans gathered on the site for ceremonies commemorating the last great victory of Indians. Robert M. Utley, former director of the park and assistant director of the National Park Service, called for "a spirit of reconciliation." Russell Means, the Sioux leader of the American Indian Movement, replied, "We bring the sacred pipe of peace."

If the Seventh Cavalry had been victorious at the battle on the Little Bighorn, probably no one would remember Tom Custer today. As it is, he is never more than mentioned in text or footnotes in works about George or the Indian Wars. Yet, in his day he was notable among the many colorful men who populated the American frontier.

What if Tom had survived? Without George, he, like Elizabeth, would have been nobody. He would likely have been relegated to the ranks of the officers and enlisted men who were symbols of the federal government's nineteenth-century Indian policies, those bygone years, of the glamorous U.S. Cavalry, of the Old West. His gruesome death with more than 250 comrades, friends, and relatives at least ensured that his name would appear in history books. He deserves more.

Tom Custer spent his short life trying to gain his brother's appreciation and approval. His waking hours were dedicated to two propositions—carefree self-indulgence and devotion to his brother. The former left him a spirited, youthful soldier who ran into predicaments that should have placed him in the fold of famous Western personalities were he not George Armstrong Custer's younger brother. The latter left him a minor member of the cast of characters in Custer's orbit. In retrospect, Tom lived his whole life in his brother's shadow.

AFTERWORD

The life and times of Thomas Ward Custer have not received the attention they deserve. One reason is the fact that many documents and resources have not been fully explored by scholars. Yet that is changing. Many Custer scholars have turned to researching the rest of George Armstrong Custer's family to shed new light on the boy general and his most famous battle, the Little Bighorn. The wealth of material about Tom Custer is growing, as evidenced by a Website on the Internet devoted to him, but the growth is slow.

Custer scholars and reviewers will criticize the choice of many of the sources cited in this book. The intent of the work has been from its inception to provide a story of Tom Custer's life, an account of the many events of his life, and to paint a verbal portrait of him as well as to impart history. For those reasons, my sources have included those Custer books which most frequently mention Tom. Some fiction works or nearly fictional secondary sources were included in order to foster a taste for the era and places in which he lived. Additionally, fiction can sometimes accomplish goals that pure history cannot achieve. And this was never intended to be about George Armstrong Custer, but at times it subjects the reader to a heavy dose of Autie's biography for the simple reason that far more is available and has been done on the elder Custer brother.

Aside from the choice of resources, the list of many other persons and sources consulted for any research on this popular topic is extensive. Since my earliest exposure to Custerana while watching Errol Flynn in *They Died With Their Boots On* with my mother as we waited late at night for my father to return home from work, I have collected or read works about the Custers. Some are classics of historical research, some are superb historical fiction, some are primary resources, some are new research including facts only recently discovered. All have added to the story of the Custers and constitute the lengthy bibliography which follows this text.

The list of persons and institutions which have helped make this work possible is also great. Over the years various staff members at the National Archives, the Little Bighorn National Historic Site, the Kansas State Historical Society, and the U.S. Cavalry Museum have earned my thanks. I am indebted to the many historians, writers, editors, and publishers who have read, commented upon, criticized, and published portions of several chapters in other forms. Many portions of my earlier short works are reflected in the preceding pages.

I am grateful to Douglas W. Sikes, publishing consultant for Turner Publishing Company, who liked what he saw when he read an unsolicited manuscript. Gratitude, too, is deserved by fellow Kansan and history writer Tom Goodrich, who never failed to ask about Tom Custer's progress and who seemed genuinely pleased to learn that these pages would finally see print.

Finally, I acknowledge my greatest debt of all—that to my wife and children who have for the best part of two decades suffered from whistled strains of the Garryowen, been dragged to museums and historical sites solely because the Custers had been there once, groaned when the television viewing was preempted because a Custer motion picture was being aired, and listened to endless rounds of Custer commentary, appearing for all the world as though they were interested. I love you all for it.

NOTES

Introduction

1. Mari Sandoz, *Cheyenne Autumn* (New York, 1953), 16.
2. Frederick Whittaker, *A Complete Life of Gen. George A. Custer* (New York, 1876), 4.
3. Robert M. Utley, "The Enduring Custer Legend," *American History Illustrated*, June 1976.
4. Mollie S. Smart and Russell C. Smart, *Children: Development and Relationships* (New York, 1972), 314.
5. Dr. Lawrence A. Frost, Letter, November 30, 1976.

One: The Formative Years

1. Lawrence A. Frost, *The Custer Album: A Pictorial Biography of General George A. Custer* (Seattle, 1964), 17.
2. The Custer name is still a common one all over the United States and in Germany as well, according to two widely used sources: Whittaker, 3-4, and Milo Milton Quaife (ed.), George A. Custer, *My Life on the Plains* (Lincoln, 1966), xi.

3. Ibid.

4. Ibid.

5. Whittaker, 4.

6. Quaife (ed.), xii.

7. Ibid.

8. Frost, *The Custer Album,* 17-18.

9. Quaife (ed.), xiii.

10. Smart and Smart, 315-16.

11. Ibid.

12. Quaife (ed.), xiv.

13. Ibid.

14. Whittaker, 4; Frost, *The Custer Album,* 18.

15. L. Joseph Stone and Joseph Church, *Childhood and Adolescence: A Psychology of the Growing Person* (New York, 1973), 607.

16. Smart and Smart, 315.

17. Stone and Church, 377.

18. Whittaker, 4; Frost, *The Custer Album,* 18.

19. Smart and Smart, 316.

20. Stone and Church, 378.

21. Quaife (ed.), xiv.

22. Frost, The Custer Album, 18-19.

23. Margaret Leighton, *Bride of Glory* (New York, 1963), 1-6.

24. Frost, *The Custer Album,* 19.

25. Ibid.

26. Leighton, *Bride of Glory,* 18.

27. Frost, *The Custer Album,* 20.

28. Leighton, *Bride of Glory,* 16.

29. Stephen E. Ambrose, *Crazy Horse and Custer: The Parallel Lives of Two American Warriors* (Garden City, 1975), 93.

30. Ambrose, 94.

31. Ibid.

32. Jay Monaghan, *Custer* (Boston, 1959), 34; Lawrence A. Frost, *General Custer's Libbie* (Seattle, 1976), 47.

Two: Military Life

1. Leighton, *Bride of Glory,* 87.

2. Ibid., 15.

3. Ambrose, 183.

4. Leighton, *Bride of Glory,* 42.

5. Paul A. Hutton, "From Little Bighorn to Little Big Man: The Changing Image of a Western Hero in Popular Culture" 7 *Western Historical Quarterly* 1, January 1976.

6. Bruce Catton, *Mr. Lincoln's Army* (Garden City, 1962), 115.

7. Ibid.

8. Ibid.

9. Bruce Catton, *The Civil War* (New York, 1960), 303.

10. Frost, *General Custer's Libbie,* 91.

11. Charles M. Robinson III, "Recipient of Two Medals of Honor, Tom Custer Died Alongside Brother George," *Wild West,* June 1996; www.thehistorynet.comlWild West/articles.

12. Quaife (ed.), xiii-xiv.

13. Frost, *General Custer's Libbie,* 91.

14. Tom Custer News & Reviews, www.users-globalnet.co.ukl-pardos/ TomCuster Rev.html.

15. D. A. Kinsley, *Favor the Bold, Volume I, Custer: The Civil War Years* (New York, 1967), 258.

16. Thomas Ward Custer Biography Page. www.civilwarhome.com/ +custerbio.html; Kinsley, *Favor the Bold I,* 258.

17. Kinsley, *Favor the Bold I,* 258.

18. Leighton, *Bride of Glory,* 98-99.

19. Frost, *General Custer's Libbie,* 122.

20. Kinsley, *Favor the Bold I,* 258.

21. Frost, *General Custer's Libbie,* 122.

22. Ibid.

23. Kinsley, *Favor the Bold 1,* 259.

24. Bruce Catton, *A Stillness at Appomattox* (Garden City, 1962), 341-42.

25. Ibid.

26. Kinsley, *Favor the Bold I,* 264; Robinson, "Recipient of Two Medals of Honor, Tom Custer Died Alongside Brother George."

27. Catton, *A Stillness at Appomattox,* 341-42.

28. Kinsley, *Favor the Bold 1,* 277-78.
29. Ibid.; Robinson, "Recipient of Two Medals of Honor."
30. Jay Scott, *Army War Heroes* (Derby, Conn., 1963), 7.
31. Kinsley, *Favor the Bold 1,* 277-78.
32. Catton, *A Stillness at Appomattox,* 370.
33. Robinson, "Recipient of Two Medals of Honor."
34. Kinsley, *Favor the Bold 1,* 277-78.
35. Double Award Winners: Congressional Medal of Honor Society. www.cmohs.org/medallhistory -links/double_award_ winners.html.
36. Medal of Honor Recipients Portrayed on Film: Blown Opportunities, Thomas Ward Custer (1845-1876). www.voicenet. com/-/padilla/custer.html.
37. Kinsley, *Favor the Bold 1,* 277-78.
38. Ibid.
39. Ambrose, 214.
40. Leighton, *Bride of Glory,* 108.
41. Ibid., 115.
42. Ibid.

Three: Intermission and Introspection

1. D. A. Kinsley, *Favor the Bold, Volume II, Custer: The Indian Fighter* (New York, 1968), 9.
2. Ibid., 8.
3. Ibid.
4. Ibid.
5. Judge Bacon to General Custer, quoted in Frost, *General Custer's Libbie,* 134.
6. Rebecca Richmond to Elizabeth Custer, quoted in Frost, *General Custer's Libbie,* 136.
7. Judge Bacon to Elizabeth Custer, quoted in Frost, *General Custer's Libbie,* 134.
8. Ibid.
9. Kinsley, *Favor the Bold II,* 8-9.
10. Frost, *General Custer's Libbie,* 137.

11. Elizabeth Custer to Rebecca Richmond, quoted in Frost, *General Custer's Libbie,* 137.

12. Ambrose, 249; Kinsley, *Favor the Bold II,* 9.

13. Ambrose, 251.

14. Marguerite Merrington (ed.), *The Custer Story: The Life and Intimate Letters of General George A. Custer and His Wife Elizabeth* (New York, 1950), 172-73.

15. Frost, *General Custer's Libbie,* 135.

16. Ibid.

17. Ibid., 136.

18. *See* Elizabeth Custer, *Tenting on the Plains* (Norman, 1971), 27-92; Ambrose, 250.

19. Merrington, 174-75.

20. Ambrose, 250.

21. Frost, *General Custer's Libbie,* 137.

22. Kinsley, *Favor the Bold II,* 16.

23. Ibid.

24. Ibid.

25. *Annual Report of the Secretary of War for the Year 1866,* 3-4.

26. Kinsley, *Favor the Bold II,* 17.

27. Frost, *The Custer Album,* 72.

28. Ibid.

29. Frost, *General Custer's Libbie,* 146.

30. Ibid.

31. Ibid., 150-51.

32. Kinsley, *Favor the Bold II,* 18.

33. Frost, *The Custer Album,* 72; Kinsley, *Favor the Bold II,* 19.

34. Frost, *General Custer's Libbie,* 152.

35. Kinsley, *Favor the Bold II,* 20.

Four: Into Kansas and Back to Service

1. Elizabeth Custer, *Tenting on the Plains,* 326-27.

2. Minnie Dubbs Millbrook, "Custer's First Scout in the West" 39 *Kansas Historical Quarterly,* Spring 1973.

3. Ralph Andrist, *The Long Death: The Last Days of the Plains Indians* (New York, 1964), 143.

4. Millbrook, "Custer's First Scout in the West."

5. Ibid.

6. Ernest Haycox, *Bugles in the Afternoon* (New York, 1943), 27-28. Haycox's work is among the best historical novels about the Custers; accounts from his work helped give color and accurate description for Tom's story.

7. Ibid.

8. Leighton, *Bride of Glory*, 138.

9. Elizabeth Custer to Rebecca Richmond, cited in Minnie Dubbs Millbrook, "Mrs. General Custer at Fort Riley, 1866," 40 *Kansas Historical Quarterly*, Spring 1974.

10. Ibid.

11. Ibid.

12. Kinsley, *Favor the Bold II*, 27.

13. Millbrook, "Mrs. General Custer at Fort Riley, 1866."

14. Leighton, *Bride of Glory*, 139.

15. Ibid., 139-40.

16. Ibid.

17. Kinsley, *Favor the Bold II*, 47.

18. Some sources spell it "Elliot."

19. John Alger, "Uncle Frank Was a Four-Bit Hero," 5 *Golden West*, July 1969.

20. Ibid.

21. Ibid.

22. Elizabeth Custer to Rebecca Richmond, cited in Millbrook, "Mrs. General Custer at Fort Riley, 1866."

23. Paul I. Wellman, *Death on the Prairie* (New York, 1934); reprinted as *The Indian Wars of the West* (New York, 1963), 75.

24. Winfield Scott Hancock, quoted in Wellman, 76.

25. Elizabeth Custer to Rebecca Richmond, cited in Millbrook, "Mrs. General Custer at Fort Riley, 1866."

26. Ibid.

27. Jack W. Traylor, Curator of Manuscripts, Kansas State Historical Society, Letter, August 31, 1978.

28. Garry D. Ryan, Chief of the Navy and Old Army Branch, Military Archives Division, National Archives, Letter, September 21, 1978.

29. Haycox, 45.

30. Frost, *General Custer's Libbie,* 158.

31. Ibid., 161.

32. Elizabeth Custer, *Tenting on the Plains,* 328.

33. S. L. A. Marshall, *Crimsoned Prairies* (New York, 1972), 45-47.

34. Ibid.

35. Ibid.

36. Roy Bird, "The Frontier Regulars in Kansas" *Kanhistique,* March 1976.

37. Marshall, 47.

38. Bird, "Frontier Regulars in Kansas."

39. Ibid.

40. Frost, *General Custer's Libbie,* 162.

41. Ibid., 163.

42. Elizabeth Custer, *Tenting on the Plains,* 631.

Five: Back on Campaign Again

1. Report of the U.S. Secretary of War, 1866-1867, Serial No. 1285, 5-19, 24.

2. Theophilus F. Rodenbaugh and William L. Haskin (eds.), *The Army of the United States: Historical Sketches of Staff and Line With Portraits of Generals-in-Chief* (Chicago, 1896), 251, quoted in Mrs. Frank C. Montgomery, "Fort Wallace and Its Relation to the Frontier," 17 *Kansas Historical Collections* (1926–1928), 211.

3. Kinsley, *Favor the Bold II,* 44-45.

4. Millbrook, "Custer's First Scout in the West"; Quaife (ed.), 33.

5. For the most definitive biography of James Butler Hickok, *see* Joseph G. Rosa, *They Called Him Wild Bill* (Norman, 1964).

6. David Nevin, *The Soldiers* (New York, 1973), 206.

7. Ibid.

8. Alger, "Uncle Frank Was a Four-Bit Hero."

9. Ibid.

10. Kinsley, *Favor the Bold II*, 45-48.

11. Ibid.

12. Ibid.

13. Ibid.

14. Ibid.

15. Ibid.

16. Ibid., 48-50.

17. Ibid.

18. Ibid., 50.

19. Ibid.

20. Albert Barnitz, quoted in "Custer Put Fort Wallace in the Spotlight," A Moment in Time Series, Kansas State Historical Society, May 25, 1998.

21. Jacob Homer, cited in Nevin, 206.

22. Kinsley, *Favor the Bold II*, 50.

23. Montgomery, "Fort Wallace and Its Relation to the Frontier"; Kinsley, *Favor the Bold II*, 57.

24. Kinsley, *Favor the Bold II*, 57.

25. Ramon Powers and Gene Younger, "Cholera on the Plains: The Epidemic of 1867 in Kansas," 37 *Kansas Historical Quarterly* 4, Winter 1971.

26. Ibid.

27. Kinsley, *Favor the Bold II*, 58-59.

28. Powers and Younger, "Cholera on the Plains."

29. Kinsley, *Favor the Bold II*, 58-59; Andrist, 144.

30. Ibid.

31. Kinsley, *Favor the Bold II*, 60.

32. Ibid.

33. For a recent discussion of the court-martial of George Armstrong Custer, *see* Leo Oliva, *Fort Wallace: Sentinel on the Smoky Hill Trail* (Topeka, 1998).

34. Kinsley, *Favor the Bold II*, 65.

35. Ibid.

36. Marshall, 50.

37. Kinsley, *Favor the Bold II,* 74.

38. Ibid.

Six: The Winter Campaign

1. Wellman, 76.

2. David Dary, *Comanche* (Lawrence, 1976), 1-2.

3. Ibid.

4. Margaret Leighton, *Comanche of the Seventh* (New York, 1957), 32.

5. Ibid., 33.

6. Ibid.

7. Ibid., 34.

8. Ibid.

9. General Phillip Sheridan, quoted in Wellman, 86.

10. For the most authoritative work on Forsyth's Frontier Battalion, *see* Orvel Criqui, *Fifty Fearless Men* (Marcelline, Mo., 1993).

11. Quaife (ed.), 271-72.

12. Kinsley, *Favor the Bold II,* 89.

13. Nevin, 206.

14. Kinsley, *Favor the Bold II,* 86.

15. Judson Elliot Walker, *Campaigns of General Custer* (New York, 1881), 41.

16. Roy Bird, "Frontier Regulars in Kansas," *Kanhistique,* March 1976.

17. Frost, *General Custer's Libbie,* 175.

18. Nevin, 207.

19. Frost, *General Custer's Libbie,* 175.

20. Haycox, 21.

21. Ibid.

22. Kinsley, *Favor the Bold II,* 88.

23. Ibid.

24. Ibid.

25. Whittaker, 634.

26. George A. Custer to Elizabeth Custer, quoted in Frost, *General Custer's Libbie,* 170.

27. Kinsley, *Favor the Bold II*, 87.
28. Alger, "Uncle Frank Was a Four-Bit Hero."
29. Kinsley, *Favor the Bold II*, 87.
30. Ibid., 89.
31. George A. Custer to Elizabeth Custer, quoted in Frost, *General Custer's Libbie*, 170.
32. Hutton, "From Little Bighorn to Little Big Man."

Seven: The End of the Winter Campaign and Kindred Matters

1. Haycox, 201.
2. Sandoz, *Cheyenne Autumn*, 110.
3. Ibid.
4. Ibid., 118.
5. Roy Bird, "Printer's Ink Ran in Their Veins," *Kanhistique*.
6. Considering the loss of Elliot's detachment, the death of Hamilton and the fact that by "Indians" Runyan probably meant warriors, this statement may well have been true. However, due to conflicting reports from the army and the Cheyenne, we will never know for sure. Bird, "Printer's Ink Ran in Their Veins."
7. George A. Custer to Elizabeth Custer, quoted in Frost, *General Custer's Libbie*, 181.
8. Kinsley, *Favor the Bold II*, 112.
9. Sandoz, *Cheyenne Autumn*, 119.
10. Ibid.
11. Leighton, *Bride of Glory*, 165.
12. Frost, *General Custer's Libbie*, 182.
13. Ibid. *See also* www.users.globalnet.co.uk/-pardos/Custer-Revs.html.
14. Walker, 42.
15. Joanna Stratton, *Pioneer Women* (New York, 1974), 203-8.
16. Lonnie J. White, "Indian Raids on the Kansas Frontier, 1869," 38 *Kansas Historical Quarterly*, Winter 1972.
17. Frost, *General Custer's Libbie*, 182.
18. Ibid.

19. Ibid.

20. Ibid.

21. Minnie Dubbs Millbrook, "Big Game Hunting with the Custers, 1869–1870," 41 *Kansas Historical Quarterly,* Winter 1975.

22. Elizabeth Custer, *Following the Guidon* (New York, 1890), 216.

23. Ibid., 218.

24. John DuMont and John Parsons, *Firearms in the Custer Battle* (Harrisburg, 1953), 20-22.

Eight: Is It True What They Say?

1. Carl Day, "The Last Will and Testament of Thomas Ward Custer," *The Guidon,* June 2000. *See also* Tom Custer News and Reviews, www.users.globalnet.co.uk/-pardos/TomCusterRevs.html.

2. Ibid.

3. Whittaker, 634.

4. Douglas C. Jones, *The Court-Martial of George Armstrong Custer* (New York, 1976), 120.

5. John Stands-in-Timber and Margot Liberty, *Cheyenne Memories* (New Haven, 1967), 199.

6. Stephen Longstreet, *War Cries on Horseback* (New York, 1970), 175-76.

7. Kinsley, *Favor the Bold II,* 94-96.

8. Sandoz, *Cheyenne Autumn,* 41.

9. Kinsley, *Favor the Bold II,* 93.

10. Ibid., 95-96.

11. E. Adamson Hoebel, *The Cheyennes: Indians of the Great Plains* (New York, 1960), 20-22; Thomas Berger, *Little Big Man* (New York, 1964), 250-53.

12. Kinsley, *Favor the Bold II,* 120.

13. Ibid.

14. Kinsley, *Favor the Bold II,* 95-96.

15. Stands-in-Timber, 199 *(n.).*

16. Sandoz, *Cheyenne Autumn,* 41.

17. Frost, *General Custer's Libbie,* 182.

18. Kinsley, *Favor the Bold II,* 126-27.
19. Ibid.
20. Ibid.
21. George A. Custer, quoted in Kinsley, *Favor the Bold II,* 85-86.
22. George Bird Grinnell, *The Fighting Cheyennes* (New York, 1915).
23. Sandoz, *Cheyenne Autumn,* 41.
24. Kinsley, *Favor the Bold II,* 126-27.
25. Leighton, *Bride of Glory,* 168.
26. Frost, *General Custer's Libbie,* 182.
27. Ibid.
28. Jones, 131.
29. Nevin, 124.
30. Rosa, *They Called Him Wild Bill,* 224.
31. Elizabeth Custer, *Following the Guidon,* 160-61.
32. Rosa, 222-24.
33. Tom Custer to Elizabeth Custer, quoted in Merrington (ed.), 242-43.
34. Sandoz, *Cheyenne Autumn,* 324.
35. Frost, *General Custer's Libbie,* 186.

Nine: A Shootout in Hays City

1. Eugene Cunningham, *Triggernometry: A Gallery of Gunfighters* (Caldwell, Idaho, 1971), 264.
2. Minnie Dubbs Millbrook, "Big Game Hunting with the Custers, 1869-1870."
3. Ibid.
4. Manhattan, Kansas, *Standard,* May 8, 1869.
5. Bern Keating, *The Flamboyant Mr. Colt and His Deadly Six-Shooter* (Garden City, 1978), 213-14.
6. Harry Sinclair Drago, *Wild, Woolly, and Wicked* (New York, 1960), 94.
7. Nevin, 206.
8. Cunningham, 264; Drago, 93-94.

9. Drago, 93-94.

10. Cunningham, 264; Drago, 93-94.

11. Drago, 94; Joseph G. Rosa, "Wild Bill Hickok—Peacemaker," 1 *The Prairie Scout*, 1973, 7.

12. *Kansas Daily Commonwealth*, July 22, 1870.

13. Junction City, Kansas, *Union*, July 23, 1870.

14. *Republican Valley Empire*, August 2, 1870. The reference to Harper refers to the article in *Harper's New Monthly Magazine* in 1867 that established Wild Bill as a celebrity.

15. Rosa, *They Called Him Wild Bill*, 157.

16. Cunningham, 264; Drago, 94.

17. Alfred Henry Lewis, "How Mr. Hickok Came to Cheyenne: An Epic of an Unsung Ulysses," *The Saturday Evening Post*, March 12, 1904, 6.

18. Nyle H. Miller and Joseph W. Snell, *Great Gunfighters of the Kansas Cowtowns, 1867-1886* (Lincoln, 1963), 128-29; Rosa, *They Called Him Wild Bill*, 157.

19. Drago, 94.

20. Rosa, *They Called Him Wild Bill*, 157.

21. Drago, 94.

22. Miller and Snell, 128-29.

Ten: Reconstructing Erring Sisters

1. John A. Garraty, *The American Nation* (New York, 1966), 435.

2. Ibid.

3. Garraty, 438.

4. Ibid.

5. Merrington, 231-32.

6. Garraty, 438.

7. Ibid.

8. Ibid., 438-39.

9. Keating, 214.

10. Whittaker, 479.

11. Keating, 214.

12. Garraty, 448.

13. Ibid., 441.

14. Garry D. Ryan, Chief of the Navy and Old Army Branch, Military Archives Division, National Archives, Letter, September 24, 1978.

15. Frost, *General Custer's Libbie,* 191.

16. Ibid.

17. Ibid.

18. Ibid., 195.

19. Ibid.

20. Ibid.

21. George A. Custer to Margaret Calhoun, quoted in Merrington, 243.

22. Tom Custer to Elizabeth Custer, quoted in Merrington, 243.

23. Ibid.

24. Leighton, *Bride of Glory,* 175-76.

25. Frost, *General Custer's Libbie,* 209.

26. Ibid.

27. Merrington, 245.

Eleven: Return to the Plains

1. Haycox, 32.

2. Leighton, *Bride of Glory,* 166.

3. Haycox, 20.

4. David Dary, *The Buffalo Book* (Chicago, 1974), 116-17.

5. Haycox, 109.

6. Alger, "Uncle Frank Was a Four-Bit Hero."

7. Ibid.

8. Kinsley, *Favor the Bold II,* 142.

9. Frost, *General Custer's Libbie,* 204; Kinsley, *Favor the Bold II,* 143.

10. George A. Custer to Elizabeth Custer, quoted in Merrington, 250.

11. George A. Custer to Elizabeth Custer, quoted in Kinsley, *Favor the Bold II,* 143; *see also* Merrington, 250.

12. George A. Custer to Elizabeth Custer, quoted in Merrington, 253.

13. Frost, *General Custer's Libbie,* 204.

14. George A. Custer to Elizabeth Custer, quoted in Merrington, 260.

15. Frost, *General Custer's Libbie,* 205.

16. Walker, 38.

17. George A. Custer to Elizabeth Custer, quoted in Merrington, 254.

18. Ibid., 256.

19. Ibid.

20. David S. Stanley, Report to the War Department, quoted in Merrington, 261.

21. Walker, 38.

22. Ibid.

23. Frost, *General Custer's Libbie,* 185.

24. Haycox, 125.

25. Ibid.

26. Frost, *General Custer's Libbie,* 145-46.

27. Ibid.

28. Ibid.

29. George A. Custer to Elizabeth Custer, quoted in Merrington, 264.

30. Frost, *General Custer's Libbie,* 146.

31. Ibid., 207; Merrington, 264.

32. Ibid.

33. Elizabeth Custer diary, quoted in Merrington, 269.

34. Frost, *General Custer's Libbie,* 208-9.

35. Sandoz, *Cheyenne Autumn,* 113.

Twelve: A Warrior Angered

1. Leighton, *Bride of Glory,* 189.

2. Frost, *General Custer's Libbie,* 208-9.

3. Ibid., 211.

4. Ibid., 211-12; Donald Jackson, *Custer's Gold: The United*

States Cavalry Expedition of 1874 (New Haven, 1966), 23.

5. Frost, *General Custer's Libbie,* 212; Jackson, 142-44.

6. Frost, *General Custer's Libbie,* 215.

7. Ibid., 212. Elizabeth Custer, *Boots and Saddles,* 299-300, cited in Frost, *General Custer's Libbie,* 212.

8. Ibid.

9. Jackson, 84-89.

10. Marsh had originally been offered the position of expedition scientist, but he declined, recommending George Bird Grinnell in his place. At General Phil Sheridan's invitation, Marsh made a trip to the Dakota Badlands later that year. Jackson, 50.

11. George A. Custer to General Terry, quoted in Frost, *General Custer's Libbie,* 213.

12. Dary, *The Buffalo Book,* 116-17.

13. Chief Red Fox, *The Memoirs of Chief Red Fox* (New York, 1971), 41-42.

14. Ibid.

15. Ibid., 42-43.

16. Leighton, *Bride of Glory,* 133.

17. Anastasio Carlos Azoy, *Paul Revere's Horse* (Garden City, 1949), 172-73.

18. Haycox, 124.

19. Walker, 44-45.

20. Ibid.

21. Haycox, 109.

22. Frost, *General Custer's Libbie,* 216-17; Leighton, *Bride of Glory,* 194-95.

23. Elizabeth Custer, quoted in Frost, *General Custer's Libbie,* 217; Merrington, 276-77.

24. Haycox, 113; Leighton, *Bride of Glory,* 194-95.

25. Andrist, 255; Leighton, *Bride of Glory,* 194-95.

26. Tom Custer telegram, quoted in Frost, *General Custer's Libbie,* 218-19.

27. Andrist, 255; Frost, *General Custer's Libbie,* 219; Leighton, *Bride of Glory,* 195.

28. Ibid.

29. Red Fox, 43; Walker, 38.
30. Ibid.
31. Walker, 38.
32. Red Fox, 43.
33. Dee Brown and Martin F. Schmidt, *Fighting Indians of the West* (New York, 1948), 112; Walker, 38; Red Fox, 43.
34. Walker, 38.
35. Ibid., 34-36.
36. Ibid.
37. Red Fox, 43.
38. Walker, 38.
39. Brown and Schmidt, 112.

Thirteen: The Last Campaign

1. Haycox, 143.
2. George A. Custer to Tom Custer, quoted in Merrington, 277.
3. Frost, *General Custer's Libbie,* 220.
4. George A. Custer to Elizabeth Custer, quoted in Merrington, 289-90.
5. Ibid., 292.
6. Haycox, 143.
7. Ibid., 174.
8. David Dary, *Finding Pleasure in the Old West* (New York, 1986), 123.
9. Haycox, 179.
10. Kinsley, *Favor the Bold II,* 196.
11. Elizabeth Custer, quoted in Kinsley, *Favor the Bold II,* 196.
12. Kinsley, *Favor the Bold II,* 198; Merrington, 206.
13. Kinsley, *Favor the Bold II,* 197.
14. Ibid.
15. Ibid., 197-98; Merrington, 206.
16. Haycox, 172.
17. Merrington, 298-99.
18. W. A. Graham, *The Story of the Little Big Horn: Custer's Last Fight* (New York, 1926), 27; Haycox, 194.

19. Ibid.

20. Dee Brown, *Showdown at Little Big Horn* (New York, 1964), 22.

21. Ambrose, 407.

22. Ibid., 418.

23. George A. Custer to Elizabeth Custer, cited in Ambrose, 418-19.

24. George A. Custer to Elizabeth Custer, quoted in Merrington, 300.

25. Boston Custer to his mother, quoted in Merrington, 301.

26. John S. Gray, "Veterinary Service in Custer's Last Campaign," 43 *Kansas Historical Quarterly* 3, Autumn 1977.

27. W. S. Edgerly to Elizabeth Custer, quoted in Merrington, 301-2.

28. Gray, "Veterinary Service in Custer's Last Campaign."

29. Ibid.

30. Kinsley, *Favor the Bold II*, 206.

31. Ibid., 198-99.

32. Mari Sandoz, *The Battle of the Little Bighorn* (Philadelphia, 1966), 18.

33. Haycox, 192; Sandoz, *Battle of the Little Bighorn*, 22-23.

34. Haycox, 195.

35. Sandoz, *Battle of the Little Bighorn*, 50.

36. Ibid.

Fourteen: The Last Battle

1. Jones, 128.

2. Stands-in-Timber, 191.

3. Paul A. Hutton, "Custer's Last Stand," *TV Guide,* November 26, 1977.

4. Kinsley, *Favor the Bold II*, 215.

5. Ibid., 217.

6. Graham, 83-84.

7. Graham, 84; Kinsley, *Favor the Bold II*, 221.

8. Kinsley, *Favor the Bold II*, 221.

9. Graham, 86.

10. Ibid., 53.

11. Ibid., 55-56.

12. Ibid.

13. Ibid.

14. John G. Neihardt (ed.), *Black Elk Speaks: Being the Life Story of a Holy Man of the Oglala Sioux* (New York, 1932), 105-6.

15. Ibid.

16. Brown and Martin, 124.

17. Ibid., 134-37.

18. Ibid.

19. Kinsley, *Favor the Bold II*, 275.

20. Sandoz, *Cheyenne Autumn*, 54.

21. Brown and Martin, 134.

22. Ibid., 138-39.

23. Sandoz, *Battle of the Little Bighorn*, 126-27.

24. Brown and Martin, 149.

25. Ibid.

26. Ibid.

27. Graham, 87-88.

28. Neihardt (ed.), 113.

29. Sandoz, *Battle of the Little Bighorn*, 126-27.

30. Ibid.

31. Neihardt (ed.), 113; Kinsley, *Favor the Bold II*, 225-26.

32. Alger, "Uncle Frank Was a Four-Bit Hero."

33. Kinsley, *Favor the Bold II*, 225-26.

34. Walker, 53.

35. Kinsley, *Favor the Bold II*, 227.

36. Sandoz, *Battle of the Little Bighorn*, 170.

37. Kinsley, *Favor the Bold II*, 228; Neihardt (ed.), 120; Sandoz, *Cheyenne Autumn*, 68.

38. Kinsley, *Favor the Bold II*, 230.

39. Charles Kuhlman, *Massacre Survivor* (Fort Collins, 1974).

Conclusion

1. Utley, "The Enduring Custer Legend."

2. J. M. Thralls, "The Sioux Wars," 14 *Kansas Historical Collections* (1923–1925).

3. Utley, "The Enduring Custer Legend."

4. Ibid.

5. Ibid.

6. Whittaker, 638.

7. Utley, "The Enduring Custer Legend."

8. Ibid.

9. Hutton, "From Little Bighorn to Little Big Man."

10. Utley, "The Enduring Custer Legend."

Bibliography

Manuscripts

Annual Report of the Secretary of War for the Year 1866.

Dallas, David. "Comanche Lives Again." Manuscript and notes for chapbook, Riley County Historical Museum, Manhattan, Kansas.

Frost, Lawrence A. Correspondence to author, concerning Captain Thomas Ward Custer, November 30, 1976.

Kansas State Adjutant General Report, 1866-1873. Archives Department, Kansas State Historical Society, Topeka, Kansas.

Mrozek, Donald J. "The Transformation of the U.S. Military Establishment." Paper delivered to departmental seminar, History Department, Kansas State University, Manhattan, Kansas, 1974.

Report of U.S. Secretary of War, 1866-1867. Serial No. 1285, 5-19, 24. Register of Sick and Wounded at Fort Riley, Kansas, November 1866–April 1867. National Archives, Washington, D.C.

Register of Sick and Wounded at Fort Hays, Kansas, July 1870.

National Archives, Washington, D.C.

Roster of the Eighteenth Kansas Volunteer Cavalry. Archives Department, Kansas State Historical Society, Topeka, Kansas.

Roster of the Nineteenth Kansas Volunteer Cavalry. Archives Department, Kansas State Historical Society, Topeka, Kansas.

Ryan, Garry D. Chief of the Navy and Old Army Branch, Military Archives Division, National Archives, Washington, D.C. Correspondence to author, September 21, 1978.

Traylor, Jack W. Curator of Manuscripts, Kansas State Historical Society. Correspondence to author, August 31, 1978.

United States War Department. *Annual Reports, 1874, 1875, 1876, 1877.* Reports of the Secretary of War. National Archives, Washington, D.C.

United States War Department. *Annual Report, 1876.* Report of the General of the Army. National Archives, Washington, D.C.

Books

Ambrose, Stephen E. *Crazy Horse and Custer: The Parallel Lives of Two American Warriors.* Garden City, New York, 1975.

Andrist, Ralph K. *The Long Death: The Last Days of the Plains Indians.* New York, 1964.

Azoy, A. C. M. *Paul Revere's Horse.* Garden City, New York, 1949.

Berger, Thomas. *Little Big Man.* New York, 1964.

Birney, Hoffman. *The Dice of God.* New York, 1956.

Brown, Dee. *Showdown at Little Big Horn.* New York, 1964.

Brown, Dee, and Martin F. Schmitt. *Fighting Indians of the West.* New York, 1948.

Catton, Bruce. *The Civil War.* New York, 1960.

___. *Glory Road.* Garden City, New York, 1962.

____. *Mr. Lincoln's Army.* Garden City, New York, 1962.

____. *A Stillness at Appomattox.* Garden City, New York, 1962.

Chandler, Melbourne C. *Of Garry Owen and Glory.* New York, 1960.

Criqui, Orvel. *Fifty Fearless Men.* Marcelline, Missouri, 1993.

Cunningham, Eugene. *Triggernometry: A Gallery of Gunfighters.* Caldwell, Idaho, 1971.

Custer, Elizabeth B. *Boots and Saddles.* New York, 1885.

____. *Following the Guidon.* New York, 1890.

____. *Tenting on the Plains.* New York, 1889.

Dary, David. *The Buffalo Book.* Chicago, 1974.

____. *Comanche.* Lawrence, Kansas, 1976.

____. *Finding Pleasure in the Old West.* New York, 1986.

Drago, Harry Sinclair. *Wild, Woolly, and Wicked: The History of the Kansas Cow Towns and the Texas Cattle Trade.* New York, 1960.

DuMont, John, and John Parsons. *Firearms in the Custer Battle.* Harrisburg, Pennsylvania, 1953.

Erodes, Richard. *The Sun Dance People: The Plains Indians, Their Past and Present.* New York, 1972.

Fougera, Katherine Bigson. *With Custer's Cavalry.* Caldwell, Idaho, 1940.

Frost, Lawrence A. *The Custer Album.* Seattle, Washington, 1964.

____. *General Custer's Libbie.* Seattle, Washington, 1976.

Fry, James Barnet. *The History and Legal Effects of Brevets in the Armies of Great Britain and the United States.* New York, 1877.

Garraty, John A. *The American Nation: A History of the United States* (5th edition). New York, 1975.

Graham, W. A. *The Custer Myth: A Source Book of Custeriana.* Harrisburg, Pennsylvania, 1953.

____. *The Story of the Little Big Horn: Custer's Last Fight.* New York, 1926.

Grinnell, George Bird. *The Fighting Cheyennes.* New York, 1915.

Haycox, Ernest. *Bugles in the Afternoon.* New York, 1943.

Heitman, Francis B. *Historical Register and Dictionary of the United States Army, 1789-1903.* Washington, D.C., 1903.

Hoebel, E. Adamson. *The Cheyennes: Indians of the Great Plains.* New York, 1960.

Hunt, Frazier, and Robert Hunt (eds.). *I Fought With Custer.* New York, 1947.

Jackson, Donald. *Custer's Gold: The United States Cavalry Expedition of 1874.* New Haven, Connecticut, 1966.

Jones, Douglas C. *The Court-Martial of George Armstrong Custer.* New York, 1976.

Keating, Bern. *The Flamboyant Mr. Colt and His Deadly Six-Shooter.* 1978.

Kinsley, D. A. *Favor the Bold—Custer: The Civil War Years.* New York, 1967.

____. *Favor the Bold—Custer: The Indian Fighter.* New York, 1967.

Kuhlman, Charles. *Did Custer Disobey Orders?* Harrisburg, Pennsylvania, 1957.

____. *Legend Into History.* Harrisburg, Pennsylvania, 1952.

____. *Massacre Survivor.* Fort Collins, Colorado, 1974.

Leighton, Margaret. *Bride of Glory: The Story of Elizabeth Bacon Custer.* New York, 1963.

____. *Comanche of the Seventh.* New York, 1957.

Longstreet, Stephen. *War Cries on Horseback: The Story of the Indian Wars on the Great Plains.* Garden City, New York, 1970.

Marshall, S. L. A. *Crimsoned Prairies: The Indian Wars on the Great Plains.* New York, 1972.

Merrington, Marguerite (ed.). *The Custer Story: The Life and Intimate Letters of General George A. Custer and His Wife Elizabeth.* New York, 1950.

Miller, Nyle H., and Joseph W. Snell. *Great Gunfighters of Kansas Cowtowns, 1867–1886.* Lincoln, Nebraska, 1964.

Millis, Walter. *Arms and Men.* New York, 1956.

Monaghan, Jay. *Custer.* Boston, 1959.

Neihardt, John G. (ed.). *Black Elk Speaks: Being the Life Story of a Holy Man of the Oglala Sioux.* New York, 1932.

Nevin, David. *The Soldiers.* New York, 1973.

Oliva, Leo. *Fort Wallace: Sentinel on the Smoky Hill Trail.* Topeka, Kansas, 1998.

Parker, Watson, and Lambert K. Wilson. *Black Hills Ghost Towns.* Chicago, 1974.

Parks, Jack. *Who Killed Custer?* New York, 1971.

Pride, W. F. *The History of Fort Riley.* Washington, D.C., 1926.

Quaife, Milo Milton (ed.). Custer, George A., *My Life on the Plains.* Lincoln, Nebraska, 1966.

Red Fox, Chief. *The Memoirs of Chief Red Fox.* New York, 1971.

Rosa, Joseph G. *They Called Him Wild Bill.* Norman, Oklahoma, 1964.

Sandoz, Mari. *The Battle of the Little Bighorn.* Philadelphia and New York, 1953.

———. *Cheyenne Autumn.* New York, 1953.

———. *These Were the Sioux.* New York, 1961.

Scott, Jay. *Army War Heroes.* Derby, Connecticut, 1963.

Sheridan, Philip H. *Personal Memoirs.* New York, 1888.

Slagg, Winifred N. *Riley County, Kansas.* Manhattan, Kansas,

1967.

Smart, Mollie S., and Russell C. Smart. *Children: Development and Relationships.* New York, 1972.

Stands-in-Timber, John, and Margot Liberty, with the assistance of Robert M. Utley. *Cheyenne Memories.* New Haven, Connecticut, 1967.

Stewart, Edgar I. *Custer's Luck.* Norman, Oklahoma, 1953.

Stone, L. Joseph, and Joseph Church. *Childhood and Adolescence: A Psychology of the Growing Person.* New York, 1973.

Stratton, Joanna. *Pioneer Women.* New York, 1974.

Sutton-Smith, Brian. *Child Psychology.* New York, 1973.

Walker, Judson Elliott. *Campaigns of General Custer.* New York, 1881.

Wagner, Glendolin D. *Old Nutriment.* Boston, 1934.

Wellman, Paul I. Death on the Prairie. Garden City, New York, 1934.

Whittaker, Frederick. *A Complete Life of Gen. George A. Custer.* New York, 1876.

Wilder, Daniel Webster. *Annals of Kansas.* Topeka, Kansas, 1886.

Williams, T. Harry. *Americans at War.* New York, 1960.

Articles

Alger, John. "Uncle Frank Was a Four-Bit Hero." 5 *Golden West,* July 1969.

Belden, Dorothy. "'Custer' Painting Hailed as Most Accurate of Battle." Wichita *Eagle and Beacon,* April 3, 1977.

Bingham, Anne E. "Sixteen Years on a Kansas Farm, 1870–1886." 15 *Kansas Historical Collections,* 1919-1922.

Bird, Roy D. "The Custer-Hickok Feud in Hays City." *Real*

BIBLIOGRAPHY

West. March 1979.

___. "Frontier Regulars in Kansas." *Kanhistique*, March 1976.

___. "Printer's Ink Ran in Their Veins." *Kanhistique*, June 1979.

Brown, D. Alexander. "Story of the Plains Indians." *American History Illustrated*, August 1973.

"Custer Put Fort Wallace in the Spotlight." A Moment in Time Series, Kansas State Historical Society, May 25, 1998.

Day, Carl. "The Last Will and Testament of Thomas Ward Custer." *The Guidon*, June 2000.

Davis, Theodore R. "With Generals in Their Homes." *Chicago Brand Book*, 1945 - 1946.

Gibbon, John. "Hunting Sitting Bull." 2 *American Catholic Quarterly Review*, April 1877.

___. "Last Summer's Expedition Against the Sioux." 2 *American Catholic Quarterly Review*, April 1877.

Graham, Stanley S. "Routine at Western Cavalry Posts, 1833–1861." 15 *Journal of the West*, July 1976.

Gray, John S. "Veterinary Service on Custer's Last Campaign." 43 *Kansas Historical Quarterly*, Autumn 1977.

Hawley, Paul R. "Did Cholera Defeat Custer?" 84 *International Abstracts of Surgery*, May 1947.

Hutton, Paul A. "Custer's Last Stand." *TV Guide*, November 26–December 2, 1977.

___. "From Little Bighorn to Little Big Man: The Changing Image of a Western Hero in Popular Culture." 7 *Western Historical Quarterly*, January 1976.

Josephy, Alvin M., Jr. "The Custer Myth." *Life*, July 2, 1971.

Lewis, Alfred Henry. "How Mr. Hickok Came to Cheyenne: An Epic of an Unsung Ulysses." *The Saturday Evening Post*, March 12, 1904.

Libby, Orin G. (ed.). "The Arikara Narrative of the Campaign Against the Hostile Dakotas." 7 *North Dakota Historical Collections,* 1920.

Menninger, Karl. "A Psychiatrist Looks at Custer." 84 *International Abstracts of Surgery,* May 1947.

Millbrook, Minnie Dubbs. "Big Game Hunting with the Custers, 1869–1870." 41 *Kansas Historical Quarterly,* Winter 1975.

___. "Custer's First Scout in the West." 39 *Kansas Historical Quarterly,* Spring 1973.

___. "Mrs. General Custer at Fort Riley, 1866." 40 *Kansas Historical Quarterly,* Spring 1974.

___. "Old Trail Plowed Under—Hays to Dodge." 43 *Kansas Historical Quarterly,* Autumn 1977.

Montgomery, Mrs. Frank C. "Fort Wallace and Its Relation to the Frontier." 17 *Kansas Historical Collections,* 1926–1928.

Owen, Freya Weaver, Pauline Austin Adams, Thomas Forrest, Lois Meek Stolz, and Sara Fischer. "Learning Disorders in Children: Sibling Studies." *Monographs of the Society for Research in Child Development.* University of Chicago Press, 1971.

Powers, Ramon, and Gene Younger. "Cholera on the Plains: The Epidemic of 1867 in Kansas." 37 *Kansas Historical Quarterly,* Winter 1971.

Robinson, Charles M., III. "Recipient of Two Medals of Honor, Tom Custer Died Alongside Brother George." *Wild West,* June 1966.

Rosa, Joseph G. "Wild Bill Hickok—Peacemaker." 1 *The Prairie Scout,* 1973.

Shulsinger, Stephanie Cooper. "The Unforgettable Custers." *Real West,* September 1975.

Slotkin, Richard. "'. . . & Then the Mare Will Go!': An 1875

Black Hills Scheme by Custer, Holladay, and Buford." 15 *Journal of the West,* July 1976.

Stackpole, E. J. "Generalship in the Civil War." *Military Affairs,* Summer 1960.

Thralls, J. M. "The Sioux Wars." 16 *Kansas Historical Collections,* 1923–1925.

Utley, Robert M. "The Enduring Custer Legend." *American History Illustrated,* June 1976.

Wade, Arthur P. "The Military Command Structure: The Great Plains, 1853–1891." 15 *Journal of the West,* July 1976.

White, Lonnie J. "Indian Raids on the Kansas Frontier, 1869." 38 *Kansas Historical Quarterly,* Winter 1972.

Newspapers

Clyde, Kansas, *Republican Valley Empire,* August 2, 1870.

Helena, Montana, *Herald,* July 1876.

Junction City, Kansas, *Union,* 1866–1870.

Manhattan, Kansas, *Standard,* 1867–1869.

Monroe, Michigan, *Commercial,* 1854–1880.

Monroe, Michigan, *Monitor,* 1862–1880.

New York *Herald,* January 1–August 31, 1876.

St. Louis, Missouri, *Globe,* 1867, 1875–1876.

Topeka, Kansas, *Capital,* 1872–1873.

Topeka, Kansas, *Kansas Daily Commonwealth,* July 22, 1870.

Websites

www.historynet.com/Wild West/articles.

www.users-globalnet.co.uld—pardos/TomCusterRev. html.

www.civilwarhome.com/tcusterbio.html.

www.cmohs.org/medal/history-links/double_award_winners.

html.

   www.voicenet.com/—/padilla/custer.html.

INDEX

with Wild Bill Hickok, 153-54, 156, 157-60, 162, 164-66; Reconstruction duty in the South, 167, 169-73, 176-78; duty in Dakota Territory, 179-93, 194-95, 203-4, 205-8; and the Black Hills, 197, 199-201; on summer 1876 campaign, 209, 211-12, 214-26; at Battle of Little Bighorn, 227-40; death of, 240, 241, 247-49; burial of, 245, 249; reputation defended by Libbie Custer, 246. *See also* Buffalo Calf; Drew, Major; Little Hair

Dakota Territory, 177, 178, 182, 191, 200, 203, 204. *See also* Department of Dakota
Darlington, S.C., 173, 179
Darrah, Dianna "Anna," 61, 69, 70, 75, 89, 123, 129, 151-52
Deadwood (Dakota Territory), 166
Denver, Col., 64, 69, 155
Denver Public Library, Western Historical Collection, 131, 133
Department of Dakota, 177
DeRudio, Charles, 188, 246
Detroit, Mich., 42
Diaz, Porfirio, 40, 55
Don Juan (horse), 37
Dorman, Isaiah, 217
Drago, Henry Sinclair, 159
Drew, Major (alias for Thomas Ward Custer), 24
Drumm, Tommy, 126, 157, 158, 160

E Company. *See* Company E
Eagle Shield (Sioux Indian), 200
Early, Jubal Anderson, 23, 30
Eastman, Dr. Charles, 248
Edgerly, W. S., 220-21
Eighteenth Kansas Volunteer Cavalry, 81, 105
Eighth New York Regiment, 30
Elizabethtown, Ky., 174, 176
Elliott, Joel, 65, 67, 80, 87, 94, 95, 104, 109, 113, 115, 117-18, 232
Ellis Station, Kans., 99
Ellsworth, Kans., 81
Emperor Maximilian, 40
Evans, Colonel, 105
Ewell, Mary, 2

Ewell, Richard S., 33, 34

F Company. *See* Company F
Fargo (Dakota Territory), 177, 204
Fifth Cavalry, 98, 105, 160
Fifth Military District (Reconstruction), 40
Finkel, Frank, 241
First Battle of Bull Run (Manassas), 19, 20
First Connecticut Volunteer Regiment, 30
First Infantry. *See* First U.S. Infantry
First Reconstruction Act, 169-71
First U.S. Infantry, 53, 59
Flynn, Errol, 253
Force Acts, 173
Forrest, Nathan Bedford, 63
Forsyth, George A., 102
Fort Abraham Lincoln (Dakota Territory), 133, 178, 180-81, 187, 188, 191, 192, 194, 195, 196, 198, 200, 202, 203, 204-5, 206, 207, 209, 210, 214, 215, 216, 218, 224, 226, 243, 244, 247, 249
Fort Bufort, N.Dak., 247
Fort Cobb (Indian Territory), 119, 121
Fort Dodge, Kans., 119
Fort Garland, Col., 59
Fort Grant, Ariz., 250
Fort Harker, Kans., 79, 81, 88-89, 90-91, 92, 155
Fort Hays, Kans., 74-76, 78, 79, 83, 88, 90, 105, 123, 124, 125, 126, 132, 133, 138, 142, 144, 150, 151, 155-56, 163, 165, 166
Fort Phil Kearny (Dakota Territory), 181, 208
Fort Laramie, Dakota Territory (now Wyo.), 198
Fort Leavenworth, Kans., 60, 74, 93, 95, 96, 97, 98, 99, 123, 134, 249, 250
Fort Lincoln. *See* Fort Abraham Lincoln
Fort McKean, 180. *See also* Fort Abraham Lincoln
Fort McPherson (Nebraska Territory), 78, 82, 83
Fort Rice (Dakota Territory), 182, 188, 209
Fort Riley, Kans., 56, 57, 59, 60, 61, 62, 63, 67, 68, 69, 70, 74, 76, 80, 89, 91, 92, 93, 165, 216, 218, 242, 250
Fort Sedgwick (Colorado Territory), 78, 86